Word, Image, Text

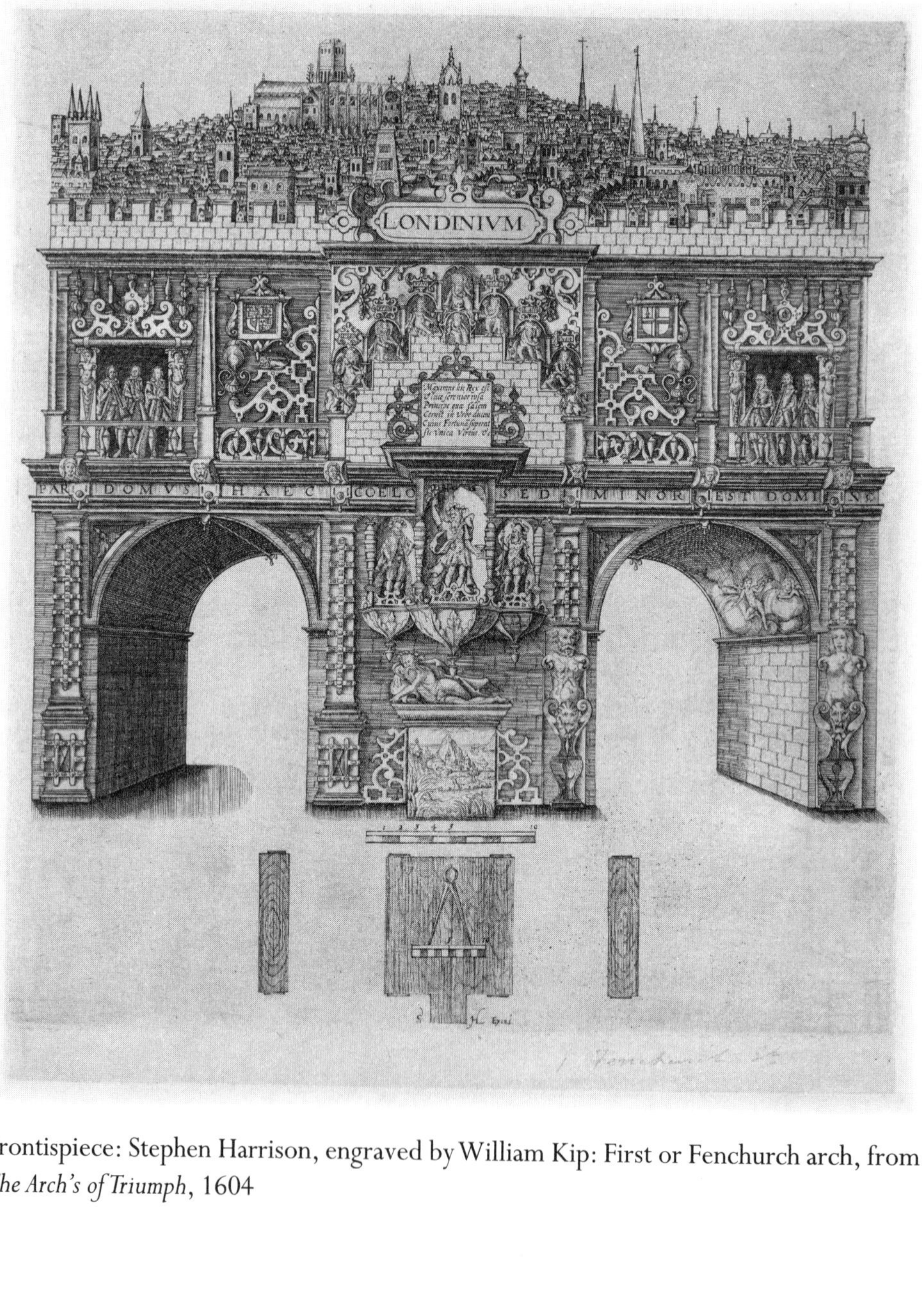

Frontispiece: Stephen Harrison, engraved by William Kip: First or Fenchurch arch, from *The Arch's of Triumph*, 1604

Word, Image, Text

Studies in Literary and Visual Culture

Editors

Shormishtha Panja

Shirshendu Chakrabarti

Christel Devadawson

Orient BlackSwan

WORD, IMAGE, TEXT: STUDIES IN LITERARY AND VISUAL CULTURE

ORIENT BLACKSWAN PRIVATE LIMITED

Registered Office
3-6-752 Himayatnagar, Hyderabad 500 029, Telangana, India
e-mail: centraloffice@orientblackswan.com

Other Offices
Bengaluru, Bhopal, Chennai, Guwahati, Hyderabad, Jaipur, Kolkata, Lucknow, Mumbai, New Delhi, Noida, Patna, Vijayawada

First published, 2009
Reprinted 2017

ISBN 978 81 250 3735 4

Library of Congress Cataloguing-in-Publication data
Word, image, text : studies in literary and visual culture / editors, Shormishtha Panja, Shirshendu Chakrabarti, Christel Devadawson. New Delhi : Orient BlackSwan, 2009.
viii, 176 p., [24] p. of plates : ill. (some col.) ; 24 cm.
PN53 .W675 2009
ISBN: 9788125037354 (pbk.) 8125037357 (pbk.)

Typeset in 10.5/13 pt Sabon

025559

Typeset by
System Graphics (India) Pvt. Ltd., New Delhi

Printed in India at
Yash Printographics, Noida

10052017

Published by
Orient Blackswan Private Limited
3-6-752 Himayatnagar, Hyderabad 500 029, Telangana, India
e-mail: info@orientblackswan.com

To
Rutajeet
Sutirtho
Christine

Contents

Preface

This collection of essays on the conceptualisation and representation of word and image and their interrelationship in literature and the visual arts is written by scholars both from western academia and India, scholars who are established experts in their field as well as young critics making an early foray in the world of scholarly research. In addition, there is an essay by a practising artist meditating on nature and time through self-portraits. The contributors come from a wide variety of locations: India, Ireland, Australia, Norway, Spain and the United States of America. The scope of the book is large: it encompasses not only the literature and art of Europe from the fifteenth through the nineteenth centuries, it also includes an examination of the art and literature of the Indian sub-continent. The verbal and visual genres examined are manifold: epyllion, comedy, epic, satire, children's fiction, travelogue, painting, sculpture, frontispiece, engraving, miniature, book illustration, cartoon, photograph.

Another important feature of this book is its interdisciplinary subject matter. Although interdisciplinarity has transformed literary research, it is, for the most part, confined to the relationship between literature and the social sciences. In comparison, the interrelationship of the arts has been a somewhat neglected domain of exploration. This is somewhat baffling since the ancient rhetoricians like Simonides and Horace and Renaissance theorists like Leon Battista Alberti and Philip Sidney often drew illustrative parallels between poetry, painting and sculpture. The *ut picture poesis* tradition kept the interaction between the literary and the visual alive in the past. In India, Rabindrananth Tagore, among others, wrote extensively on the relationship between poetry and art in his essays and letters. Moving to our times, we can see that while performance studies has provided a corrective by critically bringing together the written or printed dramatic text and its stage life, literature and the visual arts have not received similar scholarly scrutiny, particularly in India. This book is thus a bold attempt to break down the isolation of the two arts and to make parallelism an exploratory method aimed at a mutually enriching synthesis. Since ideas and tendencies acquire an irreducibly concrete life in artistic representation, examination of the same life in two different art forms deepens our understanding of it as well as of the larger issues and contexts in which the literary and visual texts are embedded.

While this is a collection of scholarly essays, there is enough here to interest the lay reader. A conscious effort has been made to eschew jargon and to make the style as pellucid and accessible as possible without in any way diluting the content. The addition of a number of valuable full-colour plates accessed from museums as diverse as the Royal Museum of Fine Arts of Belgium, Brussels, the Vatican Pinacotheca and the Victoria and Albert Museum will add to the reader's pleasure.

List of Figures

Publisher's Acknowledgments

Cover: Peter Bruegel the Elder, *The Fall of the Rebel Angels*. Copyright: © Royal Museums of Fine Arts of Belgium, Brussels / Grafisch Buro Lefevre, Heule.

Frontispiece: Stephen Harrison, engraved by William Kip: First or Fenchurch arch, from *The Arch's of Triumph*, 1604. Reproduced by permission of the Folger Shakespeare Library under CC BY-SA 4.0

Figure 1: Sebastiano Serlio, 'Arch of Constantine' from *The Five Books of Architecture, 1611. Author's collection.*

Figure 2: William Marshall, Frontispiece to Francis Bacon: *Of the Advancement and Proficience of Learning*, 1640. Reproduced by permission of the Syndics of Cambridge University Library.

Figure 3: Frontispiece to John Gerard: *The Herball or Generall Historie of Plantes*, 1633. Reproduced by permission of the Syndics of Cambridge University Library.

Figure 4: Willam Hole, Frontispiece to Michael Drayton: *Poly-Olbion,* 1622. Reproduced by permission of the Syndics of Cambridge University Library.

Figure 5: Titian, *Venus and Adonis*. Digital image courtesy of the Getty's Open Content Program.

Figure 6: The Villa Lante at Bagnaia. The Loggia of the Muses, one of a pair at the top of the garden, adjoins a colonnaded conversation area with classical benches for enlightening conversation *all'antica*. In Charles Latham *The Gardens of Italy*, Vol. 2, London: Country Life, 1905

Figure 7: Tudor Garden from Thomas Hill's *The Gardener's* Labyrinth. Wood Cut. In Reginal Blomfield and F. Inigo Thomas, *The Formal Garden in England,* London: Macmillan, 1897, p. 39

Figure 8: Painting, *Akbarnama*, Akbar tiger-hunting near Narwar, outline and portraits by Basawan, painting by Tara the Elder, Mughal, ca. 1590–95. © Victoria and Albert Museum, London

Figure 9: Painting, *Akbarnama*, Akbar punishes Hamid Bakari, outline and portraits by Miskina, painting by Sarwan, Mughal, ca. 1586–1589. © Victoria and Albert Museum, London

Figure 10: Peter Breugel the Elder, *The Tower of Babel*. Photo Credit: John W. Schulze/Flickr. Licensed under CC BY 2.0

Figure 11: Peter Bruegel the Elder, *The Fall of Icarus*. Photo Credit: Sailko/Wikimedia Commons. Licensed under CC BY 3.0

Figure 12: *Gommateshwara*. Photo Credit: Ankur P/Flickr. Licensed under CC BY-SA 2.0

Figure 12a: *A vine climbing a tree*. Photo Credit: Vincent Villafranca.

Figure 13: *The Fasting Buddha*, Mahabalipuram. Photo Credit: Vincent Villafranca.

Figure 14: John Lockwood Kipling, Illustration to 'The Sparrow and the Crow', from *Tales of the Punjab* by Flora Annie Steel.

Figure 15: John Lockwood Kipling, Illustration to 'Little Anklebone', from *Tales of the Punjab* by Flora Annie Steel.

Figures 16–20: O. V. Vijayan, Cartoons from *Tragic Idioms*, published by DC Books. Reproduced by permission of Madhu Vijayan and the publisher.

Figure 21: Raphael, *The Transfiguration*. Photo Credit: Anna & Michal/Flickr. Licensed under CC BY-SA 2.0

Figure 22: Rachel Lachowicz, *Forensic Projections (28, 58, 88)*, 1992 Reproduced by permission of the artist and Shoshana Wayne Gallery.

Figure 23: Loris Button, *Facing Time—Self Portraits, 2005–2006*. Reproduced by permission of the artist.

Figure 24: Loris Button, *Self Portraits, 2002, 2003, 2004*. Reproduced by permission of the artist.

The Renaissance in Europe

THE RENAISSANCE IN EUROPE

Speaking of poetry and painting in the same breath as allied liberal arts is, to the contemporary audience, a truism. However, this was not always the case. As Kristeller argues in his marvellous essay 'The Modern System of the Arts: A Study in the History of Aesthetics', the inclusion of poetry and painting in the scope of the liberal arts was not something that the classical world or the Renaissance did in a systematic way, although there are numerous references to the two disciplines in these periods.[1]

Plato's remarks on poets and painters are notoriously contradictory. In *Ion,* the *Apology* and in Book X of *The Republic* (*c.* 370 BC) poetry and painting are dismissed as 'representations at the third remove from reality, and easy to produce without any knowledge of the truth, because they are appearances and not realities' (*The Republic* Book X, 599).[2] Imitation is not seen as something praiseworthy for Plato. Painters and poets are mere craftsmen who presume knowledge of things about which they are profoundly ignorant. In fact, poets compose in a state of mindlessness: 'For not by art do they speak these things, but by divine power....God takes the mind out of these poets, and uses them as his servants...' (*Ion* 533C–535C).[3]

Despite these outspoken criticisms of poetry, in the dialogues Plato continuously uses poetic metaphors and conceits, the cave (*The Republic*) and the allegory of the charioteer and his horses (*Phaedrus*) being two of the best-known examples. The poets have to be banished from the Republic not because of their inefficacy but because of the power of their work and the influence they have on the masses. In the *Phaedrus* (*c.* 370 BC) the poet is admitted to be an 'inspired madman' (245): 'The third type of possession and madness is possession by the Muses. When this seizes upon a gentle and virgin soul it rouses it to inspired expression in lyric and other sorts of poetry…' (*Phaedrus* 245).[4]

Aristotle, however, picking up the argument where Plato leaves off, clearly sees imitation as something worthy of closer scrutiny in the *Poetics*. He admits that this is the basis for the comparison between poets (no distinction is made between poets and dramatists in the *Poetics*) and painters as is their attempt to galvanise the emotions of the spectator. There are a few scattered analogies in the *Poetics* between the work of poets and painters like Zeuxis and Polygnotus (*Poetics* chapter 6).[5] At one point, the poet is told to follow the 'example of good portrait-painters, who reproduce the distinctive features of a man, and at the same time, without losing the likeness, make him handsomer than he is' (*Poetics* chapter 15). It is in imitation, *mimesis*, that poetry and painting are compared: 'The poet being an imitator just like the painter or other maker of likenesses' can represent people 'either as they were or are, or as they are said or thought to be or to have been, or as they ought to be' (*Poetics* chapter 25). Aristotle squarely picks up the gauntlet where Plato has left it and claims that the world of art has its own independent existence. It must be judged by its own laws and not by laws of fidelity to the real world: 'It is to be remembered, too, that there is not the same kind of correctness in poetry as in politics, or indeed any other art' (*Poetics* chapter 25). It is more heinous for the artist to fail in his/her artistic attempt than not to be lifelike. The latter error 'is not in the essentials of the poetic art' (*Poetics* chapter 25). Like Plato, Aristotle admits, albeit fleetingly, so concerned is he to present the composition of poetry as a demystified science, that the poet has a touch of madness in him.

The comparision between poetry and painting continues among the Roman writers as well. *Ut pictura poesis*, as in painting so in poetry, has been popularised by Horace but traced back by Plutarch to Simonides's statement, 'painting is mute poetry and poetry a speaking picture.' Horace in his *On the Art of Poetry* (12–8 BC) writes:

> A poem is like a painting: the closer you stand to this one the more it will impress you, whereas you have to stand a good distance from that one; this one demands a rather dark corner, but that one needs to be seen in full light…; this one only pleased you the first time you saw it, but that one will go on giving pleasure however often it is looked at. (337–96)[6]

In the Renaissance, unlike the Middle Ages, when according to Kristeller, there was no coherent system of the fine arts, there was some attempt, although not as methodical as the attempt made in the eighteenth century, to raise the stature of both poetry and painting, particularly the latter, above the mere status of a craft to that of inspired creation and a justified member of the liberal arts. That is why Alberti in *On Painting* (1435–36) insists on devoting the whole of the first book to mathematics, particularly geometry, already an accepted member of the quadrivium. The quadrivium consisted of arithmetic, geometry, astronomy and music and the trivium of grammar, rhetoric and logic and these formed the basis of Medieval education. Poetry and music were taught in schools but painting was not. Painting, sculpture and architecture did not at this point form part of the trivium or the quadrivium. It comes as no surprise then that Alberti is at pains to insist that the painter must be well-educated and well-trained: 'Perfection in the art will be found with diligence, application and study' (*On Painting* Book III, 91).[7] The painter must keep in the company of respected individuals like poets (at the time poetry obviously enjoyed a higher reputation and rhetoric was also a part of the trivium). Alberti gives the example of the classical painter Phidias who claimed to have learned more from Homer than from other sources. At the centre of Alberti's work, the first example of serious theorising about the visual arts, lies the concept of *istoria*. Even the use of the word, akin to Aristotle's notion of plot as the principle which holds the work of art together and around which all its other attributes adhere, suggests a literary or at least narrative parallel. It is *istoria* that determines the decorous use of *copia*; it is *istoria* that helps all parts of the painting to be appropriate; it is *istoria* which enables the work of art to 'merit both praise and admiration' and 'capture the eye of whatever learned or unlearned person is looking at it and... move his soul' (*On Painting* Book II, 75). It is in the perfect composition of the *istoria* that poets can aid the painter according to Alberti:

> For their own enjoyment artists should associate with poets and orators who have many embellishments in common with painters and who have a broad knowledge of many things. These could be very useful in beautifully composing the *istoria* whose greatest praise consists in the invention.... Therefore I advise that each painter should make himself familiar with poets, rhetoricians and others equally well learned in letters. They will give new inventions or at least aid in beautifully composing the *istoria* through which the painter will surely acquire much praise and renown in his painting.
>
> (*On Painting* Book III, 91)

It was the *studia humanitatis* or the humanism project that once more linked the painter/sculptor and the poet. Leonardo da Vinci in his *Paragone* (literally test or trial,) a section of his *Trattato della pittura* (*Treatise on Painting* pub. 1651) in which Leonardo wittily defends painting against poetry, music and sculpture, put together by Manzi in 1817, playfully insists on the superiority of painting over poetry. It was also common to argue about the relative merits of sculpture versus painting, Leonardo understandably opting for the latter. Both painting and poetry were seen to have their uses. Castiglione in Book I of *The Courtier* (1528) has Count Lodovico Canossa, a friend of the painter Raphael, extol the virtues of painting, saying that the courtier must have a knowledge of the art 'although nowadays it may appear mechanical and hardly suited to a gentleman' (*The Courtier* 96).[8] This was the disrepute that painting suffered that Alberti, Vasari and Castiglione fight against. They wanted painting to get rid of the old reputation of being a lowly craft, a mechanical thing done with the hands and therefore not worthy of respect. Castiglione cites the example of the ancient painter Fabius, who insisted on signing himself as 'pictor' even though he came from an illustrious family, after decorating the walls of the Temple of Salus (*The Courtier* 97) as an example of the value given to painting in the ancient world. Castiglione also points out the usefulness of painting—the courtier can sketch citadels and fortresses and thereby use his art in the service of war. (One may recall that Leonardo da Vinci also boasted of his prowess in the creation of cannons, bombardments and armoured vehicles when he was trying to get a job from Ludovico Sforza of Milan around 1480 and mentioned his artistic gifts as an afterthought). As a final word of commendation, Castiglione compares God and Nature to painters of no mean talent: '...the very fabric of the universe...can be said to be a great and noble painting, composed by Nature and the hand of God' (*The Courtier* 97). And the Count does not hesitate to add his opinion on the great *mimesis* debate: 'And in my opinion whoever can imitate it deserves the highest praise. Nor is such imitation achieved without the knowledge of many things, as anyone who attempts the task well knows' (*The Courtier* 97). The last is a direct rebuttal of Plato's observation that the poet and painter, blindly imitating the imitation of an imitation, have no true knowledge. The Count also enters briefly into the debate between painting and sculpture with the sculptor Giovan Christofero Romano, saying that while painting was the superior art, sculpture and painting came from the same source: 'good design'. Just as *mimesis* was a common ground for the discourse about poetry and painting, *disegno* or design, referred to time and again by Giorgio Vasari in his *Lives of the Poets* (1550; second edition 1568) came to be the means by which art could be legitimately institutionalised. Kristeller points out that it was through Vasari's insistence and the support of Cosimo de' Medici that the *Accademia del Disegno* (Academy of Art) came up in 1563 in Florence to provide institutional support and training for artists. It was the first of its kind and proved a model for similar institutions in Italy and elsewhere. Literary academies were already in existence. In the Preface to the *Lives,* the first example of art history and another important element in the project to raise the status of art from a mere mechanical thing to be done with ones hands and therefore to be despised, Vasari writes, speaking of sculpture and painting, 'I would say that design, the basis of both arts, or rather the very soul which conceives and nourishes within itself all the aspects of the intellect, existed in absolute perfection at the origin of all other things when God on High, having created the great body of the world...and shaping man, discovered in the pleasing invention of things the first form of sculpture and painting.'[9] Invention and design became a means of bringing the arts together and of diminishing the conflict between them that Leonardo in his Paragone had aggrandised.

One can observe many of the same concerns as the Greeks, the Latins and the Italians when one looks at Sir Philip Sidney's *Apology for Poetry* (pub. 1595).[10] Very early in the work Sidney draws a parallel between poetry and painting, when he speaks of the 'meaner sort of painters (who counterfeit only such faces as are set before them)' and those who 'painteth the outward beauty of such a virtue' as that of 'lamenting' Lucretia raped by Tarquin (*Apology* 20). Similarly there are good poets and bad ones. The very definition of poetic composition abounds in analogies drawn from the world of painting: 'Poesy therefore is an art of imitation...that is to say, a representing, counterfeiting, or figuring forth—to speak metaphorically, a speaking picture—with this end, to teach and delight' (*Apology* 18). Rather than 'rhyming and versing' it is 'the feigning notable images of virtues, vices...with that delightful teaching' which is the true identification, the 'right describing note to know a poet by' (*Apology* 21). It is the 'perfect picture' of the poet that works better than the 'wordish description' of the philosopher to persuade the reader to rightful action (*Apology* 27). Poets like Xenophon 'paint [ing] men' (*Apology* 58) like the heroic and virtuous Cyrus so that the example can 'pierce' and 'possess the sight of the soul' (*Apology* 27) and thereby breed more Cyruses. In the battle between the philosopher, the historian and the poet, a battle begun by Plato and sustained by Aristotle, it is the painter who is the poet's ally rather than antagonist. It is not rhyme but 'feigning notable *images* that maketh a poet' (*Apology* 21) (emphasis added). It is ironic that while Alberti, Castiglione and Vasari and even, to a certain extent, Leonardo da Vinci, stress the analogy between poetry and painting in an effort to raise the status of the latter, Sidney mentions the parallel between poetry and painting to answer the charges against poetry, particularly in his own nation, which he terms a 'step-mother' to poets: '...methinks before I give my pen a full stop it shall be but a little more lost time to enquire why England (the mother of excellent minds) should be grown so hard a step-mother to poets...' (*Apology* 68). Sidney claims that 'from almost the highest estimation of learning' poetry is 'fallen to be the laughing stock of children' (*Apology* 5). Of course the difference here is that Alberti and Vasari wish to lift up the status of painting to a position it has never enjoyed while Sidney wants poetry to reclaim its lost glory. As Alberti and Vasari had claimed a divine quality in the work of painters ('Painting contains a divine force' *On Painting* Book II 63,) Sidney too compares the work of the poet to that of God: 'the heavenly maker...having made man to His own likeness...which in nothing he showed so much as in poetry, when with the force of a divine breath he bringeth things forth far surpassing her [Nature's] doings' (*Apology* 17). Nature's 'world is brazen, the poets only deliver a golden' (*Apology* 15).

Thus we see that poetry and painting enter the arena as rivals and as allies, the points of comparison being *mimesis*, invention and humanism. At times it is painting that falls into disrepute and has to be elevated by a comparison with poetry, at times it is poetry that suffers the slings and arrows of outrageous fortune and has to be rescued by a comparison with painting. Despite the paragone, Leonardo da Vinci's half-playful tussle between poetry and painting, the two arts are more often seen in close conjunction as opposed to the art of the historian or the philosopher in the great Renaissance enterprise of elevating the liberal arts for the purpose of *studia humanitatis*. More, they are crucial to the expression and explication of theories of representation. They are the media through which the early modern theoreticians of art can argue forcefully for the usefulness, sweetness and beauty of the liberal arts in the fashioning of an ethical and moral individual. In Sidney's words, citing Aristotle, 'it is not *gnosis*, but *praxis* must be the fruit' (*Apology* 37). Art can 'lead and draw us to as high perfection as our degenerate souls, made worse by their clayey lodgings, can be capable of' (*Apology* 22) and it is in this vital project that both poetry and the visual arts come to the aid of humans.

The essays in this section of the book deal with many diverse aspects of the relationship between word and image in the sixteenth and seventeenth centuries. Stuart Sillars writes of the frontispiece of two works, Inigo Jones' design for *Salmacida Spolia* (1640) and Shadwell's *The Tempest, or The Enchanted Island* (1667) and how the arch they depict is one of the key cultural forms and performative tropes of the early modern period. Theatre, statecraft, political and intellectual hegemony and cultural appropriation are played out in this multifarious set of relationships between word and image that the arch on the frontispiece represents.

Shormishtha Panja analyses two works by Shakespeare, *Venus and Adonis* and *The Rape of Lucrece,* in conjunction with two paintings by Titian, *Venus and Adonis* and *Tarquin and Lucretia,* in an attempt to see if one can evolve a common vocabulary to talk of word and image. Panja attempts to address the questions of space and time: do they transmute in familiar ways in painting and poetry? Can one speak of visual syntax in painting as one speaks of *ekphrasis* in poetic narrative? The essay also explores poets and painters' approach to problems of *mimesis* and self-reflexivity: is nature's world brazen and can the poets and painters deliver a golden?

James Yoch examines the destabilising of time in Shakespeare's *As You Like It* through the discussion of agrarian seasons (labour), aristocratic festivals (leisure) and divine eternity (salvation). Blending old vernacular religious drama with fashionable Italian designs of country houses, *As You Like It* moves, Yoch argues, past the desperate eroticism and greed of earthly time to the promise and comfort of eternal recompense.

Maria Antonia Martì Escayol writes of Antoni de Montserrat's account of his travels to the Mughal emperor Akbar's court and how he tries to come to terms with the flora and fauna and topography of a strange land through continual comparisons with the European counterpart mixed with a healthy respect for difference. The endeavour she sees is in contrast to the Hispanic monarchy's attempts to suppress all juridical, political, linguistic and territorial particularities of the Catalan country in the Catalonian Renaissance.

Davinder Mohini Ahuja discusses the use of adagia and aporia in the works of Rabelais and Pieter Bruegel. Narrative time in both literary and visual texts, she argues, is made discontinuous with startling effect as both painter and author resist the recuperation into a Christian community.

Notes

[1] P. O. Kristeller, 'The Modern System of the Arts: A Study in the History of Aesthetics,' *Journal of the History of Ideas,* 12 (1951): 496–527. JSTOR. 16 Sept. 2008 <http://www.jstor.org/search>. I am greatly indebted to this essay.

[2] Plato, *The Republic* trans. Desmond Lee (1955; Harmondsworth: Penguin, 1974). Book and line references are mentioned.

[3] Plato, *Ion, Great Dialogues of Plato* trans. W.H.D. Rouse, (New York: Mentor Books, 1956), 13–27. Line references are mentioned.

[4] Plato, *Phaedrus & Letters VII and VII*, trans. Walter Hamilton (1973; Harmondsworth: Penguin, 1977), 19–103. Line references are mentioned.

[5] Aristotle, *On the Art of Poetry* trans. Ingram Bywater (1920; Oxford: Clarendon P, 1967).

[6] Horace, *On the Art of Poetry, Classical Literary Criticism* trans. T.S. Dorsch (1965; Harmondsworth: Penguin, 1977), 77–95. Line references are mentioned.

[7] Alberti, *On Painting* trans. John R. Spencer (New Haven: Yale UP, 1966).

[8] Baldassare Castiglione, *The Courtier* trans. George Bull (1967; Harmondsworth: Penguin, 1983).

[9] Giorgio Vasari, *The Lives of the Artists* trans. Julia Conaway Bondanella and Peter Bondanella (1991; Oxford: Oxford UP, 1998).

[10] Sir Philip Sidney, *An Apology for Poetry* (Indianapolis: Bobbs Merrill, 1970).

1. Image, Word and Authority in the Early Modern Frontispiece

Stuart Sillars

In 1574, Henri III of France visited Venice. His entry to the city was marked by the erection of a triumphal arch designed by Palladio, modelled on the Arch of Constantine. This was not unusual: the use of classical arches of triumph, based on the Arch of Constantine or sometimes the Arch of Trajan, had been a recurrent feature of early modern statecraft since the beginning of the sixteenth century. What makes this particular event remarkable is that it was the subject of a painting by Andrea Vicentino, now in the Palazzo Ducale, Venice.[1] The painting shows all the features of the triumphal arch as a fundamental component of early modern thought. A massive, tangible emblem of imperial statecraft and the idea of hierarchical order, the arch demonstrates a unity of ideology, structure and word in a single composite text. Already a part of state ceremonial throughout Europe, it would later become a physical and narrative component of court and public theatre; and, as an oral culture moved increasingly towards print, it would become a key element of the printed book. All these elements make the arch, as revealed in this remarkable painting, one of the key cultural forms, and performative tropes, of the early modern period.

Before leaving the painting, it is worthwhile to point out how all the later significances are, to a later eye, quite implicit within it. The arch is a complete unification of word and image, the tablet above the arch being inscribed with an appropriate moral or laudatory statement to the honour of the person passing through it, while the proportional perfection, in the balance of circle and square of the arch's structure, is a complementary statement of perfection through number. From this will grow the emblematic proscenium that both frames the action of a play and synoptically presents it through carvings and paintings on its three plane surfaces. At a further level, it is innately performative, the arch defined by the process through it, which leads it to dramatic use; and the movement through the arch to the loggia behind it suggests its role as a prelude or boundary to a performed text. Again the proscenium is evident as the prelude to later action—most especially, perhaps, the emblematic arch through which the courtly masquers would walk to take part in the concluding round dance. Finally, the structure of the arch, its two columns supporting a central tablet above a central space, lends itself perfectly to the design of a title-page, the central space being reserved for a portrait of the writer, the tablet for the title, and the columns for a synopsis, in visual form, of the book's contents—that would, of course, be reached by the reader's metaphorically passing through the arch towards the loggia, or body of the text. All of these subsequent incarnations have one further element in common: they all depend on a close, and in some cases indissoluble, relation between word and image.

Just how this works in practice may be seen by looking at two arches that were produced nearly a century later. In 1640, Inigo Jones designed the last of his court masques, *Salmacida Spolia*. His extensive account of 'The Subject of the Masque' includes a full description of 'the border that enclosed the scenes and made a frontispiece to all the work.' Far more than a mere proscenium, this frame is a prefiguration of the action of the masque and its emblematic significations of power and the divine right of kings. In achieving this, it combines the design of the Teatro Olimpico in Vicenza with the drawings of Serlio and Scamozzi, all of which Jones had seen. A few months later, in 1641, Richard Braithwait's volume *The English Gentleman and the English Gentlewoman* appeared with a title page in which the title was flanked by simple depictions of its two idealised characters, and surrounded by sixteen simple depictions of the attributes of these ideal citizens.

The two figures demonstrate the absorption of genuinely transnational visual structures into English cultural forms that demonstrate and extend the verbal-visual relationships characteristic of the structure in two widely separate social echelons. Jones uses arcane emblems to demonstrate the ideology of aristocratic power resting on neo-platonic ideas of divine right, in a framing of the masque that reveals it as a final statement of royal power. By contrast, the Braithwait offers a pragmatic construction of national identity through codes of individual behaviour, resting on bourgeois socio-economic power visualised through accessible naturalism. The growth of the triumphal arch into such diverse forms, and the conceptual exchange that each generates, can be traced across nation-states and cultural centres throughout the sixteenth century and for most of the seventeenth, involving texts from theatre, state spectacle and print, in a process that is far from linear in its growth but instead is genuinely rhizomic in temporal and demographic extent. It is also one in which the relationship between word and image is explored, exploited and held up to question in ways that typify its examination throughout Europe at least since the middle of the preceding century. All this would seem to be reason enough to consider the frontispiece, in all its forms and meanings, as one of the key structures of the early modern period.

As an arch synoptically enfolding the masque's action, the *Salmacida Spolia* 'frontispiece' unites all the functions of the structure, translating the temporal extent of verbal narrative into the synchronically-configured space of a planar construction. Physically, it offers an arch through which the court masquers will enter to participate in the final dance; itself embodying the platonic order Charles I was still anxious to project, and reflected also in the mathematical harmonies of its design. It also demarcates a larger conceptual border: as the façade of the final Caroline masque, it represents a cultural threshold between the ideological exclusiveness of an absolutist, transnational aristocracy and the shared power structures of a parliamentary government that would increasingly manifest itself aesthetically through print culture, represented and furthered by frontispieces accessible to a far wider, citizen readership. That this border is not so much porous but vulnerable to popular appropriation is shown in the printed frontispiece to Braithwait's work. Accessible to the new literate 'middling sort', it offers in its ostensible readership a synopsis to the book's contents. While these offer an instant statement of the welcome into the status of gentlefolk that the text lays out, the arch is a point of induction into this new order, so that the franchise is extended in the words of the text, the images of the arch, and the iconographical reference of the arch itself as a mark of welcome entry. Both of these arch forms make clear, in different ways, the powerful political dynamic from which they arose.

An index of this change, from presentational to printed and from elite to popular, is offered by another theatre design, the frontispiece for Shadwell's *The Tempest, or The Enchanted Island*, first performed on Thursday 7 November 1667. No illustration survives, but the stage direction preceding Act 1 makes plain the design:

> While the Overture is playing, the curtain rises, and discovers a new frontispiece, join'd to the great Pilasters, on each side of the Stage. This Frontispiece is a noble Arch, supported by large wreathed Columns of the Corinthian Order; the wreathings of the Columns are beautifi'd with Roses wound round them, and several Cupids flying about them. On the Cornice, just over the Capitals, sits on either side a Figure, with a Trumpet in one hand, and a Palm in the other, representing Fame. A little further on the same Cornice, on each side of a Compass-pediment, lie a Lion and a Unicorn, the Supporters of the Royal Arms of England. In the middle of the Arch are several Angels, holding the Kings Arms, as if they were placing them in the midst of that Compass-pediment.[2]

This description essentially catalogues the key features of the frontispieces, whether entry arch, theatrical fabric or the first page of a book. The use of columns—most often Corinthian, but frequently Doric or Ionian—is widespread. They instantly inflect the structure with a classical dignity, but they also define a central space, which functions as a portal for the monarch, an acting area, or a space to contain the book title, often in an elaborate font that echoes the dignity of the columns. In printed frontispieces, the roses wound around the columns of the Shadwell design find counterparts in foliage or strapwork, often of a highly formalised geometrical nature that may have a ritual or nationalistic significance in reflecting mathematically the hieratic harmony of the state. Flying Cupids are often introduced as a way of filling space on either side of the pediment, generally to crown with laurel a portrait or statue. Coats of arms are another common feature, supported as in *The Tempest* proscenium by royal beasts or other emblematic devices; and the figure of fame further reinforces the status of monarch, patron, or author. Angels add religious authority to that of the state, and are especially important in entry arches. In *The Tempest*, the impression is one of state power transferred to the theatre: while the iconography of royalty is used, this must be seen within the period's political circumstances. The use of the royal arms is far more than a statement of the granting of a Patent to the Drury Lane Theatre: it is a political imprimatur that proclaims the cultural hegemony of the royal court restored little more than a year before. The frontispiece is a complex verbal-visual statement of the narrative, action and symbolism of the play as the entry to which it functions: but that it needs explanation in Shadwell's direction, and commentary in the foregoing paragraph, reveals a problem implicit within the design of such structures, to which I shall return. This is their dependency on an audience highly educated in decrypting their meanings, without which they would paradoxically demand a verbal text to explain their elaborately inscribed visual meanings.

One other key difference separates the frontispieces of Jonson and Shadwell. One was produced for an elite concentration of onlooker-participants, the other for a theatre that, though patronised by a select group, was nonetheless public and defined by income rather than birth. Furthermore, the audience remains as passive spectators to the very end; there is no terminal communion in the grand dance, and no royal appearance: as so often in the process of cultural change, the form has been subtly shifted towards the larger demographic group, the culture now determined by parliament and commerce rather than monarch and court. At the same time, the shift to the verbal becomes more marked, in the use of a theatrical script far more extensive than that of the masque.

The supple traffic between theatre, progress and print is already evident much earlier in the trajectory of the form's growth. Structures celebrating the entry of a ruler into a town or province had been fashionable since the fifteenth century, largely making use of Biblical typology to show the stature of the prince or incorporating street theatres mounted by the guilds, in a clear line of descent from mediaeval mystery plays. The shift to a renaissance sensibility occurred in Italy, when the use of the Roman imperial entry took over as the basis of the referential imagery. Even at this stage, the elision between event and print was strong, with Petrarch's *I Trionfi* (1488) establishing the pattern of allegorical figures drawn in cars that was developed and in part satirised in Francesco Colonna's *Hypnerotamachia Poliphili*, one of the first books printed by Aldus Manutius, in 1499. By the mid-sixteenth century, the emphasis changed from the triumphal car to the triumphal archway. Henry II's entries into Lyon in 1548 and into Paris in the next year were made through classical arches designed on the geometric principles of the new architecture. From its first use, the new form gave structural inscription to ideological statements that were fundamental to contemporary notions of order and idea. The arch *à l'antique* simultaneously inflected the royal progress with classical authority and revealed it as an embodiment of harmony and just proportion through the mathematical principles on which the designs rested. At the same time, the panel above the central archway offered an ideal space for inscriptions of welcome, authority or allusion, that would offer a parallel statement of the arch's ideological and diplomatic purpose. In this way the columnar form, the mathematical symbolism and the verbal inscription fused together to present a single compound text of authority and rule.

That the growth of the triumphal arch was roughly contemporary with the development of print culture ensured close relations between state events and their inscription in word and image. The visual imprint of the triumphal arch spread rapidly throughout Europe in the architectural manuals of Alberti, Vitruvius and Serlio. Of these, the last is probably the most significant. Book III of the *Architettura* of Sebastiano Serlio was first published in Venice in 1540, and was quickly translated into French, German and Dutch. Such was the transnational nature of the printing trade that the blocks used for the editions printed in Antwerp and Basel were used again for the English version printed for Robert Peake in London in 1611, itself a translation from the 1606 Dutch version by Pieter Coecke van Aelst. The fourth chapter of Book III devotes many pages to the reproduction and discussion of classical arches, among which the account of the arch of Constantine is representative. (see Figure 1). Serlio's account describes it as 'wonderfull rich of Ornaments, Images, and divers Histories' and continues to give an accurate account of its measurements beginning 'the breadth of the greatest Arch is 22. Palmes and 24. minutes.'[3] The dedicatory text that appears on the main pedestal is introduced as follows: 'The Letters which stand here, are above the Arch, in the place marked A. besides many others, which stand in divers places of the Arch.' Implicit here is that a script is an essential component of the arch not only in print but in stone: the rhetoric of state is architectural, but it is also grammatical. In pragmatic political terms, this acts to impose the power of the nation on those witnessing the triumphal entry through the arch; aesthetically, it reveals the arch once more as a compound text designed to be read through a composite of verbal, mathematical and iconographical decryption; and at the same time it proleptically reveals the arch as a trope ideally suited for the 'entry' to a printed book through the form of a visually synoptic frontispiece.

Serlio's account delineates the three elements through which the arch constructs its meanings and cultural force: visual forms, either representational or emblematic;

proportions that are ideological as much as physical; and engraved texts extolling their patron. It is matched by a drawing of the arch, the significance of which lies as much in what it does not do as in what it does. Like almost all of the arches discussed, it is shown from directly in front, but in outline only, with the images, emblems and engraved texts omitted. In leaving the design blank, Serlio has facilitated its appropriation by other designers for use as another kind of entry—that which is provided for a book by an emblematic title page. That the arches are drawn not as architectural elevations, but in perspective, is also significant. Serlio's Second Book contains a discussion of perspective that includes the celebrated stage settings for Tragedy, Comedy and Pastoral which were so influential in scenography, first in Italy and then through the whole of Europe, influencing among many other designs those of Inigo Jones for Jonson's masques. Through the work of Serlio and others around the middle of the sixteenth century, the triumphal arch is established as a form that, developing in parallel with the new science of stage design, has all the necessary components of the emblematic frontispiece.

In 1604, a series of triumphal arches were designed by Stephen Harison or Harrison, which survive in the form of a remarkable collection of engravings with accompanying descriptions. They are amongst the most ornate of their kind, and again demonstrate the truly transnational nature not only of their design and iconography but of the aristocratic caste and its ideology that they inscribe. John Peacock describes them as 'teeming farragos of infelicitous detail, their chaos emphasised by a busy, rebarbative Flemish mannerist style.'[4] From an art-historical standpoint this is perfectly valid, but in terms of the larger cultural significance it diverts attention away from the fundamentally transnational nature of the arch, its use of visual conceits and references from a wide range of sources. As well as the emblematic devices, for example, the first arch (see Frontispiece), erected at Fenchurch Street, has a large panoramic view of the city of London, of a kind, earlier familiar from representations of cities in emblem books and travel literature, showing the crossover between state ritual and print culture: its inclusion here predates anything that would be presented on stage for many decades. It also further erased the boundaries between state ritual and popular theatre in visual and verbal manifestations: one of the niches contained not a sculpture but the living form of Edward Alleyn, who came forward and delivered a speech of welcome to the King. Harison's intricate and lovely drawings of the arches present them with no appreciable difference between live figures and statuary. What matters here is not only that the two forms are conjoined, the arch of state becoming the theatrical frontispiece or background against which heavily allegorical action or declamation takes place: in addition, there is the *sprezzatura* of the miraculous transformation of the statues into live musicians and speaking images, itself a frequent trope of Renaissance stage, epic and aesthetic theory, and now made real in a public celebration of kingship. Supple and imaginative though its unity of word and image is, the arch represents far more in symbolic terms: it is the word of divine kingship made manifest.

Another axis of cultural appropriation is shown in Harison's arch known as *Nova Fœlix Arabia*, which replaces the usual classical columns with obelisks in an 'Arabic' style. These were most likely borrowed from similar devices used for the entries of Henry II, and were later seen also in a number of printed frontispieces. As late as 1640 they were used as the flanking structures in William Marshall's design for Bacon's *Of the Advancement of Learning* (see Figure 2), surmounting plinths engraved with the words 'Scientia' and 'Philosophia'. This reveals a fascination with Eastern European iconography and belief, disclosing an unexpected but no less valid dimension of the transnationality of the period's cultural forms, and their assimilation into print culture as a visual synopsis of the book's verbal and conceptual structures.

Other forms introduce a similarly double overlap between aristocratic progress and print culture, word and image. One of the most remarkable examples of the triumphal arch is itself not an actual arch but a printed representation. In about 1512, Johannes Stabius, philosopher and astronomer to Maximilian I, engaged Albrecht Dürer to produce an image of an arch from 192 wood-block prints, measuring just under 3.5 x 3 metres (nearly 13 by 10 feet). The arch is covered with allegorical scenes, images of saints, and passages from the Bible. It has three portals, and at the focal point of the centre tower is a figure of Christ in Glory. Stabius himself wrote a prose key which, in a modern English translation, takes up over six pages of a double-column folio, clearly a different kind of relation between the twin texts.

The very extent of the annotations and the arch's visual symbolism betrays one of the key features of a triumphal arch which is to the present day onlooker most puzzling: what is the purpose of such complex statement, in both word and image, if it can only be understood through elaborate annotation in the single, less elevated medium of explanatory prose? Ben Jonson's explication of Harison's arches concludes that the emblems and devices

> ...might, without cloud, or obscurities, declare themselves to the sharpe and learned: And for the multitude, no doubt but their grounded judgements did gaze, said it was fine, and were satisfied.[5]

Discussing this passage, D. H. Gordon lays stress on the simple power of 'the appeal of mysteries and wonders.'[6] This is plainly true of an age where ballads and broadsheets record mysterious and miraculous happenings, but Jonson's statement has more to reveal about the social and political frame of these cultural objects. In a society where hierarchy is a primary organising principle, it is a logical inevitability that those of the lowest rank will not comprehend the complex visual allegories produced for the elite. The very sense of proportion implicit within the geometry of the arches is emblematic of the fact that, for the great mass of the people, its truths will be incomprehensible. The same principle may be seen in another architectural structure similar in form to many triumphal arches: the *eikonostasis* or icon-screen from the Greek Orthodox church, which itself moved across national and theological categories to become the screen and rood-screen in Catholic and

Protestant churches. One of its purposes was to display icons as objects of veneration and intercession, transformed in western Europe into carvings of saints; but its other key purpose was to maintain the mystery of the Eucharist.

This doubleness is apparent in the triumphal arch. While celebrating the divine power and grace of the ruler, it conceals the nature of this power—the heritage from which it derives, the typology that has anticipated it—from those most likely to see it. This is not necessarily an impediment to popular appreciation: the splendour remains while the allusions are unheard. The parallel between church and state, implicit in the use of arcane allusion and iconography, is another reinforcement of the divine right of rule; and the cultivation of a holy mystery generates a proper distance from the masses. It operates through a curious syllogistic proof of divine right: we do not understand, they do, therefore they have the right to power. Not for nothing did the concept, as well as the etymology, of propaganda originate in the Papal court. What is striking about the Dürer arch, of course, is that it was never seen by the masses since it was never an architectural structure. As Walter L. Strauss points out, producing the arch on paper had two clear advantages: 'It was much less costly, and it could be "constructed" simultaneously in many locations.'[7] Approximately 700 copies were produced over a two year period, and distributed throughout the Holy Roman Empire.

This is not to say that all such structures worked through elaborately restricted codes of meaning. The Arch of Constantine is echoed in the outdoor stages erected for the *landjuweels* or popular, open air theatrical performances in the Low Countries.[8] In addition, whereas these theatre designs are the sites of *tableaux vivants*, with actors holding static poses to represent important events or myths, Harington's arches include spaces for musicians or performers who come forward to deliver speeches at the appearance of the king: the same visual identity is consequently embedded in quite different patterns of movement. The Dutch stagings are often reproduced in books that record performances, offering another kind of stasis: the same is true of the arches, which Harington reproduced as engravings. Interestingly, they show no difference between the statuary and the living performers. All are enfolded into a single emblematic and performative actuality held together by underlying conceit or myth. One other point is significant. It is remarkable not only that the forms echo those of the Low Countries as well as the more formal triumphal arches, and their implied rhetoric of power, of the Italian city-states, but that a fundamentally similar structure is adopted by a genuinely popular form of street theatre, which in turn is adopted by the city guilds. Aristocratic, bourgeois and folk culture are thus briefly aligned through the shared structures of the arch or frontispiece.

While carved ornaments, emblems and statues are dominant, some arches convey the historical schemes from which they gain power through painted narratives. In so doing, they are moving across yet another medial boundary, that between three-dimensional action or representation—the live orator or its carved simulacrum—and its two dimensional presentation. This marks a key shift from a primarily theatrical mode—the varieties of tableau vivant—to one innately pictorial and static. The significance here is in its preparing the way—opening the door, so to speak—for the pictorial, narrative frontispiece that will come to dominate, as an entity separate from the title page, and lacking in all but a tiny minority of cases its emblematic or synoptic nature, from the eighteenth century.

One of the reasons for the abundant possibilities of transmediation and thematic application of the frontispiece is the basic structure of the triumphal arch. The existence of the central arch is not only a means of ceremonial entrance but, on different scales and in different media, a performance space and an ideal location for typography. The classical Roman origin of the arch, stressed in accounts from Serlio to Ogilby, invites the presence of familiar architectural formations of plinths, columns or caryatids: the presence of figures in niches allows all kinds of allegorical embodiments that can readily be adapted to a range of purposes in a printed book. It is this pattern that allows for the most variation and allusiveness. Once the pattern is established, in a sense every printed frontispiece is an iconographical reference to the arch of triumph, providing a rich source both of serious allusive textural amplification and ironic and satiric undermining.

All of this meant that, through the development of the triumphal arch as an elite form expressive of rule and order, the use of its geometrical structures offered an ideal way of imposing the power of the book as a prestigious cultural object upon the reader, conferring upon him or her the right of ducal entry into its contents and intellectual possession of its arcane secrets. One of the earliest and finest examples of the traffic between arch and page is provided in an edition of the *Bucolica* of Virgil produced in1481 for the Venetian Agostini family by Antonio di Bartolommeo Miscomini.[9] The page presents an architectural figure, based on a triumphal arch, with two columns rising from square plinths and a large pediment all embellished with foliage and natural forms. At the foot, a group of putti is shown in profile; the whole is produced in thin washes of stone colour, to further the impression of a solid architectural form. Yet even in such an early instance of the form, play is made on the generic identities that are being elided. The text that occupies the space between the columns is presented as if inscribed on a large banner suspended by two crimson ropes from the corners of the pediment. The impression is of a painted representation of an actual triumphal arch itself impinging on the identity of a text, and this is heightened by the presentation of a border of clear blue sky on the right hand side of the page. While this is not a title-page as such, it appears near the very opening of the volume, and clearly suggests the idea of an entry. The notion of the wealthy collector entering the domain of the antique text just conquered is embedded quite appropriately within the imagery of the imperial entry into the newly-subjugated town. Given the mercantilist interests of the Agostini, the link between cultural object and annexation is doubly fitting: the book becomes an object of possession as well as an *objet de vertú*.

Once begun, the tradition of title pages as imperial architectural forms, with or without allusion to dramatic action, continues throughout Europe for the next two centuries, reaching the climax of visual and verbal complexity in the seventeenth century. The structure's adaptability is demonstrated, for example, in the frontispiece to John Gerard's *The Herball or Generall Historie of Plantes* (London, 1633) (see Figure 3). The title is presented in a central cartouche, flanked by Corinthian columns outside which are niches occupied on the left by Theophrastus and on the right by Dioscorides, Ceres and Pomona above, and elaborate displays of flowers and herbs beneath, with the author's portrait between them, complete the design. The link with the entry lies in the presentation in visual terms of the key elements of the book, offering a conceptual way in to its contents. Echoes of theatre are manifest in the facing figures in the two niches, who stand as if having just entered from the tiring house of an early baroque stage. The design is infinitely adaptable: Æneas with Anchises (*The XII Æneids*, 1632) and a skeleton and an anatomical study (*The Workes of that famous Chirurgeon Ambrose Parey*, 1634), are significant but by no means unusual examples of the way in which the oppositional columnar structure can be manipulated to express a tension or guiding principle of the book, often with emblematic details that convey its content in concentrated form.

Sometimes the avoidance of the pattern of classical columns or allegorical figures can be significant in itself. The edition of Horapollion's *Hieroglyphiques* produced by Pierus (Lyon, 1615) replaces the columns with two obelisks on plinths, one topped with a crescent moon and the other with a sun, both embellished with geometric strapwork. This not only conveys immediately the content of the volume, described in the subtitle as a *commentaire des lettres et figures sacrées des Ægyptiens and autres nations,* but immediately asserts the value of such cultural objects as equivalent to those deriving from classical origins. The presence of semi-naturalistic images of rulers from the four continents in the corners of the page, and a portrait of the author at the top centre, furthers an established pattern, in the process drawing the exotic within the ambit of the familiar. The central plaque, occupying the space of the entry arch, gives the title and subtitle. Such was the influence of this that Nicolaus Caussin's *Polyhistor Symbolicus*, published in Paris in 1618, adopts a near-identical structure of the two obelisks, again topped by a sun and moon. Here, though, the thrust of the book is again related to a European concept of an Egyptian belief-system, transationalism is demonstrated not through dynastic interweaving but through the power of intellectual and mercantile colonialism.

The most effective printed versions of the arch formula are those that play on the two formal identities within which they operate. The 1623 edition of *Les Oeuvres de Pierre Ronsard* for example, presents the figures of Venus and Mars leaning against pairs of Doric columns, to embody love and war, the two major concerns of the writer and the text found through the arch. Before the pediment, beside Ronsard himself and crowning him with laurels, sit Homer and Virgil. What is striking here is not only the transmediation of the architectural form: it is also the presence of Venus and Mars as *trompe l'oeil* real figures, not sculptures in niches but actual figures presented as characters acting before a high Renaissance stage, while the two classical writers sit above, watching as befits two literary giants, from the gods. The whole is a meticulous balance between self-reflexive wit and classical decorum, all achieved within the medial fusions of the arch tradition.

A more direct allusion to the entry as such is found in the emblematic frontispiece designed for Michael Drayton's *Polyolbion* by W. Hole (see Figure 4). This approaches in complexity the elaborate arches erected for European rulers, but its critical apparatus is more compact: a short poem in decasyllabic couplets names the figures, to which are added glosses and commentary notes. What is striking here is not the presence of Albion, allegorically portrayed as a Ceres-Astræa figure in the centre, or the figures of her historical rulers— Brute, Caesar, Hengist and King James—in place of the columns and above the pediment. The link is made explicit by the poem's opening:

> Through a *Triumphant Arch*, see *Albion* plas't,
> In *Happy* site, in *Neptunes* armes embras't,
> In *Power* and *Plenty*, on hir *Cleevy* Throne
> Circled with Natures Ghirlands, being alone
> Stil'd *th'Oceans Island.*[10]

In a printed frontispiece, the allegorical representation of the nation is placed identically with the monarch at the moment of entry into the city through the arch—the moment of the assumption of power. That this is not an actual but an allegorical monarch in no way diminishes this power: a cornucopia in one hand and the sceptre of state in the other, clothed in a robe embellished with mountains, trees, rivers and buildings to emblematise the state, two cupids laying a wreath of laurel on her head, while another representing fame flies across above; the figure is a compendium of Renaissance visual devices of rule. That the two lowest figures have their feet extended just over the plinths on which they stand is a further transmedial play: it suggests that these are real figures placed within the arch, in the manner in which musicians and actors were located in the arches of Stephen Harington and others. State, stage and page are all brought together in this hieratic visualisation of the entry into a literary kingdom.

It would, of course, be absurd to pretend that all title-page frontispieces followed this pattern. Many of the most effective deliberately reject it. Aldus Manutius, the finest Renaissance typographer and book designer, followed the earlier style of having a very simple typographic title page, instead using his famous dolphin and anchor colophon at the end of the volume as imprimatur. His edition of *Hypnerotomachia Polyphili* —the first, published in 1499—contains extremely elaborate figures based on triumphal arches, fountains, obelisks and other structures that would later be used frequently in emblematic title-pages, but as wood cut illustrations within the text, not as an entry through which the reader must pass towards it. Clearly, the phenomenon is not universal: but in its transnational currency, that extends beyond the pan-European to embrace iconographies for Ottoman and Egyptian conventions, and frequently makes self-referential play with the generic elisions of theatre, stage and print, the frontispiece constitutes one of the major forms of the period in its multivalent interactions of theatre, statecraft, political and intellectual hegemony and cultural appropriation. And within it remains a mysterious, and multifarious, set of relationships between word and image, in whatever physical form and political frame it appears.

Notes

1 *Arrival of Henri III at Venice*. c.1593: Venice, Palazzo Ducale, Sala della quatro porte.

2 *The Tempest, or the Enchanted Island*, by Thomas Shadwell. *The Complete Works of Thomas Shadwell*, edited by Montague Summers. 5 Vols. (London: The Fortune Press, 1927). Vol. 2 199.

3 Sebastiano Serlio. *The Five Books of Architecture: An Unabridged Reprint of the English Edition of 1611*. (New York: Dover, 1982). The third Booke, f.54 verso.

4 *The Stage Designs of Inigo Jones: The European Context*. (Cambridge: Cambridge UP, 1995) 63.

5 *B. Jonson his part of King James his Royall and Magnificent Entertainment through his Honorable Cittie of London, Thursday the 15. of March. 1603. Ben Jonson*. Edited by C. H. Herford and Percy and Evelyn Simpson. (Oxford: Clarendon UP VII, 1941). 91.

6 'Roles and Mysteries', *The Renaissance Imagination: Essays and Lectures by D. H. Gordon*, collected and edited by Stephen Orgel. (Berkeley, Los Angeles and London: U of California P, 1975) 14.

7 Walter L. Strauss, *The wood-cuts and Wood Engravings of Albrecht Dürer* (New York: Abaris Books, 1980), 55.

8 These are fully discussed in Kernodle, George Riley. *From Art to Theatre: Form and Convention in the Renaissance*. (Chicago : U of Chicago P, 1944, rev. 1947).

9 *Prima (-decima) egloga della bucolica di V. B. pulci di latino in vulgare traducta*. Anthonium Bartholomei Miscomini: Florentie?, 1481. British Library, London, shelfmark IA.27156 The volume is also known under the title of a later edition, *Bucoliche elegantissimamente composte da B. Pulci*.

10 *Poly-Olbion. Or A Chronographicall description of Tracts, rivers, Mountaines, Forests, and other Parts of this renowned Isle of Great Britaine...Digested in a Poem By Michael Drayton, Esq.* London: Printed by H. L. for Mathew Lownes; I. Browne; I. Helme, and I. Bushe, 1613. Quotation from 'Upon the Frontispiece', ii.

2. Titian's *Poesie* and Shakespeare's Pictures

Shormishtha Panja

In spite of the paragone, or rivalry of the poets and painters and the claim by Lessing that the two have distinct areas of operation, the painter spatial and the poet temporal 'in its imitations painting uses completely different means or signs than does poetry, namely figures and colours in space rather than articulated sounds in time,'[1] if we look at Alberti or Sidney, it is more common to see the historian and philosopher posited as rivals to poets rather than painters. The painters and poets, if anything, are seen as allied professionals (and the Renaissance was the age in which the whole idea of professionalism in the arts was initiated) with much to learn from one another. Alberti, the renowned Renaissance *uomo universale* and probably the first Renaissance theorist of art, advises artists in the third book of his treatise *On Painting* (1435–36) to consort with poets in order to better their 'invention,' the source of beauty, pleasure and renown: 'Phidias, more than the other famous painters, confessed that he had learned from Homer, the poet, how to paint Jove with much divine majesty' (Alberti 91). At the core of *On Painting* lies Alberti's notion of the *istoria* and the very use of the metaphor links art to narrative. Alberti's *istoria* is to art what Aristotle's plot is to tragedy: it is the unifying principle that links all the different elements of a work of art together so that it has the maximum effect on the viewer, even the untutored one. It incorporates variety in moderation, dignity, excites pleasure and wins the creator praise and admiration.[2] Sidney in his *Apology for Poetry* (1595) speaks of poetry as 'an art of imitation, a representing, counterfeiting or figuring forth—to speak metaphorically, a speaking picture—with this end to teach and delight' (*Apology* 18). Sidney adds that just as a long gown does not make one an advocate, similarly mere 'rhyming and versing' do not make a poet; rather, 'it is that feigning notable images of virtues, vices, or what else, with that delightful teaching, which must be the right describing note to know a poet by' (*Apology* 21). Once again Sidney uses the metaphor of the artist to describe the characteristic features of the poet—'counterfeiting or figuring forth', 'feigning...images.' The sustainer of both painting and poetry is life, nature, but nature is also their most alarming enemy. Can a juxtaposition and analysis of the verbal and the visual in any way illumine problems of mimesis and representation, of the poets and painters' awareness of the constructedness of their work? Can an overlapping vocabulary, be it in terms of visual syntax, ekphrasis, verbal chiaroscuro, overlap or visual metaphor and metonymy better equip one to read paintings and view literary texts? How does the frozen image free itself in painting and approach narrative, and how does a poem's image clusters provide a meditation on nature and time? Does the analysis of the interrelation of the visual and the literary yield any commentary on artistic scope and function? These are some of the issues explored in this essay.

This essay deals with two poems and two paintings: Shakespeare's *Venus and Adonis* and *The Rape of Lucrece* and Titian's paintings, *Venus and Adonis* and *Tarquin and Lucretia.* Both poems and paintings are companion pieces, in that they are two parts of a pair.

Shakespeare's poems are addressed to the same patron and composed within a year of each other (1593, 1594). The dedication of the first to Henry Wriothesley, Earl of Southampton reads:

'Right Honourable, I know not how I shall offend in dedicating my unpolished lines to your lordship, nor how the world will censure me for choosing so strong a prop to support so weak a burden. Only, if your honour seem but pleased, I account myself highly praised, and vow to take advantage of all idle hours till I have honoured you with some graver labour.'

The promised 'graver labour' is *The Rape of Lucrece* which appears the following year. The ardent tone of dedication is very different from the diffident tone of the *Venus and Adonis* dedication:

'The love I dedicate to your lordship is without end, whereof this pamphlet without beginning is but a superfluous moiety.... What I have done is yours; what I have to do is yours, being part in all I have, devoted yours.'[3]

The series of paintings of mythological subjects composed between 1550–62, Titian termed his *poesie* or *favole*. The *Venus and Adonis* along with the *Danae* and four others were made for Philip II of Spain. In a 1554 letter to his patron, Titian writes that he wants *Venus and Adonis* and the *Danae* to be seen as companion pieces:

'And as the Danae which I have already sent to your Majesty is seen from the front, I wanted to vary it in this other *poesie*, showing the figure from a different view; thus the room they are to hang will be more appealing.'[4]

In the *Danae* (1553–54) the female form is seen from the front (modelled on Michelangelo's *Night* in Medici Chapel 1524–33) and in *Venus and Adonis* it is seen from the back (in a Mannerist rather than High Renaissance manner).

Venus and Adonis

The source for Shakespeare's epyllion is mainly Ovid's *Metamorphoses* X. Arthur Golding's English translation which appeared in 1567 says that this book is 'reproving most prodigious lusts.' Shakespeare's poem, however, is quite dissimilar to Ovid. The overt physicality of Venus is never stressed in Ovid. In fact, initially, mimicking Adonis's liking for the hunt, Ovid's Venus resembles Diana in her garb and pursuits. There is no hectic and, more importantly, one-sided amorous pursuit. Adonis and Venus share a few quiet moments together, spent mostly in telling stories. Adonis never resists Venus' overtures. As is the case with many Renaissance adaptations of classical sources, in Shakespeare the Ovidian tale is combined with medieval erotic poetry. Here, the Petrarchan motif of the cold, unwilling, distant recipient of the lover's ardour is included, but with a twist. In Petrarchan sonnets, it is the female beloved who resists her male lover. Here, it is the green and callow Adonis, more boy than man, who frostily but resolutely repulses the advances of none other than the goddess of love, albeit a sweating, melting and dissolving goddess of love. He of 'the heavy, dark, disliking eye' (l.182) would much prefer, he tells her, to 'hunt the boar with certain of his friends' (l.588): 'the…boy…blushed and pouted in full disdain/ With leaden appetite, unapt to toy' (l.32–34).[5] Shakespeare's Venus uses the stock Petrarchan image of the deer to represent the hotly pursued beloved: 'I'll be a park, and thou shalt be my deer' she tells Adonis (l.231), but she is obviously much more than the soft green grass he'll graze on: if he's the deer, she's the hunter.

Shakespeare comically twists another Petrarchan convention, the catalogue or blazon of the mistress's charms by the dazzled lover. Here, it is Venus who does her own cataloguing and blazoning:

> Were I hard-favoured, foul, or wrinkled-old,
> Ill-nurtured, despised, rheumatic, and cold,
> Thick-sighted, barren, lean, and lacking juice,
> Then mightst thou pause, for then I were not for thee.
> But having no defects, why dost abhor me? (l.139–143)[6]

As is evident from this declaration, it is Shakespeare's Venus who is the real eye-opener. She encompasses everything and is, true to her mythical nature, a bundle of contradictions. She is so light that the flower stems are like tree trunks that hold her up ('Witness this primrose bank whereon I lie,' she confides to Adonis, 'These forceless flowers like sturdy trees support me…' (l.151–52)); she is so brawny that she thinks nothing of tucking Adonis under her arm before moving swiftly to a better location for dalliance: 'Over one arm, the lusty courser's rein; Under her other was the tender boy' (l.31–32). Her fingers are as white and fragile as lilies but her grip is a grip of iron: 'And whence from thence he struggles to be gone, She locks her lily fingers one in one' (l.227–28).

Shakespeare puts his classical learning to good use in the portrait of Venus. If we examine the mythical etymology of this figure we will see that contradiction is Venus's middle name. In one of the earliest references, Pausanius' speech in Plato's *Symposium*, there is a reference to two Venuses and not one:

'And am I not right in asserting that there are two goddesses? The elder one, having no mother, who is called the heavenly Aphrodite—she is the daughter of Uranus; the younger, who is the daughter of Zeus and Dione—her we call common; and the love who is her fellow worker is rightly named common, as the other love is called heavenly' (*Dialogues of Plato* 177).[7]

Amor Vulgaria is the name given by Ficino in his *Convito* to Venus Genetrix, the Venus related to nature and honourable procreation. He thought lust too debased an emotion to be associated with Venus.[8] The other Venus was given the name Venus Coelistis.

If we look at Titian's *Sacred and Profane Love* (1514), at times attributed to both Titian and Giorgione, his guru, we see two women, one sumptuously dressed and the other partially clothed in wispy drapes. While the dress and posture of the two vary, we are struck by the facial resemblance. Panofsky argues that they ought to be called the twin Venuses.[9] The two Venuses, sacred and profane, are closely related. Note the contrast in dress and in landscape behind either figure—Panofsky terms it *paysage moralisé*—behind one (Profane) a fortified town with a hare and a rabbit symbolising procreation and fertility, behind the other (Sacred) a church spire and a flock of sheep. It is not just the facial resemblance but also the attitude of one towards the other that is significant: Panofsky observes that the celestial Venus does not regard the other with disdain but rather with an air of gentle persuasion. There is no dichotomy between the two Venuses—they but represent two orders of being. Although the two figures are reminiscent of Hercules's choice between good and evil in paintings such as Carracci's *Choice of Hercules* (*c.* 1596); in such paintings Virtue is fully clothed, unlike Titian's portrayal of Sacred Love as partially naked. Both Titian and Shakespeare are alike in that they do not condemn the Venus associated with physicality and with procreation. Shakespeare sees her drives as natural as the many woodland creatures she identifies with: the jennet, the courser, the hare and the eagle. In the work of Titian there is a similar naturalness, an immediacy, in the approach to Venus. In his *Venus Anadyomene* (*c.* 1520) Venus is like any rustic young woman, drying her hair after a bath. The curve of the body is more pronounced and more realistic, given her action, than that of the composed and elegant classical *Cnidian Aphrodite* by Praxiteles. Titian's Venus's naturalness becomes clear in contrast with Giorgione's *Dresden Venus* (*c.* 1501) or Sleeping Venus—Kenneth Clark famously described Giorgione's Venus as a bud, while Titian's *Venus of Urbino* was a full-blown rose.[10] Fritz Saxl calls Giorgione's figure a classical marble statue lying on the grass, remote, eyes shut, lost in her own reverie.[11] Titian's *Venus of Urbino* (1538) is, by contrast, wide awake, brazenly looking out at the viewer. Her body weighs down the rumpled sheets: it does not float above them. This is a woman, not a goddess, completely demythologised and naturalised. Saxl rightly compares her to a woman at her toilet, her fully dressed attendants hovering in the background.

Let us turn now to Titian's *Venus and Adonis* (1553–54) (see Figure 5). More than thirty painted and engraved versions of this survive today. Some were painted by Titian himself; others were produced by members of his workshop. Panofsky suggests that this painting is a source for Shakespeare's poem, saying that it was unusual to depict Venus and Adonis as parting, and that Titian was the first to paint this. Shakespeare may have known of the painting. Philip II of Spain was the consort of the English Queen Mary I (in a 1554 letter to Titian, Philip complained of paint being scraped off in transit) and prints were made of it by Guilio Sanuto (1559) and Martino Rota (*c.*1520–83) and widely circulated.[12] Certain lines in *Venus and Adonis,* Panofsky claims, are an exact description of the Titian scene:

With this he breaketh from the sweet embrace
Of those fair arms which bound him to her breast,
And homeward through the dark laund runs apace,
Leaves love upon her back, deeply distressed. (l. 811ff)

However, scholars have pointed out that the 'Leave taking of Adonis'[13] motif goes all the way back to classical art. John Doebler mentions one of the sources: a high relief from a second century AD Roman sarcophagus in the Lateran Museum.[14]

How does visual image encompass narrative, free rather than freeze time? Let us look at the painting more closely. Panofsky calls this a night scene, but actually day is breaking. There is tremendous movement incorporated within an apparently static image. The twisted torso of Venus is seen from the back in a typically Mannerist fashion. As she twists around, her leg overturns a jug of wine. The fact that the jug is empty suggests that they have spent the night together and now Adonis will depart for the hunt. The scene is one of disarray. Note the detail of the overturned jug. It is an integral part of the visual syntax—Venus has overturned it as she spins around to detain Adonis. The jug is empty, suggesting the end of revelry. Titian does not even bother to show Venus from the front—even though she is the goddess of beauty. Note the dirty soles of her feet—again this detail is part of the visual syntax that suggests the duration of the time the two have spent together. The dirty soles are also part of the naturalising, demythologising process.[15] The sleeping Cupid figure is another sign of time's duration: Cupid has fallen asleep in the process of watching over his mother and Adonis.

Apart from visual syntax there is visual metaphor. The three large hounds straining at their leash suggest the conflict within Adonis. One hound is eager to leave: he looks outward, while another dithers, facing the ground. Similarly, Adonis' face looks down at Venus, but his body is already turned to go. In both painting and verse, one notes a naturalness and immediacy of observation—there is none of affectedness of Lyly, for example, in Shakespeare's portrayal of Venus or the classical 'marble' appearance of Giorgione's *Dresden Venus* in Titian's painting. And one of the ways in which this naturalness finds expression is in the use of animals.[16] As one critic puts it, in this poem we can sense the Warwickshire loam sticking to Shakespeare's shoes. Venus asks Adonis to hunt the 'dew-bedabbled wretch' the hare, not realising that he too will become as helpless and frantic a victim once the boar attacks him:

How he outruns the wind, and with what care
He cranks and crosses with a thousand doubles. (l.679–80)

When Venus glimpses Adonis' bloody bruised body, her horrified recoil is like that of

...the snail, whose tender horns being hit
Shrinks backward in his shelly cave with pain,
And there, all smothered up, in shade doth sit...
So at his bloody view her eyes are fled
Into the deep dark cabins of her head (l.1033ff)

Apart from visual metaphors in the poem, there are also visual symbols in the painting. Sleeping Cupid in Titian's painting represents not just cold love but Adonis' doom as does the pronated arm of Adonis.[17] As Rosand suggests, the leashes biting into the flesh of Adonis's arm suggest Christ's arms twisted and tied to the cross as in Bellini's *Crucifixion* c. 1455–60. The association with love and a tragic, early death made it quite common for the figures of Adonis and Christ to be compared. In Shakespeare's poem, the Christian frame of reference is hinted at when Venus turns at the end of the poem from Amazonian lover to frail, discarded nymph, from a yearning romantic to a *mater dolorosa*—a grieving mother, modelled on Mary at the time of Christ's crucifixion and death. She cradles the purple anemone that rises from Adonis's blood in place of the lost beloved:

Here was thy father's bed, here in my breast,
Thou art the next of blood, and 'tis thy right.
Lo, in this hollow cradle take thy rest;
My throbbing heart shall rock thee day and night. (l.1183ff)

The Rape of Lucrece

The last section of this essay discusses Shakespeare's long poem *The Rape of Lucrece* and Titian's *Tarquin and Lucretia* (before 1571). In two other visual representations of Lucrece, one by Cranach in 1533 and the other by Artemesia Gentilleschi *c.* 1611, both depict Lucrece at the moment of suicide, the suicide that was critiqued by St. Augustine.[18] However, Titian chooses to focus on the rape. Shakespeare, too, does not elide the moment of rape in his poem, unlike his two literary sources, Ovid in *Fasti* and Chaucer in *The Legend of Good Women*. In Titian's painting, the scene is presented as an artifact. Titian wants the viewer to be aware of the reflexive quality of the work. The scene is staged, surrounded by thick curtains, and there is even a viewer. The young boy is perhaps Tarquin's page, holding the drapes up, or a frightened peeping Tom who cannot tear his eyes away from the frightful scene. Tarquin is fully dressed, Lucretia is naked, emphasising her vulnerability. Tarquin's hose is bright red, the colour associated with blood and fire, therefore representing through visual metaphor Tarquin's turbulent, uncontrolled passion.[19]

While Titian's depiction of the scene *is* a painting, in Shakespeare's poem based on the same story, after being raped by Tarquin, the distraught Lucrece observes, 'a piece/ Of skilful painting' (l. 1366–67) of the Fall of Troy. None of the sources of the poem, Livy's *History*, Ovid's *Fasti*, and Chaucer's *Legend of Good Women*, contain ekphrasis. Ekphrasis which can be defined in James A. W. Heffernan's neat formulation as a 'verbal representation of visual representation,' (Heffernan 3) a representation that is 'dynamic and obstetric; it typically delivers *from* the pregnant moment of visual art its embryonically narrative impulse' (Heffernan 5).[20] There are a number of techniques used by Shakespeare in this ekphrastic passage that mimics the art of the painter. One is in the use of overlap. Gombrich quotes a passage from Philostratus' *Imagines* which elucidates the trick of the artist to mimic the movement of the eye. Explaining why the men around Thebes are represented in bits and pieces, Philostratus writes, 'some are seen in full figure, others with the legs hidden, others from the waist up, then only the busts of some, heads only, helmets only, and finally just spearpoints. All that, my boy, is just analogy for the eyes must be deceived as they travel back along with the relevant zones of the picture.'[21]
In *The Rape of Lucrece* we have the lines

For much imaginary work was there;
Conceit delightful, so compact, so kind,
That for Achilles' image stood his spear,
Grip'd in an armed hand; himself behind,
Was left unseen, save to the eye of the mind:
A hand, a foot, a face, a leg, a head,
Stood for the whole to be imagined. (l. 1422ff)

In this use of metonymy, a verbal figure, ('That for Achilles' image stood his spear') we have an exact verbal correspondence of the visual technique, overlap. Overlap, then, is a kind of visual metonymy.

There are other ways in which the visual and the verbal correspond. If we can speak of visual syntax in Titian (more prevalent in *Venus and Adonis* than here), we can speak of verbal chiaroscuro in Shakespeare. Speaking of the Trojan mothers seeing their young sons in armour, Shakespeare writes

And to their hope they such odd action yield
That through light joy seemed to appear
(Like bright things stained) a kind of heavy fear (l. 1433–35)

The use of the word 'light' emphasises the mirroring between visual and verbal—light can mean light-hearted, but it can also suggest luminosity—a pride that brightens the mothers' faces, irradiates them from within. Thus the mingling of joy and foreboding on the mothers' faces has a similar effect both in technique and in the emotive effect of the work sought to be created by the painter's use of chiaroscuro.

One of the earliest examples of ekphrasis is, of course, Homer's description of Achilles's shield in the *Iliad* (Bk. 18, l. 478ff).[22] Let us examine this description for a moment. Homer describes a number of scenes depicted on the shield by Hephaestos. One scene melts into the next, like a sequence of images in a film, until the reader is fully immersed in the little stories told by those images, for those images also contain narrative, and is momentarily oblivious of the larger narrative of which this shield is a tiny part: the story of the Trojan war. What techniques does Homer use to create a sense of movement within apparent pictorial stasis? One of the ways is by spanning out and then zooming in to a tiny little detail—combining telescopic vision with microscopic vision.[23] The young men and young girls 'holding hands at the wrist' depicted on the shield (line 394) share space with 'the tireless sun and the moon waxing into her fullness' (line 484). Shakespeare employs a similar technique in the ekphrastic passage in *The Rape of Lucrece*:

> Perjured Sinon, whose enchanting story
> The credulous old Priam after slew;
> Whose words like wildfire burnt the shining glory
> Of rich built Ilion, that the skies were sorry;
> And little stars shot from their fixed places,
> When their glass fell wherein they viewed their faces. (l. 1521–26)

The vastness of the sky shrinks into the intimate looking glass of the little stars. Here, telescopic vision is not just juxtaposed with microscopic: telescopic vision narrows down to the microscopic.

This technique is not the only one. What is most arresting of the techniques used is the frozen image which then liquefies and turns into narrative. In Homer we have movement suggested through the continuous use of participle and other -ing forms—bellowing, reaping, singing, dancing, setting, 'happily watching,' urging, 'holding hands at the wrist.' This sense of swirling movement catches us up in the movement of each scene, each story on the shield, be it of grape-gatherers, farmers, women scattering 'white barley' 'for workmen to eat' young men and women dancing—to the extent that we forget that the scenes are fixed. The marriage scene blends into that of the marketplace, full of bustling, quarrelling people; this is followed by and by with scenes of herdsmen with their flocks and ploughmen tilling the land. The sudden inclusion of details of gold and tin and blue enamel—the materials used to make the shield—wrench us into an awareness of narrative yielding to frozen image, verbal movement yielding to visual stasis. ('There they sat down in place shrouding themselves in the bright bronze' l. 522; 'The earth darkened behind them and looked like earth that has been ploughed/though it was gold' l. 548–49). Why does Homer deliberately shatter the moment of verisimilitude which he has so carefully wrought? Is it to make us aware of the shield as an artifact and of the workman's skill ('Such was the wonder of the shield's forging' l. 549)? This underlining of the artistic skill required to create the scene is reminiscent of the use of drapery in Titian's painting—Titian frames bedroom scenes with heavy drapes and includes a viewer—these details call attention to the painting as an artifact and underline its reflexive quality. In *Tarquin and Lucretia* with the use of the drapery he calls deliberate attention to the scene as a staged, carefully arranged, moment of violence. In the *Iliad* the reflexive quality of the artistic work calls attention through the highlighting of Hephaestus's skill to Homer's own expertise. But it can also serve another purpose. This becomes clear when we look once again at Shakespeare's poem.

In Shakespeare's poem, the frozen image of Sinon is juxtaposed with the narrative of Troy's fall. In fact, Shakespeare wrenches the reader out of the chronological account of the fall of Troy to dwell on the image of Sinon:

> In him the painter laboured with his skill
> To hide deceit, and give the harmless show (l. 1506–7)

Why does Shakespeare do this? Sinon is certainly not the central figure in the story of Troy. The simple answer is of course the one given in the poem—the duplicity of Sinon reminds Lucrece of Tarquin's deceit:

> So fair a form lodged not a mind so ill.
> And still on him she gazed, and gazing still,
> Such signs of truth in his plain face she spied,
> That she concludes the picture was belied. (l. 1530–33)

Could there be another reason? Could it be that Shakespeare is talking about the function of art and its limitations here? The use of the word 'deceit' reminds one of Sidney's use of the word 'counterfeit' to describe the poet's creations: 'Poesy therefore is an art of imitation...that is to say, a representing, counterfeiting, or figuring forth' (*Apology* 18). The word 'counterfeit' suggests a discrepancy between what is on the surface and what lies within. The word 'counterfeiter' meant both imitator and deceptive imitator from the fourteenth century onwards. Puttenham, for example, calls the poet both maker and counterfeiter. Questions about the truth value of art have been posed from the time of Plato's *Republic*. Aristotle argued for art's organic existence and intrinsic value. The rules of art governed it, not the rules of life. Sidney worked his way around it by stating that, 'Now for the poet, he nothing affirms, and therefore never lieth' (*Apology* 57). However, one can argue that the poet's skill too is a kind of deceit, a deceit that tries to convince us that the artefact is real and natural: 'In scorn of nature, art gave liveless life,' (l. 1374) as Shakespeare writes in *The Rape of Lucrece*. The struggle of art with nature and time continues. For all Sidney's talk of the golden world of the poet which renders nature's world brazen, there is a nagging anxiety, a doubt at the back of his mind that his poetic creation is a mere bubble, a 'figuring forth' without any real substance.

It is no accident that Sinon in Shakespeare's ekphrasis is a teller of tales, much like Sidney's poet who 'with a tale…holdeth children from play and old men from the chimney corner.' (*Apology* 38):

Perjured Sinon, whose enchanting story
The credulous old Priam after slew; (l. 1521–22)

The contrast between Sinon's outward appearance and the inner truth of his character could be a sign that art, be it poetry or painting, can be said to be 'belied' i.e. untruthful. It is significant that it is not the detractors of poetry and painting who say this but the very practitioners themselves, and the most skilled ones at that. The reflexivity of artists serves the function of not just drawing attention to the artist's skill but to the 'liveless' quality of art. In this, poet and painter are not rivals but partners, alike frustrated by nature's effortless abundance and variety. As is painting so is poetry, *ut pictura poesis*.

Notes

1 See G.E. Lessing, *Laocoon: An Essay on the Limits of Painting and Poetry* trans. Edward Allen McCormick (Indianapolis: Bobbs Merrill, 1962), 78.

2 See Alberti, *On Painting* trans. Herbert T. Spencer (New Haven: Yale UP, 1966).

3 Muriel Bradbrook refers to the 'aristocratic boldness and freedom' of the dedication (see Muriel Bradbrook, 'Beasts and Gods: the Social Purpose of *Venus and Adonis*' in *Muriel Bradbrook on Shakespeare* (Sussex: Harvester Press, 1984, 54,) but to me it suggests an ardent, perhaps intimate, relationship.

4 Quoted by David Rosand in '*Ut Pictor Poeta:* Meaning in Titian's Poesie' *New Literary History* 3 (1972): 527–46, 535.

5 See William Shakespeare *The Poems* ed. John Roe (1992; Cambridge: Cambridge UP, 2006). All quotations are from this edition.

6 See Katherine Eisaman Maus's introduction to the poem in *The Norton Shakespeare* eds. Stephen Greenblatt et al. (New York: Norton, 1997) 601–6.

7 *Dialogues of Plato* trans. Jowett (1951; New York: Washington Square P Inc., 1963).

8 See John Doebler, 'The Reluctant Adonis: Titian and Shakespeare' *Shakespeare Quarterly* 33 (1982): 480–90, 483.

9 See Panofsky's *Studies in Iconology: Humanistic Themes in the Art of the Renaissance* (New York: Harper Torchbook, 1967), 129-69.

10 See Kennth Clark's *The Nude* (London: John Murray, 1956), 64-112 and 113-129.

11 See Fritz Saxl, *A Heritage of Images: A Selection of Lectures by Fritz Saxl* (1957; Harmondsworth: Peregrine, 1970) 71–88.

12 See Doebler 486.

13 See Doebler 487.

14 See Doebler 488.

15 Interestingly, according to his enemy Baglione, Caravaggio's *Madonna di Loreto* (c1603–6) shocked the viewer because of the dirty soles of the peasants in the painting; this was seen

as a sign of disrespect to the Madonna and too mundane a detail to be included in a religious work of art.

16 Muriel Bradbrook says the animals in the poem are 'conceived in full naturalistic detail' and very different from artificial creatures in works of Lyly, e.g. See Muriel Bradbrook 'Beasts and Gods: the Social Purpose of *Venus and Adonis*' in *Muriel Bradbrook on Shakespeare* 53.

17 See Rosand 539. I am indebted to Stuart Sillars here.

18 Augustine in *The City of God* Book I argued that if Lucrece's will remained steadfast, she was innocent, inspite of the rape; if she consented to the rape, then she was guilty. Augustine questioned Lucrece's suicide if indeed she was innocent. See Coppelia Kahn's sensitive analysis of Lucrece's sense of shame, a feeling completely independent of her innocence, in 'Publishing Shame: *The Rape of Lucrece*' in *A Companion to Shakespeare's Works: The Poems, Problem Comedies, Late Plays* eds. Richard Dutton and Jean E. Howard (Oxford: Blackwell, 2003) 259–274.

19 The term 'visual metaphor' is used by Gombrich in a different context in *Reflections on a Hobby Horse and Other Essays on the Theory of Art* (1963; London and New York: Phaidon, 1978) 12–29.

20 See James A.W. Heffernan, *Museum of Words: The Poetics of Ekphrasis from Homer to Ashbery* (1993; Chicago and London: U of Chicago P, 2004). Heffernan goes on to examine in detail the ekphrasis in *The Rape of Lucrece* (74-90,) drawing parallels between Lucrece's violated body and the invaded city of Troy depicted in the painting Lucrece observes. The image, Heffernan argues, 'refuses to cooperate with the rhetoric of seduction' that the verbal account of the rape enacts (90). See also Judith Dundas, 'Mocking the Mind: the Role of Art in Shakespeare's *Rape of Lucrece*' *Sixteenth Century Journal* 14.1 (1983): 13–22. Dundas calls the ekphrais in the poem Shakespeare's 'most explicit account of how art works' (15).

21 See E. H. Gombrich, *Art and Illusion:A Study in the Psychology of Pictorial Representation* (1960; London: Phaidon P, 1977), 176–77. Gombrich cites the passage from *The Rape of Lucrece.* As S. Clark Hulse points out, Shakespeare could have read Philostratus if not in Greek (remembering Ben Jonson's taunt) then in any of the five Latin translations that appeared in print between 1517 and 1550. See S. Clark Hulse, ' "A Piece of Skilful Painting" in Shakespeare's "Lucrece" ' *Shakespeare Survey* 31 (1978): 13–22.

22 All quotations from the *Iliad* are from Richmond Lattimore's translation (Chicago and London: U of Chicago P, 1951).

23 See Hulse 13–22.

3. Radically Incomplete: Shakespeare's Codes for Time and Place

James Yoch

Influential Renaissance Italian critics of the drama attempted to contract the image of nature on stage into the unities of earthly time and space. Although classically minded authors like Ben Jonson imported these precepts into England, Shakespeare resisted them in his comedies and eventually came to mock them explicitly in his romances. This paper explores Shakespeare's experiments breaking out of critical boundaries specified in fixed and one-dimensional concepts of the universe. He first tested characters in the mysterious groves of *As You Like It* (1599) and later in the tumultuous seas of *Pericles* (1608). In both plays, observers must sort through fragments of diverse times and spaces. The resulting litter of possibilities offers meaning only to the wise interpreter, like the Duke in *As You Like It,* who 'Finds tongues in trees, books in the running brooks, sermons in stones, and good in everything' (2.1.16–17).[1] By the last act, the complications have led to a tangle of desires that require the help of sensible Rosalind to shape them into an agreeable conclusion. Developing this guiding role of the interpreter further in his later play, Shakespeare reintroduced the Chorus in *Pericles*. From his all-knowing position, Gower solves the puzzles of conflicting data and fills in the audience regularly on meanings for the events they are watching. He invites listeners to follow him through the 'stages of our story' (4.4.9).[2] These plays expand the audience's perceptions through forests and over seas by having an agent, like a scientist exploring chaos, pointing to patterns hidden in the *mêlée* of probabilities.

This paper divides into four parts. The first on time and the second on space contrast classical Italian theories with Shakespeare's practice in favour of an observer facing multiple dimensions and perspectives. The third part explores gardens in Italy and England as analogies to the drama offering simple and complex visual texts to the visitor for interpretation. The fourth section connects the evaluation of varied times and spaces in Shakespeare's plays with the observer measuring probabilities in modern physics.

Time

Why were the unities of time and space so important that they merited many pages of discussion in sixteenth-century Italy? 'Time' appears as a subject thirty-seven times and 'place' eleven in Weinberg's compendium of *Literary Criticism in the Italian Renaissance*.[3] Did this iteration show dutiful subservience to Aristotle, or presumed Aristotle? Did it indicate a need for comforting rules? In a period of great civil and religious dissensions, did the unities give an illusion of control over a fundamental element of life? Was this an affirmation of secular time in contrast to sacred eternity? Or was it a literary fundamentalism sprung from Italian staging practice?

Critics of varied backgrounds established the unities. The linguist Lodovico Castelvetro's *Poetica d'Aristotele Vulgarizzata Et Sposta* (Vienna, 1570, Basel, 1571) argued for the unity of time by drawing on the writings of the soldier, cataloguer of plants and sometime physician Julius Caesar Scaliger in his *Poetices Libri Septem* (1561). Behind the theory is the presumption Castelvetro made that he was updating Aristotle's *Poetics* for an unimaginative audience whom, as Weinberg summarised, he saw as the 'ignorant multitude, which has no knowledge, no imagination, no memory, and which demands that its comfort be respected.'[4] Accordingly, he wanted to see actions that could be accomplished in 'the revolution of the sun,' that is, twelve hours.[5] Castelvetro was still following ancient sources in calculating from the earth-centered view of the sun rather than changing to accommodate Copernicus' dangerous view, published in 1543, that the earth went around the sun.

Castelvetro's specification has less to do with Aristotle than with his calculation of the amount of time the audience could actually spend comfortably in the theatre listening to poetry. Castelvetro conceded that after twelve hours, 'the necessities of the body, such as eating, drinking, excreting the superfluous burdens of the belly and the bladder, sleeping, and because of other necessities, the people cannot continue its stay in the theatre beyond the aforementioned time.'[6] English authorities would not have allowed such squandering of time in a public theatre, for the London ordinances demanded that performances last no more than three hours.[7]

Yet Castelvetro, who had to flee the Inquisition for his heterodoxy, also dared to offer a route to freedom within these boundaries of time he so carefully specified. He took issue with Aristotle's suggestion that the action be single, Aristotle's only 'unity', and preferred instead a plot that allows 'several actions of a people' and even 'many actions of many persons or of many peoples.'[8] Calling for greater variety and emancipation from the supposed unities in the generation following Castelvetro, the humanist critic Paolo Beni in his *Discorso Sopra Il Pastor Fido* (Venice, 1600) carried the taste for multiplicity to the extreme by proposing that:

> dramatic plots represent not events which are invariable and which have determined and certain causes and means, or even those of slight inconstancy and variety, but happenings full of variety and inconstancy, crowded with strange and unexpected accidents, in which therefore enter the marvellous, peripeteia or change of fortune ...[9]

Beni described an ideal design that quickly became the fashionable and popular practice in Italy and England, particularly in the new genre of the pastoral tragicomedy, where writers could exercise the most invention and freedom from conventional rules.

In England, the debate over using and then discarding the unities began with their affirmation by the neoclassicist Philip Sidney. Venerated for his sophisticated tastes in literature and his gallantry on the battlefield, he argued with panache in his *Apology for Poetry*, written and circulated in 1583, then published in 1595, that even the esteemed vernacular play, *Gorboduc*, is 'faulty both in place and time, the two necessary companions of all corporal actions. For where the stage should always represent but one place, and the uttermost time presupposed in it should be, both by *Aristotles* precept and common reason, but one day, there is both many dayes, and many places, inartificially imagined.'[10] In England, Ben Jonson demonstrated his devotion to the imported unities in his play *Volpone*, written and played just a few years before *Pericles*. Jonson's Prologue boasts that the play:

> . . . presents quick comedy, refined,
> As best critics have designed,
> The laws of time, place, persons he observeth,
> From no needful rule he swerveth. (Prologue, 29–32).[11]

Jonson's classical fastidiousness did not appeal to audiences as much as Shakespeare's diversity, and Jonson complained about audience's preferences for:

> No doubt some mouldy tale,
> Like *Pericles*, and stale
> As the shrieve's crusts, and nasty as his fish-
> Scraps, out of every dish
> Thrown forth, and raked into the common tub,
> May keep up the play-club: (*The New Inn,* 'Ode to Himself,' 21–26).[12]

The long-remembered anger of these lines, a generation after *Pericles* first appeared, indicates both Jonson's spleen and the continued, galling popularity of Shakespeare's play. How did Shakespeare come to write a play so contrary to neoclassical prescriptions about time? In his England, time had many shapes. Audiences experienced and measured its passage in various schedules, including agricultural (astrological, astronomical), literary (*The Shepheardes Calender, The Rvines of Time*), solar (pre-Copernican and post-Copernican), secular (sitting of courts, the monarch's reign), religious (Anglican and rival feasts old and new), and familial (ancestors, spouses, children). Not all these systems were harmonious. Elizabeth I had continued the use of the Julian calendar despite its obvious disjunction with the solar calendar, and so England moved increasingly ahead of all those who had followed Pope Gregory XIII's remedy of removing ten days from the calendar in 1582. Ricardo Quinones argued that Shakespeare exalted progeny as offering 'some possibility of temporal response and renewal' in his sonnets and history plays but most centrally in the final romances.[13]

In 1599, he wrote *As You Like It,* his most famous excursion into the pastoral, a genre often set out of time's way. Instead, time in various forms becomes a recurring motif in the words of the characters. In the second act, the melancholy and cynical Jaques scorns the simple calibrations of someone he observed checking a pocket watch or sundial saying:

> ... very wisely, 'It is ten o'clock.
> Thus we may see,' quoth he, 'how the world wags.
> 'Tis but an hour ago since it was nine,
> And after one hour more 'twill be eleven.
> And so, from hour to hour, we ripe and ripe,
> And then from hour to hour we rot and rot,
> And thereby hangs a tale.' When I did hear
> The motley fool thus moral on the time ...
> I did laugh *sans* intermission
> An hour by his dial. (2.7.22–29, 32–33)

A few lines later, Orlando wonders more subtly that the courtiers exiled in the forest

' . . . lose and neglect the creeping hours of time' (2.7.112) and Jaques concludes the riff on mortality with his aria on the seven ages of man that ends:

> In second childishness and mere oblivion,
> *Sans* teeth, *sans* eyes, *sans* taste, *sans* everything. (2.7.166–67)

In the third-act banter, Rosalind, disguised as a boy, meets her beloved Orlando to train him for when he can eventually court Rosalind face to face. When her dutiful student asks what she would like to do, she replies by asking 'What is't o'clock?' (3.2.291). He rebuts her from another temporal system, 'You should ask me, what time o'day. There's no clock in the forest' (292–93). In response, Rosalind rhapsodises that 'Then there is no true lover in the forest, else sighing every minute and groaning every hour would detect the lazy foot of time as well as a clock.' (294–296). Then follows a routine where she lists the different paces of time for those who amble, trot, gallop, and stand still (299–302). Finally, in the fourth act, Rosalind dollies forward from a panoramic vision of time, 'The poor world is almost six thousand years old' (4.1.86–87) to a poignant focus on months,

> . . . men are April when they woo, December when they wed. Maids are May when they are maids, but the sky changes when they are wives. (4.1.137–39)

These passages playfully expand the meanings of time until the whole game collapses when Orlando fails to arrive at his appointed two o'clock and sends Rosalind instead his bloodied kerchief from a fight with a lioness.

Eight years later in *Pericles*, Shakespeare concluded his story with calibrations of time in new perspectives. Various natural clocks announce the many years that have passed since the beginning of the play: Pericles' marriage, the birth of his daughter, her coming of age, his beard growing untended for fourteen years to mark the time when he thought she had died. When Marina meets her father she portrays herself as long lost in time:

> But time hath rooted out my parentage,
> And to the world and awkward casualties
> Bound me in servitude. (5.1.94–96)

Most complexly, Pericles embraces his newly recovered wife, Thaisa, in an inspired love lyric on death and resurrection far from the cynicism of Jaques' musings on temporal decay in *As You Like It*:

> ... You shall do well
> That on the touching of her lips I may
> Melt and no more be seen. O come, be buried
> A second time within these arms. (5.3.41–44)

This short passage, dissolving time into an intense present on the edge of life and death, revises painful antitheses in earlier plays like *Romeo and Juliet* and predicts the finales of the later romances, especially *The Winter's Tale*.

Shakespeare's variations on the theme of time as a structural and verbal component consistently escape consistency. Human reason, careful preparation, and exact time continually give way on stage to the pressures of real life and unexpected changes. These include in *As You Like It* unscheduled encounters with snakes and priests in the forest and in *Pericles* storms and wonder-working physicians. In both plays, the most powerful characters who transcend time's usual effects and bring about salvation in the conclusion are young women, Rosalind and Marina. Exiled from home and battered by fortune, Rosalind saves herself through difficult times by means of disguise and charm. Even more forlorn and attacked furiously by lustful men, Marina stands outside of conventional time by means of her arts of music and sewing and most importantly by her fervent virginity echoing eternally rewarded Christian martyrs. The mutability of time shapes the vast emperies both vertical and horizontal within which to judge these characters.

Further amplifying time with recollection, the heteroglossia of other texts, *As You Like It* and *Pericles* encode additional dimensions. Geoffrey Bullough accounted for many of these in his evaluation of sources, particularly in Greek novels and in medieval drama, which scholars have extended to include morality and miracle plays beyond original listings.[14] Echoes of Shakespeare's own practice occur in these plays. *Pericles* recalls the sea-divided family of his first play, *The Comedy of Errors*. Shakespeare might have found the story of Pericles especially appealing, for he could then write a sea pastoral to match his land one, *As You Like It*. In this way, he could participate in the witty international practice of writing piscatory variations, such as Antonio Ongaro's *L'Alceo,* called in Italian, the *Aminta bagnata* for its watery and fish-filled version of Tasso's great *Aminta*. But the play *Pericles* goes to extremes in jumping over the customary boundaries of time. Like the hero Pericles himself, the audience might well despair of seeing more than fragments of a now lost template in the times of the play were it not for the contexts Gower points to beyond mere temporality itself. Pericles in the storm of the third act prays:

> The god of this great vast rebuke these surges
> Which wash both heaven and hell. (3.1.1–2)

Shakespeare's figure here, combining vertical spiritual dimensions with horizontal earthly ones, positions earthly events within the spacious geography of eternity.

Space

Castelvetro in 1571 proposed that, 'tragedy... must have as its subject an action accomplished in a small area of place and in a small space of time.'[15] Despite opposition from critics like Alessandro Piccolomini, the interpreter and translator of both classical and scientific books, who credited the audiences with an imagination that recognised stage action as metaphoric not literal,[16] some later commentators expanded the rule for unity of location to all genres. Importing this idea into England, Philip Sidney complained about vernacular drama with 'many places, inartificially imagined . . . where you shal haue *Asia* of the one side, and *Affrick* on the other.'[17] In the generation after Sidney, Ben Jonson proudly observed the 'laws of time, place' (*Volpone*, Prologue.31).

Shakespeare, however, did not. Although aware of the unities, he most often took a contrary stance, even in dramas that seem superficially to observe them, such as *The Tempest*. In *As You Like It*, the settings shift constantly. Shakespeare divided the scenes between the court in town and the forest of Arden, which shatters into many kinds of natural locales including 'desert', 'desert inaccessible,' 'sheepcote', 'uncouth forest', 'skirts of the forest', and 'purlieus of this forest'. The settings invoke Mediterranean olives and lionesses as well as English willows, oaks and a green snake. Even Arden, the name of the woods, has a double dimension. It combines both the Ardennes, the site of the action Shakespeare found in his source, Thomas Lodge's novel *Rosalynde*, as well as his mother Mary Arden's family name and her still somewhat wooded property. Here in the forest and pastures many of her Catholic relatives had taken refuge from Protestant persecution.[18] Both continental and English, Arden eludes simple nationalism to link Shakespeare's homeland to realms divided since the Reformation.

Drawing on his experiments with varied pastoral locations in the circumscribed environments of *As You Like It*, Shakespeare in *Pericles* chose a much more chaotic and unpredictable set of locations. The action takes place in six coastal cities: Mytelene and Ephesus in western Turkey (to give the locations in modern terms), Tarsus and Antioch in southern Turkey, Tyre in southern Lebanon, and Cyrene in Libya on the north coast of Africa. There are also eight voyages, as well as a storm and a shipwreck, that keep characters moving long distances, sometimes radically off course.

These dramatic places shimmer with associations that enlarge them beyond mere physical dimensions. Christians recognise readily the sites of St. Paul's travels. John Gower's rendition of the story as Apollonius of Tyre presented his fourteenth-century readers with a pagan story in which true love survived against odds:

Fortune, thogh sche be noght stable,
Yit at som time is favorable
To hem that ben of love trewe. (*Confessio Amantis,* 8.2013–2015).[19]

Shakespeare embellished the religious background for these locations into a broader range of Christian and pagan associations, far more than his source stories provided. *Pericles* contains twenty-six 'heaven/heavens', fourteen 'fortunes,' and twenty-one invocations of classical gods including Diana, Zeus, Neptune, and Juno.[20] Moreover, the play also ties into distant scenes Greek, Italian, and English. The poses of courtly melancholy from Sidney's romance *Arcadia* echo in Myteline where Pericles' ship arrives with 'banners sable, trimmed in rich expense' (Act 5.Chorus line 19). Christian, pagan, and English reverberations add multiple dimensions to the locations of the play and require a well-informed audience to appreciate and interpret the heteroglossic meanings.

The enlargement of scenes in *As You Like It* and *Pericles* geographically and literarily broadens the virtual scenery throughout the plays. Such rich associations aggrandising the verbal sets for the background seem likely to diminish if not supplant attention to the achievements of human enterprise.[21] However, the spacious environment of the forest and the wildly chaotic tumult of the seas make all the more extraordinary the achievements of the young women who take control of action and draw from the disparate scenes a benign solution. Rejecting the virtù, ingenuity, and trickery, by which Italian heroes and heroines flourished, both English plays arrive at conclusions where unfortunate women in exile from their families triumph with verbal skill, imagination, artistry, sympathy, patience, and fortitude. This unexpected achievement in the midst of dislocation and multi-location goes beyond the geometrical peripeteias Aristotle recommends. Shakespeare expanded dramatic meanings into gendered and theological dimensions available in old Christian stories, including Gower's moral exemplum Apollonius of Tyre, the Acts of the Apostles, and the Legends of the Saints. Marina mirrors the heroic fortitude under torture of virgins such as Sts. Agnes, Cecilia, and Catherine of Alexandria.

To reinforce further connections to Christian contexts outside the frenzied flow of earthly life in *Pericles*, Shakespeare fashioned Gower into the stable, wise choric leader who guides the audience through the scenes of the play. Classical in origin, the device of the observer who measures out meanings from the action comes more immediately from medieval dramas, still played in Shakespeare's time in rural areas of England, where it survived even the attempts at suppression by agents of Elizabeth I. Called the presenter in the dramas of the Middle Ages, he 'introduces and recapitulates each scene, apologises for breaks and leaps in the action, but most importantly, acts as moral interpreter to the audience.'[22] Gower helps the audience keep up with events and assigns them well-measured moral evaluations, a method analogous to scientific observations in later times.

Impossibilities of space and time abound in *Pericles*, and Gower encourages the audience to participate in following this disjointed course with him, as did the Chorus in *Henry V* a decade earlier. Discarding conventional limits, Gower promises the play will 'long leagues make short' as it flies 'from bourn to bourn [border], region to region' (4.4.4). The moves are so quick in the 'fast-growing scene' (Act 4 Chorus line 6) that he needs to give a hand filling in the missing pieces:

> . . . I do beseech you
> To learn of me, who stand i'th'gaps to teach you
> The stages of our story. (4.4.7–9)

As Philip Edwards in his *New Penguin Shakespeare* edition of the play pointed out, several nautical events described could not have occurred in the spaces and times allotted.[23] For example, Thaisa's casket, jettisoned from Pericles' ship outside of Tyre, arrives so quickly at distant Ephesus that a physician can revive her fresh corpse. This navigational routing, alas, is not geographically correct. Castelvetro and Sidney might have cared about this bold violation of the rules. Shakespeare's willfulness is all the more surprising because staging sea voyages is notoriously demanding, especially in a theatre without the financial resources and artistic talent of the court masques. These revelled in wave machines and ships. The performance critic Peter Holland believes that 'Placing a voyage on stage is, of course, a direct route to dramaturgical difficulty. The readiest way of demonstrating the limitations of the stage is to move spaces.'[24] The great success of *Pericles* in Shakespeare's time demonstrates that his approach was convincing, his audiences pleased with his appeal to their imaginations and the play's affirmation of spiritual over physical dimensions.
Shakespeare, by inventing difficulties and then having Gower call attention to them, embellished the role of the observer in his experiments testing characters in shifting settings. The multi-faceted forest of *As You Like It* and the diverse seas and ports of *Pericles* rely on interpreters to make sense of their variety, so far beyond the unity of place.

Gardens: The Nexus of Time and Space

With enthusiasm for verisimilitude and control familiar in critics arguing for the unities in drama, Renaissance Italian princes made models of nature where time and space performed in the garden theatres of the ruler. The archetypal commander observing the field; he surveyed dramatic narratives on the ground that are analogous to those Shakespeare built with words in the theatre. In Italy's famed projects showing control over the physical world, architects and rhetoricians designed scenes, fountains, statues, grottoes, and automata as exhibits illustrating the power of the prince, who from his villa terrace could survey the lofty scene. Discipline organised the programmes of these gardens, perhaps most famously at the Villa d'Este at Tivoli well on its way to completion in the mid 1570s, although by then the commissioning Cardinal Ippolito d'Este had died.[25] From the entrance, a central walkway begins at the bottom of the garden, which Venus rules, and rises to the upper levels where Hercules (a d'Este ancestor), Hippolytus (a figure of chastity appropriate to the builder-cardinal with the same name), Pegasus (inspiring thoughts heavenward), and the Tiburtine Sibyl (modelling wisdom) all illustrate virtue here in the employ of the prince. From the topmost terrace, the cardinal could look over the play of fountains amongst the sculpture and allées of his domain, where all elements of creation—particularly time and space—were in harmony. This display came with considerable cost and pain. The cardinal's workmen pulled down numerous farms, houses, and churches and in some cases drove the owners away. To make the fountains play, engineers rerouted the river Anio and raised it to the level of the topmost garden, a display of power perhaps comforting to the cast-aside cardinal, who had lost his campaigns to be pope. Did he smile when visitors admired his large-scale model of the city of Rome? At his signal, gardeners opened valves that shot jets of water over the observers. Shakespeare, in contrast to this villa's spacious assertion of authority, emphasises the evanescence of rule, usurped and discarded in *As You Like It*, thunderstruck and burned in *Pericles.*

Instead of the absolutism ruling the scene at Tivoli, another villa in the same decade shows a more relaxed mix of control and wilderness. The Lante family, losing most of their money and their villa on the Janiculum hill above St. Peters in Rome, fled to the countryside. Sixty miles north of Rome, they built a new Villa Lante at Bagnaia. Here, too, as at the Villa d'Este, a central axis runs through the garden. But it starts high on the hill rather than low, its wildness gradually changing to disciplined order. Beginning at the top, a rustic stream tumbles into a woodland pool between two small dining pavilions, runs down the centre of a table where it chills wines and floats plates, divides into many jets for a water theatre, goes underground to emerge from the horns of plenty of two reclining river gods, runs underground between two small *casini*, and then fills the basins of a tidily squared water parterre where a central statue holds up the cardinal's coats of arms. Throughout the garden, prankish sprays of water catch the unwary—from the roofs of the dining pavilions, in the steps of the walks, under the seats alongside the table. A hunting forest embraces the tamed portion of the estate in a plan that resembles a brain, with only a small side section devoted to order. Edith Wharton admired Lante in her 1904 *Italian Villas and their Gardens* for its restraint in shaping nature, for its little *casini* seem not to dominate the scene.[26] Similarly, the extensive natural contexts of scenery in *As You Like It* and in *Pericles* imply the lack of power humans have in this world (see Figure 6).

The principal features of both these Italian gardens invited explorations of a spiritual nature beyond their physical delights. The Cardinal d'Este set learned topics for his five hundred courtiers to discuss on their perambulations, and at the Villa Lante, curved classical benches at the top of the slope invite conversations *alla romana.* Reflections on the meaning of life in the perspective of nature rather than human swagger suited these exiled but once powerful churchmen. Shakespeare assigned similar speculations to the usurped duke in the forest of Arden and to Pericles, a magistrate, who came to discover how insignificant his powerful office was when faced with real events in life. Recognising the double-dimensioning of gardens as terrestrial and celestial, the Platonic Professor Francesco Vieri published in 1586 his description of the famed Medici garden at Pratolino, which he saw as both 'an earthly paradise... an expression of princely magnificence' and 'a means whereby philosophers were able to express the truths of the universe.'[27]

In England, princely exhibitionism under the Tudors followed a more primitive course. Henry VIII displayed his chivalric badges throughout the garden he confiscated from Cardinal Wolsey, and under Elizabeth I, England remained isolated from Italian practice.[28] Thomas Hill's popular *The Gardener's Labyrinth*, first published in 1577 republished in 1594 (and still in print), spent almost all of its pages on the 'workmanlike' tasks of digging, manuring, and planting in the garden.[29] Instead of physically reshaping the scene into a model of nature, the English relied on words rather than stone and water to form the dominant architecture within which to understand the forces of nature (see Figure 7). Articulate observers measure the experience and assess it within allegorical formulas. In *The Tragedy of Richard II* (1599), Shakespeare showed a lamenting queen and a rueful gardener explicating a garden differently through a range of emblematic meanings that change with the observer (3.4). In his pastorals, details within a repertoire of reactions establish meaning. Characters in *As You Like It* describe the play's various scenes primarily in generic terms: desert, forest, and sheepcote. These display a mix of emblematic plants from various climes including palms (martyrdom), willows (for abandoned lovers), and oaks (despair).

But with the accession of James I and Anne of Denmark to the throne of England, images of larger vistas over the physical world began to appear. On the court stage, masques represented this scenery *all'italiana* with painted temples, prospects, avenues, and rolling seas. Gardens for great courtiers like the Earl and Countess of Arundel imitated Italianate villas on their estates. Sir Henry Wotton recollected the new powers given to the privileged owners in 1624, when he noted the advantages of 'A well chosen *Prospect*: which I will call the *Royaltie* of *Sight* . . . There is a *Lordship* likewise of the *Eye* which being a raunging and Imperious, and (I might say) an *usurping Sense*; can indure no narrow *circumscription*; but must be fedde, both with extent and varietie.'[30]

For his theatre Shakespeare, unlike the masque designers and the peers of the realm, could not command realistic scenery for forests and seas. Instead, Gower in *Pericles* models a different princely habit, and like Shakespeare from his earliest play, invites all observers to develop their own Lordship of the Eye, spiritually ranging and morally imperious in order to escape the limitations on wood, paint, stone, and life itself. Shakespeare reinforced long perspectives outside the borders of space and time in *As You Like It*'s sudden infusions of converting grace, and in *Pericles'* tolling lines that acknowledge the fragility of life in 'rough seas, that spare not any man' (2.1.132) and in the avenging 'fire from heaven [that] came and shrivelled up/Their bodies even to loathing' (2.4.09). Nature, understood, leads characters to submit before divine, not princely, authority.

Shakespeare, Theology, and Quantum Mechanics

Barbara Everett asks how one is to account for the success of *Pericles* in the face of its outdated moral interpreter, a character already antique in Shakespeare's time. 'What remains to be explained about the play is how it can so ironically alienate, and yet in the end prove perhaps the single most intensely moving or feeling work, in its fragmentary way, in Shakespeare's career.'[31] In addition to the answers she offers, the enthusiasm for the play in our time may also depend on its harmony with other methodologies representing rhythms of time and projections of space.

Modern physics and mathematics are adept at explaining the chaotic forms of earthly life in which they discover wondrous patterns. Quantum mechanics lays out the formulas for study, which requires 1. a set of probabilities and 2. an observer. Finding this sequence relevant to the nature of the human mind, Stephen Barr in *Modern Physics and Ancient Faith* (2003) explains that with the birth of quantum mechanics:

> Suddenly the theories of physics could not even be formulated, it seemed without reference to observers. Suddenly—as Heisenberg said—knowledge entered the picture, and—as Peierls said—'some one who knows' entered with it . . . The knower appears in the framework of the theory in a logically different way, on a different level, as it were. Is this not what the non-materialist would have led one to expect?[32]

The location of this shaping knower, 'the observer perturbs the system' as a friend in science said, seems most obviously connected to the prince parading on the terrace above his controlled demesne. Shakespeare's Prospero for much of *The Tempest* has such taming powers until he tosses them into the sea. In *As You Like It* and in *Pericles*, Shakespeare designed observers of spirit who deftly evaluate and arrange probable outcomes in their scenes. Rather than raw physical power or even magical tricks, he assigned subtle grace to the loving Rosalind in *As You Like It*, whose disguise separates her from the scene and gives her control in Arden, and even more to the benevolent Gower, who stands outside the action in *Pericles* to explain it for the audience. Both characters function as observers necessary in experiments whose outcomes they help determine.

Discussions about observers have led to questions Shakespeare's faith-based 'Pericles' expressed by showing ultimately benign forces of love and grace rebutting Dame Fortune's whimsy and evil human designs. Bakhtin, the master of heteroglossia, was a critic sensitive to the dense traffic of literary connections across time and space. So it is surprising to find him arguing positively on behalf of reduction of time to one dimension. He praised Rabelais' task 'to purge the spatial and temporal world of those remnants of a transcendent world view still present in it, to clean away symbolic and hierarchical interpretations still clinging to this vertical world, to purge it of the contagion of 'antiphysis' that had infected it.'[33] In contrast to Bakhtin's rage for the simple and immediate, many modern scientists have come to recognise that materialism is not a sufficient explanation for natural events. They argue that the 'very acts of 'knowing' that give rise to these theories [equations, laws] cannot be described by them.'[34] In *As You Like It,* Rosalind and Gower in *Pericles*, leading interpreters of action, illustrate a similar tension between the probabilities of the observed events and the determinations of the observer.

In the romances he turned to, as sources for both *AsYou Like It* and *Pericles*, Shakespeare found a radical contrast to the Italian strictures on the unities of time and space. Bakhtin wrote that in the Greek romances, both time and space were without character. 'Not historical time but what is important is to be able to escape, to catch up, to outstrip, to be or not to be in a given place', in settings where 'all adventures [are] governed by an interchangeability of space.'[35] Drawing on the instabilities of admired models, including Ovid's *Metamorphoses* and Apuleius' *The Golden Ass,* Shakespeare invented forests and seas without any markers or with many conflicting beacons of meaning, uncertain swirlings from which mysteries and surprises emerge. Even the venerable Gower does not always enter on cue. He consistently gives the prologue of each act, but he also drops in without prediction into 4.4 and 5.2. In these intrusions, all structure seems to be breaking down with late-Beethoven abrasiveness to form a dramatic world in which the audience is at moments lost and bewildered.

Shakespeare's subject is exiles shoring up their experience, like the wandering characters in *The Odyssey* or *Star Wars.* His wide-ranging variety of spatial and temporal models brings his practice closer to the fluidity and instability of real life affirmed in Heisenberg's Uncertainty Principle (the inability to know exactly both time and location). Similarly rejecting the illusion of human mastery, Gödel's Proof (that the proof of a famed mathematical problem could not be both consistent and complete; and could not prove itself consistent without proving itself inconsistent) affirms that at the heart of being lie meanings that no human proof will ever completely contain. Behind the settings of *As You Like It* and of *Pericles* lies uncertainty about England as home, not yet fully defined as nation or empire, adrift from much of its past, and severed from the continent.

Heisenberg and Gödel empowered the knowing observer, an analogue to both Shakespeare and God. Barr recalls that 'Creation in its deeper meaning refers to the divine act whereby God gives being to everything that exists.' As St. Thomas expressed it, 'God is to all things the cause of being.' Thus, every finite thing that exists, including every part of space and time, exists because God causes it to exist ... The physicist Stephen Hawking famously asked about the laws of physics, 'What is it that breathes fire into the equations and makes a universe for them to describe?' The theist answers, 'God.' St. Augustine observed that God is outside the time of the universe.[36] In Shakespeare's theatre, it would be hard to ignore such contexts, since the players performed between the heavens represented on the baldachin above and the hell of the understage below. Moreover, the plots of medieval morality and miracle plays made explicit the theological dimensions of eternity and infinity in the theatre. Following his familiar practice of giving antique formulas new life,[37] Shakespeare turned limits into swaggering assertions of power, since he was confident in the imaginations of his audience. Thus, he anticipated structures combining observers and their experiments, a relationship now central to scientific method. Rather than a simplistic tired tale, *Pericles* gave Shakespeare the opportunity to explore cosmic tensions between fundamental forces of time and space, which he refused to see boxed into the unities. Instead, through the testing experiences of new times and spaces, characters show their strengths and define themselves in new spiritual shapes. Sailing well beyond his usual disregard of limits, he composed audaciously, with what seems dashing haste, fragments of scenes like asteroids from an exploding planet of ideas. Seeing these travelling through the space and time of the theatre frees the audience to share in imaginings, with the help of Gower, of probabilities in tune with great Creation itself.

Notes

1 All quotations from *As You Like It* are from the *Arden Shakespeare: Third Series* edited by Juliet Dusinberre (London: Arden, 2006).

2 All quotations from *Pericles Prince of Tyre* are from the New Penguin edition edited by Philip Edwards (New York: Penguin, 1981). (I wish to acknowledge the authorship discussions about *Pericles*. (i) According to many, including Suzanne Gossett's 2004 Arden edition and Roger Warren's 2003 Oxford edition, the play is by Shakespeare and perhaps George Wilkins in a team effort where Shakespeare was principally responsible for the last three acts. or (ii) Shakespeare is the sole author as Doreen Del Vecchio and Antony Hammond claim in the 1998 New Cambridge edition. Efficient reviews of the authorship musings appear in David Beringtou's *The Complete Works of Shakespeare* (New York: Harper, 4th. ed. 1992), 1398–99.

3 Bernard Weinberg, *A History of Literary Criticism in the Italian Renaissance* (Chicago: U of Chicago P, 1974).

4 Weinberg 69.

5 Weinberg 505.

6 Weinberg 505.

7 See A. Hart, 'The Time Allotted for Representation of Elizabethan and Jacobean Plays' *Review of English Studies* 8.32 (1932) 395.

8 Weinberg 509.

[9] Weinberg 1098.

[10] G. Gregory Smith, *Elizabethan Critical Essays*. Vol. 1 (Oxford: Oxford UP, 1964) 197.

[11] G. A. Wilkes, ed., *The Complete Plays of Ben Jonson*. Vol. 3 (Oxford: Oxford UP, 1981).

[12] Wilkes, IV.

[13] Ricardo Quinones, *The Renaissance Discovery of Time* (Cambridge: Harvard UP, 1972) 435.

[14] Geoffrey Bullough, *Narrative and Dramatic Sources of Shakespeare,* Vol. 6 (New York: Columbia UP, 1966) 352–53.

[15] Weinberg 509.

[16] Weinberg 547.

[17] Smith 197.

[18] For information regarding Edward Arden and Shakespeare's Catholic lineage see Michael Wood, *Shakespeare* (New York: Basic Books, 2003) 20, 46, 74.

[19] John Gower, *Confessio Amantis* (Kalamazoo: University of Rochester Medieval Institute Publications, 2006). See also references to Gower in Bullough 423.

[20] See Linda McJannet, 'Genre and Geographys: The Eastern Mediterranean in *Pericles* and *The Comedy of Errors*' *Playing the Globe: Genre and Geography in English Renaissance Drama* John Gillies and Virginia Mason Vaughan eds. (Madison: Fairleigh Dickinson UP, 1998) 98.

[21] See Barbara Everett, 'By the rough seas reft,' *Times Literary Supplement* 11 Aug. 06: 15.

[22] Howard Felperin, 'This Great Miracle: *Pericles*' *Pericles: Critical Essays* ed. David Skeele (New York: Garland Publishing: 2000) 115.

[23] Philip Edwards ed. *New Penguin Shakespeare: Pericles* (New York: Penguin, 1981) 12.

[24] Peter Holland, 'Traveling Hopefully: The Dramatic Form of Journey in English Renaissance Drama,' *Travel and Drama in Shakespeare's Time*, ed. Jean-Pierre Maquerlot and Michèle Willems (Cambridge: Cambridge UP, 1996) 160–161.

[25] For a detailed background on the Villa d'Este, see David R. Coffin. *The Villa d'Este at Tivoli* (Princeton: Princeton UP, 1960) and David R. Coffin. *The Villa in the Life of Renaissance Rome* (Princeton: Princeton UP, 1979).

[26] Edith Wharton, *Italian Villas and their Gardens* (New York: Century, 1904).

[27] Roy Strong, *The Renaissance Garden in England* (London: Thames and London, 1979) 82.

[28] Strong 70.

[29] See Thomas Hill, *The Gardener's Labyrinth* (Oxford: Oxford UP, 1987).

[30] Henry Wotton, *Elements of Architecture* (Charlottesville: U of Virginia P, 1968).

[31] Everett 15.

[32] Stephen Barr, *Modern Physics and Ancient Faith* (Notre Dame: Notre Dame UP, 2003) 254.

[33] Mikhail Bakhtin, *The Dialogic Imagination* trans. Caryl Emerson and Michael Holquist (Austin: U of Texas P, 1981) 168.

[34] Barr 254.

[35] Bakhtin 91,100.

[36] Barr 261-62. See also St. Thomas Aquinas, *Summa Contra Gentiles* (Garden City: Image Books, 1955), Bk. 2, 46.

[37] 'In *Shakespeare's Festive Comedy* (Princeton: Princeton UP 1958), Barber showed how obsolescent social customs influenced Shakespeare's comic form.' See R. W. F. Martin, rev. of *The Whole Journey: Shakespeare's Power of Development*, *The Review of English Studies*, n.s. 40.159 (1989): 414–416. See also C. L. Barber, *Shakespeare's Festive Comedy* (Princeton, Princeton UP, 1959).

4. Antoni de Montserrat in the Mughal Garden of Good Government: European Construction of Indian Nature

Maria Antonia Martí Escayol

There are two large-scale models for approaching the study of nature. One would be objective, which is to say, the study of 'real' alterations in the natural environment. The other would be 'subjective', which is to say, the study of the social meanings subjects attribute to the environment in their dialogue with nature through perceptions, ethics, laws, identity, scientific knowledge, economic interests and myths. The aim of this essay is to analyse the environment as a structure of meanings using the account of the journey made by Antoni de Montserrat (Vic, Catalonia 1536 – Salsete, India, 1600) and, in addition, to analyse the political significance of the control of nature furthered by the policies of Emperor Akbar.

Antoni de Montserrat, who was born in Catalonia, spent the early years of his priesthood in Portugal and travelled to India in 1574, where he was one of those chosen—together with Francisco Henríquez and Rodolfo Aquaviva, nephew of Jesuit superior general Claudio Aquaviva—to enter into conversations with Emperor Akbar (1556–1605). Akbar invited them in 1579 with the object of holding a debate on religion, but the cultural exchange between them went further. The Jesuits brought to the court examples of European culture; illustrated books, engravings by Raphael, Michelangelo and Dürer and oil paintings. These Renaissance works had an influence on attempts to adopt perspective and Christian themes on the part of court artists. For this reason it is said that the Jesuit mission brought the Renaissance to the Ganges.[1] For his part, Antoni de Montserrat had the opportunity to update classical knowledge of the territories visited, focussing on ethnological, cultural, natural and geographical aspects.

His book, written in Latin and entitled *Mongolicae Legationis Commentarius,* records the notes taken on his journey across India, Pakistan, Afghanistan and the Himalayas. Leaving from Goa on 17 November 1579, the Jesuit mission travelled through Chaul, Daman, Navsari, Surat and Mandu. Acquaviva and Henríquez arrived at the Mughal capital, Fatehpur Sikri—location of the conversations—on 27 February 1580, and Antoni de Montserrat, delayed by a mild illness, arrived on 4 March. A year later, Antoni de Montserrat was invited to accompany the emperor on a military expedition, during which he visited Agra, Mathura, Delhi, Ambala, Kangra, Riwat and Kabul. From Kabul, he continued on to Riwat, Rotas, Lahore and Ambara, returning by the same route to Goa.[2]

Dialogue with Renaissance Nature

Antoni de Montserrat's book is an account of journeys promoted by the Jesuits and framed within the objective of the Jesuit community to create a corpus which would provide a new image of the regions of the world. Montserrat justifies his work in precisely these terms: 'Many have followed this exemplary diligence, travelling by land or sea, and in their devotion to the excellent studies of geography, navigation and history they have generously enriched the treasures of the Republic of the Arts. For this and other reasons, the custom of recording all of these facts has been established in la Society of Jesus.'[3]

Antoni de Montserrat was Catalan and for him as a European the discovery (America) and rediscovery (Asia) of new territories was parallel to the discovery of nations themselves. He is situated in the group of authors who between the fifteenth and seventeenth centuries made up a powerful Renaissance nucleus in Catalonia. The description and study of nature was a key point for all of them. And for those who were dedicated to the immediate environment (Catalonia), their aim was to construct a coherent vision of the country, destined to generate elements of identity and alterity within the decisive context that was the shaping of modern states. The importance of their intellectual labour is borne out by jurists' and politicians' use of their arguments until 1714 to establish Republican projects as a counterpoint to the absolutist Borbon politics of the Royal Court, and their nineteenth-century revival within the context of the configuration of nationalities.

For the case of the study of India, Pakistan, Afghanistan and the Himalayas, Antoni de Montserrat's work may be summarised in five suppositions. First, it puts his ideas in context, relating them to a prior tradition of written knowledge deriving from the habitual or instinctive feeling which considers that nothing that has been said can be omitted. Secondly, it introduces modifications to written tradition by means of an exercise which compares what has been read to what has been seen, allowing the author to have a running dialogue with reality. Thirdly, it enters a dialogue with 'real' nature, viewed always with the standard of 'real' European nature, allowing him to classify the environment positively or negatively. Fourthly, he maintains an open mind towards the indigenous peoples' knowledge, science and technology, which leads to a complex intellectual reciprocity in the process of creating the image of nature. And finally, he reveals the political significance of territorial control, interaction with the environment and the domestication of nature.

As a starting point, the author uses previously made statements constructed by classical authors and compares them with his own knowledge of the region, based on direct experience, thereby creating an opening for intellectual discourse. This opening is a challenge both for him as a writer—he must evaluate the validity of previous discourse and incorporate information—and for the sixteenth and seveneeth-century European reader, who must make a decision regarding the veracity of the multiple conflicting statements of the age. 'Correct, explain and reconcile' are the three words chosen by Montserrat in the preface to the work to describe his working method when attempting to 'provide a service for the scholars in our schools'.[4]

The author is aware of the challenge, as he explains in the preface and at various stages of the work with phrases like: 'At least I have had an advantage over other authors: I have been able to see the mountains with my own eyes.'[5] He therefore follows the Renaissance precepts which exhorted scholars to walk on the land, climb into the mountains, visit rural workshops or houses, all in the name of creating empirical knowledge. Using this method, Montserrat's language not only gives the reader an impression of the testimonial nature of his observations but also brings the past into the present. Indeed, the author presents himself as a direct witness of something he is seeing at the very moment he describes it. This approach is an example of the Renaissance 'now,' a description of something which is happening at a defined instant. What is more, by describing what he has seen at a specific time, he brings objectivity and veracity to the text.[6]

Antoni de Montserrat is aware that he is using his observations to demonstrate the deficiencies of geographical knowledge accepted in the world of learning. To this end, he creates a dialogue between practical knowledge—that which he has seen and talked about with the natives—and theory—that which is written—correcting texts by Pliny, Strabo, Quintus Curtius Rufus and Diodorus Siculus.

There can be no doubt that the map drawn up by the author is the maximum exponent of this corrective task. It is based on contemporary rather than classical descriptions and, for this reason, shows greater accuracy and rigour than the maps of India created up to that time. On his map, geographical features are classified in four groups: cities, rivers, mountains and regions. All of these are oriented according to the four cardinal points and positioned on a grid of latitude and longitude. The measurements were taken daily by Antoni de Montserrat himself during the journey from Chaul to Fatehpur Sikri and later on the journey to Kabul while accompanying Akbar, during which he was encouraged by the emperor himself, who was interested in them. The details are fairly close to reality, although a correction of 39° must be applied to longitude, since the meridian of reference used by the author was located on the eastern coast of Brazil, in accordance with the Papal Bull *Inter Caetera* issued Alexander VI in 1493.

Of particular interest among the contributions of the map are the description of the Himalayas—it is the first map on which the outlines of the different mountain ranges in the Himalayas are drawn—and the upper reaches of the rivers of the Punjab, as well as the extraordinary accuracy of the drawing of the Indus and its sources. It is also the first European map that includes Lake Mansarowar, highlighted in black with the accompanying phrase 'hic dicuntur christiani habitare' (it is said that Christians live here).

Our objective here, however, is to analyse the text. One important challenge posed by the text is the correction of place names through the replacing of names of rivers, mountains and cities with the updated 'current' name, which is to say, the one decided by the inhabitants of the region themselves.[7] In the same respect, his aim is to situate each natural element in the 'correct' place that he has observed. For both types of corrections he adopts the language of geographers, as he admits on various occasions, understanding nature as an inert and regular thing which is susceptible to be subjected to geometrical analysis, in line with the Italian Renaissance model.[8]

Other updating relates to flora[9] and fauna. We must highlight in this respect the correction made with regard to the elephant, without doubt one of the subjects which most attracts, surprises and stimulates the author. This animal is subjected to precise biological and etiological scrutiny through his own observations and, both particularly and significantly, through dialogue with the native keepers. As he does with all other flora and fauna, he describes the elephant using the European standard. Thus, he writes that a group of them resembles a herd of bulls or that they belong to the type of animal which likes water, such as the buffalo and the pig. He corrects Strabo and Pliny, who declared themselves, according to the author, confused by 'lies and legends' that elephants did not have joints, nodules or ligaments. With an ethologist's eye, he describes the behaviour of these animals in their natural environment, establishes the life stages of an elephant, its principal illnesses and its 'social' behaviour: how they interrelate, their clans and group hierarchies. The majesty and beauty of the elephant fascinate the author and, in particular, from a purely anthropocentric viewpoint, he is amazed by the fact that man is able to domesticate such a powerful animal: 'With the intention of allowing the domestication and training of these enormous beasts, God the creator of all things made to serve man and man to serve Him has established that the elephant should have two weak points in its body ....'[10]

But the most interesting thing about this animal is the symbolic significance that it takes on in the description. According to Montserrat's notes, it was the king who promoted their domestication, financed their upkeep and organised their preparation for the needs of the army. It was the king who possessed this element of military power and who, in turn, subordinated it to his will. Like the rest of the flora and fauna, and like the human population itself, everything within Akbar's reign was domesticated in order to maintain, perpetuate and aggrandise his sovereignty. The powerful physique of the domesticated elephant is the symbol of the absolute power of the king and the submission of a population that sustains that power.

Emperor Akbar's full power can be seen in Basawan and Chatar's painting 'Akbar Tames the Savage Elephant, Hawa'i, Outside the Red Fort at Agra', included in Abul Fazl's book *Akbarnama*. On the right-hand side of the painting, witnesses watch on as Akbar tames the elephant Hawa'i, who, on the left, is chasing another elephant across the rickety boat bridge over the Jamuna River. In the image, Akbar restrains Hawa'i, takes command of the chase and saves the people from an uncontrolled elephant. The composition of the painting itself shows Akbar's strength. The main scene crosses the 'focal point' of the miniature, in the top right section, and it does so through the drawing, volume and colour of the animals.

The image shows a certain influence of European renaissance art. Akbar, fascinated by the art samples he received as gifts from the Jesuits, wanted some of his own artists to learn the European techniques. Basawan had even familiarised himself with these techniques before the arrival of the Jesuit missions. European methods were actually of such interest to Basawan that along with his son, Manohar, and Kesu Das, that he became a specialist in the representation of Christian images. This interest in European art can be seen in his miniature through the different perspectives, the depth of the landscape, the three-dimensional nature of the objects, the blue gradations suggesting distance in the river and the way some of the boats are smaller to suggest that they are farther away. The Emperor's strength is also suggested in another miniature 'Emperor Akbar Crossing the River Ganges in 1567' where he is seen riding elephants and horses along with some of his men. In both cases he is fighting against the elements of nature and in both cases Akbar wins through thanks to his powers of domestication.

The Dialogue between Macrocosms and Microcosms

Among the corrections proposed by the author we find one aimed at Pliny with regard to whether the origins of silk are animal or vegetable. Once again he compares the worms of the region with the ones he knows best, those from Tarragona (Catalonia)[11] as it is precisely this Mediterranean and European region, the known, which is the standard used to define everything seen. In fact, Montserrat constantly sees Europe reflected in everything he observes. He tends to identify animals, plants and environmental characteristics in the areas he travels to with that which he knows and for this reason subordinate phrases of comparison and exceptions are constant throughout the text. He therefore describes those animals which are hunted as the same as the European, except in the case of the 'blue bull (*Neelgai* Antelope)', which he describes as similar to the deer but bigger; or he describes the process of hunting similar to the European with the difference that instead of using dogs they use panthers,[12] or how the 'long tailed sheep' of Samarcanda resemble 'a type of goat' called a *dumbi*.[13]

Establishing the European standard also allows him to classify what he has seen. Thus, with exceptions, admiration or aversion is marked by the contrast with the author's known environmental reality. That which most resembles the European standard is positive and that which least resembles it is negative. A paradigmatic case of negative classification due to contrast with the standard befalls any wild 'fauna' unknown to the author. It is considered harmful, due to the immediate danger predators represent for human life and the little utilitarian interest provoked by animals which are not subject to domestication.

A key subject when comparing India with the European standard is the climate. An ideal climate is considered to be one which most resembles the European. Underlying this is the environmental consideration of Hippocratic medicine predominant until the end of the eighteenth century and according to which, due to the system of sympathy between micro- and macrocosms, the climatic situation, the earth, the air and the water determine both individuals' health and character. The macro–microcosms analogy therefore distinguishes that which is healthy from that which is not, in as much health depends on the balance between the four terrestrial qualities through the extent to which this can maintain or disrupt the balance of the four human humours. The correlation between micro- and macrocosms means that throughout the text there is an indissoluble relationship between nature and inhabitants or nature and culture, in all its manifestations.

The obligatory mental presence of the European reference together with the environmentalist conception of the surroundings lead the author to consider the most positive climate to be a mild one,[14] where a maximum balance is achieved between the four atmospheric qualities (heat, cold, wetness and dryness).[15] This climate is marked by latitude, or the space between two parallels. Those regions which are closer to the European latitude are healthier and therefore receive greater praise. Apart from this, the climate is also determined by the elevation or depression of the earth, its proximity or distance from the sea,[16] its location with regard to the wind,[17] and divine providence: 'The merciful Creator has given those parts of the country rays of Sunlight which, despite being surrounded by snowy peaks, provide warmth and make the earth as productive as that of regions more distant from the snows.'[18] Milder regions with low humidity are for Montserrat the most suitable for settling and finding immediate means of survival. These regions are the ones considered to be more apt for human living and have products adaptable to the tastes and basic requirements of the European diet.

The Dialogue between Climate and Religion

The environmentalist theory of the Hippocratic tradition was also the basic physiological theory from ancient times to the beginning of the eighteenth century, when Buffon and Montesquieu concretely established that certain nations had certain temperaments and that each space acquires specific medical conditions and has inhabitants of a specific character. This led to the theory of the differentiated identity of each space according to its environmental conditions. Montserrat uses the characteristic language of Hippocratic medicine, characterising certain people as melancholic, choleric, sanguine or phlegmatic.[19] In the same respect, environmental surroundings favour certain religious practices. This is how he explains the hermits of Beedaulat, where the extreme austerity of cells excavated from the rock propitiates retreat and penitence, practised by Saint Bartholomew in this place known to the ancients as India *Citerior* or Hither India.[20]

As with the flora and fauna, the inhabitants are also classified according to the European standard. Thus, as with the majority of descriptions of cultural or religious practices in America or Asia, rejection of indigenous practices is linked to their differences to the basic precepts of Christian religious morality. The 'mistaken' character attributed to some attitudes is the product of a conscious rejection of any cultural standard different to the European and Christian. Nevertheless, we must stress the effort made by Montserrat, in the most typically Jesuit fashion, to analyse and describe these practices. The author concerns himself with analysing the origins and characteristics of a culture he does not know, even though he does always end up denouncing practices he considers improper. It is not our objective to judge the sense in the dual exercise of interest and rejection, only to note the Jesuits' awareness of the antiquity and complexity of the civilisation they described. And it is precisely this awareness that obliges them to familiarise themselves with indigenous ideas in order to develop an indirect preaching method to evangelise Asian lands.[21]

The European standard is the place where the author feels most comfortable in analysing the aforementioned religion. Thus, he searches for the origins in classical western antiquity, in order to at times understand, at others pardon or justify indigenous behaviour. In addition, as is commonplace in descriptions of the age—and as José de Acosta does for America—he attributes 'idolatry' to actions of the devil. Thus, Montserrat describes tree consecrations[22] or Indian theories on the origins of Europeans[23] as attitudes worthy of study and dissemination in order that European readers might have 'pity' on the ignorance of the authors of these practices.[24]

On occasions, this critical posture towards Asian religious practices leads to a paradox within the work. For example, the author strongly criticises the Paixtus for consulting fortune tellers and witch doctors and following their astrological predictions before going into battle.[25] In another chapter, however, we find the same author, as a man of his age and for the same reason as the union between micro- and macrocosms, interpreting the lunar eclipse on 31 January 1580 as a portent of the death of Henry of Portugal and as a premonition of ill fortune and calamity for that country.[26]

The Dialogue between Civilisation and the Domestication of Nature

The relationship between climate and the fertility of the earth is also a recurrent theme. The author establishes a system of cause and effect for milder regions which, in his view, are more fertile, provide more crop diversity and a balance between agriculture and livestock and therefore allow for a greater network of imports and exports and maintenance of a larger population.[27] Among the regions he singles out for praise are those between Ravi and Sandabalis (Chenab)[28] and the region of Hazara,[29] whereas regions farther from a milder climate are those which suffer from the rigours of cold or heat, where the air is unhealthy and thick, causing disease, and where there is the wildest and most dangerous flora and fauna.[30]

We observe attempts to produce a panoramic vision of India's nature which we are unfortunately impeded from completing due to the fact that part of the author's manuscripts have been lost. Despite this, we find evidence of this in the description of the kingdom of Zelaldin,[31] where a southern region with 'fruits resembling those on the Indian coast' is differentiated from a northern region with 'fruits resembling the European'.[32] The most significant thing about the description of agriculture is the relation established by Montserrat between agriculture and the emperor's power. In Montserrat's book, cultivation is described as a form of territorial control that functions through a complex, diversified and continuous flow of agricultural revenues that are transferred from the fields to the political centre with the object of maintaining the whole imperial machinery.[33]

Another feature which stands out is the author's admiration for the indigenous inhabitants' diligence and technological resources for domesticating nature and making infertile land fertile by building, for example, complex irrigation systems. The most outstanding examples of this domestication and control of nature[34] are places such as gardens 'designed in very artistic ways,'[35] pools and fountains[36] and private zoos, or activities like hunting, falconry, as well as bird watching,[37] pigeon training,[38] or, on a more specific level, the transformation of opium by means of the *Baba Kapur* potion produced with capsules soaked in water[39] (from the seventeenth century onwards, transforming opium would in fact become a means of altering vegetation which would have greater ecological consequences for the region).[40]

There can be no doubt that this domestication of nature is seen as positive by the author due to its being subject to a European mental framework where the intellectual and spiritual meaning acquired by cultivated earth is a key subject for the economy from the sixteenth century onwards. Within this framework farming equates to civilisation, and agricultural progress therefore equates to personal, social and national progress.[41] The paradigm of connection between farming and civilisation is especially strong in America, where the aim of naturalists' regulation of wild products is to convert desert (understood to be a 'wild' place, uncontrolled with no useful species) into a garden. Part of this conception comes from authors who recovered the literature of Virgil[42] and for whom a country is not developed when it is not inhabited or has few inhabitants, no cultivated lands, no self-pride and no praise from its own citizens or foreigners. By contrast, a nation is mature and deserving of praise when it is populated and cultivated.

There can be no doubt that the classical revisionist method imposed on the Renaissance together with the exhortation to 'feel reality' generated a clear advance in the perception of natural phenomena. Nevertheless, at the end of the sixteenth century the excessive rhetoric of humanist education generated a new attitude towards the environment, characterised by commercial interests and the prioritisation of productive work. A new method for approaching nature was born. In fact, geographical discoveries, the perspective of new markets and 'inexhaustible' energy sources together with the politics of the greater glory of the state propagated by the 'great modern states' generated a new mental framework which promoted expansion in productivity, extended life expectancy and legitimised mechanical work. This mentality acquires its maximum theoretical expression with Francis Bacon (1561–1626), who advocated the need to understand the world in order to transform it and domesticate it.[43] In this way the attribution of productive work qualities were generally imposed.[44] We move from a theological and organic mental schema to one which is mechanical and causal; that is to say, we move from a contemplative to an active science, where the human being is not a spectator but an active element.[45] In this respect, we must not lose sight of the fact that Montserrat's Jesuit mission was closely related to Portugal's economic and commercial interests. It is clear that the literary genre of Renaissance travel is structured according to the practical interests of merchants, soldiers and royal officials.[46] The conquest of the Great Mughal territories was not considered possible at the time, although it was at least hoped that Jesuit presence in the court would make Akbar more amenable.[47] For this reason Montserrat's description has remained, whether intentionally or not, an extremely useful instrument for European states in their attempts to appropriate a territorially strategic region, filled with natural resources and energy sources.

It is in this vein that two key elements of the author's description should be interpreted. On the one hand, the description of nature as an obstacle—an extremely useful instrument for Europeans in the choice of the correct route for travelling into the Indian mainland—and, on the other hand, the indigenous inhabitants' use of nature to defend themselves—an instrument to combat the country's resistance. In both cases, Montserrat bears witness to Akbar's territorial control. The organisation of the territory acts as a metaphor for sovereignty to the extent that space is organised, measured and divided in order to make evident and effective the absolute control and grandeur of the Emperor. No territorial space remains outside his power, and this reinforces the subordination and hierarchical organisation of political space.

In the first case, the analysis of nature as an obstacle, the bases of the author's interpretation are, first and foremost, a clear attention to paths. He indicates whether these are passable or not, the appropriate transport required to this end or for transporting goods and the characteristics of the surrounding landscape (its fertility[48] or the surrounding vegetation being advantageous as a place for replenishing stocks or disadvantageous as a place where bandits may hide).[49] One of the various times when the author praises Indian culture is worthy of mention here. On the journey to Kabul, the author describes how the king has the distance travelled measured each day using a measurement of ten feet, thereby allowing him to verify the size of his domain and the distances between cities, where ten feet times two hundred is equivalent to a '*coroo*' in the Persian language or a '*cos*' in the

Indian language, this being two miles. A very useful measurement, the author admits, for knowing how long messages or official visits would take.[50] This is precisely one of Akbar's most important accomplishments: the measuring of his lands, of great importance to the English in the nineteenth century.[51]

Antoni de Montserrat had the opportunity to be an eyewitness to these measuring methods upon being invited to accompany Akbar in 1581 on an expedition to Kabul to fight against Mirza Hakim Muhammad.[52] He describes the deployment of forces for the occasion, with an army made up of horses, elephants, camels, men and women. The Jesuit relates how Akbar conceives of war as a hunt (this is how he refers to the military expedition)[53] and to the hunt as a method of military training. In organising both the march and the encampments, a detailed ritual is followed that theatricalises the hierarchical order of power. The different characters are placed to the front, to the rear, to the right or to the left according to their family, social or political relation to the emperor.

The army followed the foothills of the mountain ranges where more water and animals could be found while the sappers and labourers laid out the roads according to Akbar's wishes. During the hunt itself, no one could be stationed in the line of advance of the king—as a metaphor for his sovereignty, the king preferred to keep far away from the crowd and to have sole charge of the entire process. The practice also served to avoid acts of treason and to keep from frightening off the prey.[54] He used hungry panthers for the occasion, carried, with eyes blindfolded, on the backs of horses, and he had himself surrounded by horsemen with falcons on their wrists, not for hunting, but as a symbol of royal dignity. The hunt continued along the entire route and all of Akbar's power was exhibited, punishing those who slowed things up or did not collaborate skilfully enough and were thus considered inadequate for fighting.[55] In addition, this great demonstration of power over the natural world enabled the army to maintain its subordination of the population wherever it passed. Those villages that showed submission and supplied the army with food and gifts were rewarded with exemption from taxes and were not molested, but those that did not cooperate were severely punished. In this way, Akbar made his way, feeding his army with demonstrations of vassalage and negotiating treaties of friendship with kings intimidated by such a show of force.

The significance of hunting can be appreciated in another miniature by the Indian painter Basawan, 'Akbar slays a tigress which attacked the royal entourage', included in the *Akbarnama* (see Figure 8). In the main scene of the painting, the positions of the objects suggest a clear circumference. Everything is so intimately connected through the drawing that a complete entity is formed. In the upper area of the circle, Akbar, on horseback, wounds the largest and most detailed tiger. The Emperor dominates the domesticated animal (the horse) and the wild animal (the tiger) and chronologically and spatially breaks the infinite circuit of the circle. There is major plasticity in the scene, the gestures are fierce and the faces are expressive, almost grotesque, inspired by classical Indian paintings.[56] The painting is also inspired by classical art: the violence of wild nature, in which the stronger animals attack the weaker ones, is placated by a superior power, by the power of law, order and the Emperor's strength. So, in the miniature, hunting is an inherent attribute of a ruler, is a characteristic of the ideal leader, is a method of military training and is, therefore, not only a pastime for a king.

Similarly, in another miniature 'Akbar engaged in *shikar* (hunt) near Lahore' (see Figure 9) by artists Muskin and Mansur, the scene is focused on the discharge of energy involved in hunting and on its political significance. Akbar, in the centre, the most three-dimensional and best illuminated part of the image, domesticates the chaos of nature. In the miniature, neither is time precise nor is space specific. On the contrary, time and space form part of different sequences. There are different chronological moments and different localisations in the same scene. Akbar moves in reality, and therefore his power is omnipresent in his kingdom just as it is in this miniature and this guarantees the proper administration of justice. For this reason, the upper part of the painting shows how Hamid Bakari is punished for his offence against a court official. The inclusion of this exemplary punishment in a hunting scene becomes a symbol of Akbar's exercising of justice.

Mughal Gardens

Much as with the hunts, Akbar's gardens also acquired political significance. They were the physical representation of the ideal of good government and, at the same time, the representation of territorial control and of a prosperous government enjoying an eternal spring.[57] In this sense, Montserrat cites the fountains and trees planted in the temple of Firoz Shah, in Delhi, as having the triple function of beautifying the countryside and showing off the currents of architectural design, contributing to the public good by offering shade to visitors and, above all, demonstrating the magnificence of power.[58] He also relates how, during the first few days of March 1582, Akbar took advantage of *Norouz*—according to Montserrat, the moment when the beginning of spring is celebrated, when 'the countryside smiles, dyed in green' and the people visit the fields and gardens—to celebrate his military victories.[59] The coincidence took on great significance by equating a moment of political prosperity with the rebirth of nature and making the entire population participate in this coincidence through a celebration. The author also mentions, although without any description, the garden of the residence of Humanyun, *Dinpanah* in Delhi (present-day *Purana Quila* or old fort) and the artificial lake at Fatehpur Sikri, the setting of a work by the painter Narsingh where Antoni de Montserrat, Rodolfo Acquaviva and Emperor Akbar appear deep in debate with the Muslim doctors of the court. On the upper left edge of the image, the sky is an allusion to an element that is common to the entire globe and acts as a symbol of dialogue between religions. The characters are situated in an exterior space, where the floor is decorated with natural motifs, and form part of a harmonious and geometrically ordered garden. As in miniature of gardens, there is a predominance here of straight lines, angles and the union of objects with architecture as an organic whole. The civilised nature represented by the garden is substituted here by the idea of civilisation through religious debate.

Both along the road to Kabul and during the rest of Montserrat's journey, as far as rivers are concerned, these are not only obstacles but also sources of supplies and natural routes. He details their route with extraordinary precision, not only in the drawing of them on the map, but also in their description in the text, as in this example: 'Such is the strength of the river's current that elephants can only cross it with great effort. Beyond this point it widens between Nilabh and Arachosia, and not very far from here it receives waters from the Coas and the Suast, which have formed one single current shortly before this point. From this point onwards the river gets bigger and flows in a southerly direction until finally emptying into the sea through three different outlets.'[60] He demonstrates a special interest in this matter in knowing original sources and points where the rivers empty, the seasonality of the swells, the strength of the currents, the quality of the water, the quality of the fauna and flora, the infrastructures for overcoming the river (boats or bridges) or the safety of the river beds.[61] But what Montserrat is most concerned with is observing the indigenous inhabitants' use of nature in overcoming these obstacles. And it is in this matter, now free from the rigidity imposed by the observation of religious practices, that we find true sentiments of admiration for the natives' work, particularly in their construction of bridges and Akbar's thorough dedication to maintaining and constructing an efficient infrastructure.[62]

For Antoni de Montserrat, mountains are accidents to be overcome, and he details routes through them, but they are also a source of supplies and riches. Indeed, the author has a positive view of mountains and this sets him aside from common medieval theory persistent in the sixteenth and seventeenth centuries, according to which God created the earth flat and mountains were therefore dangerous, repulsive places which were the sign of terrestrial degeneration. From the Renaissance onwards, according to intellectuals, the earth and nature were mortally wounded. Nicolás de Cusa (1401–1464) speaks of universal destruction and Luther (1486–1546) was convinced that the end of the world was imminent. There is an abundance of literature which speaks with fascination of natural degeneration where mountains are the principal evidence of this. Montserrat's positive view of mountains fits perfectly with the theoretical formulations constructed at the University of Coimbra, where the author studied, and are perfectly explained in the *Comentarii Colegii Conimbricenses* or *Curso Conimbricense*, a commentary to Aristotle's *Libri Naturales* (384–332). The author no doubt sides with Coimbra theory, where it is accepted that the Earth had been created with mountains and they were praised for their economic usefulness and beauty.[63]

In the second matter, the use of nature for defence, the author is a privileged spectator when he is able to accompany Zelaldin on the military expedition to Kabul. En route, Montserrat admires how the people symbiotically adapt to their environment to defend themselves. This relationship between warrior and nature can be seen perfectly in the representations of battles in the different miniatures shown in the *Akbarnama*. Each group in the composition has its own natural setting and serves to highlight the different scenes or levels as part of a single miniature, thus converting nature into a receptacle for each figure or group of figures.

On the text, Antoni de Montserrat admires the fact that some areas have neither a cavalry nor an artillery but make up for this deficiency with their environment, with the jungles, cliffs, vegetation and rocks which become walls and trenches for both defending themselves and attacking,[64] whilst at the same time being perfect spots for replenishing supplies from the surrounding area in the case of a siege.[65]

The European Construction of Nature in America, Asia and Europe

In the early modern age, one of the points which changes our perspective on an approach to nature is the scientific concern born of Renaissance Humanism. On a temporal level, the intellectual rupture of the Renaissance and conceiving of new paradigms in fields such as philology, history, archaeology, epigraphy, literature,[66] geography, art[67] and natural science have awakened a renewed interest in the study of the natural environment. Also, on a geographical level, discoveries bring us news from parts of the world as yet mostly or completely unknown to Europe. Both of these factors prompt the need for fundamental reviews, extend the reach of ancient ideas and knowledge and reveal human and environmental diversity. What is more, geographical discoveries and the attainment of large markets and 'inexhaustible' sources of energy configure a new mental framework which promotes expanded productivity, extends life expectancy and legitimises mechanical work. In parallel with this, the sixteenth century is also the century which witnessed the appearance of the 'great modern states', based on politics which advocate the greater glory and prosperity of the state where nature becomes an icon of identity and, at the same time, of an alternative world view.[68]

As a final point we must ask what relational elements can be established between the environmental perceptions in sixteenth and seventeenth-century descriptions and the characteristics of the territorial apprehension and invasion of America, Asia or Europe. Antoni de Montserrat's modus operandi is similar to that of authors who described other regions, although budgets and attitudes differ considerably.

In America, the 'New World,' previous classical discourse had to confront lands which had hitherto neither been imagined nor witnessed and where Europeans rapidly dominated the native peoples because the discourses were dominated by the 'Eurocentric belief' in the evident superiority of European civilisation, culture and technology.[69] In America, almost immediately nature was reconstructed according to European commercial interests: generating a market of American resources to be incorporated into the European commercial dynamic asymmetrically constructed on the basis of north-west European manufacturing specialisation and where the rest of the world was a supplier of foodstuffs, raw materials or precious metals.[70]

Objectives in America meant that during the colonisation process the landscape was constructed without taking into account its own particularities. This generated a distorted image of its 'model society' and consequently led to it suffering a process of Europeanisation of the environment, with serious ecological consequences: the trophic and agricultural and ecological networks were altered due to substitution of the pre-Hispanic agricultural systems by intensive European agriculture, thus accelerating systematic degradation of the land.

For America, postcolonial studies suggest that the incorporation of new knowledge allowed definition of the territorial identity of the environment to aid the colonisation process. But these same descriptions will also be useful in configuring the theoretical elements necessary to justify the Creole identity in the nineteenth century. That is to say, sixteenth and seventeenth century descriptions of America will define the way in which Creole society would structure itself in the nineteenth century[71] and, in addition, from these descriptions would arise a large part of the dominant perceptions of the environment in contemporary Latin American societies and they would become the 'ideological' justification for long-term systematic environmental depredation.

Significantly, the use of American descriptions from the sixteenth and seventeenth centuries in nineteenth century Creole political constructions has a parallel process in Europe, where descriptions of your own territory are true icons of identity which are recovered and used as a basis for national constructions in the nineteenth century, a time when Renaissance descriptions are rediscovered and reedited and proposals for improving the territory are studied and indeed applied.

The process in Asia has both similarities and differences. For the Europeans, in contrast to America, Asia was a familiar place, due to ancient religious conflicts and historical commercial routes. In Europe there exists a knowledge and awareness of the economic, social and political complexity of the region, where the native peoples have stable and efficient commercial networks.[72] In Asia, the religious behaviour of analysing beliefs to 'change from within' has a parallel in the natural environment. Renaissance descriptions could not proposes changing territory but correcting the ancient texts and creating an image of the real territory, understanding the social, economic and political complexity of the region adapting to the routes, uses and customs of inhabitants of the region in their coexistence with nature.

Obviously we cannot generalise in this matter to include all of Asia. Attitudes in India, Japan, China[73] or the Philippines,[74] for example, doubtless had their own nuances. Nevertheless, we can say that in Antoni de Montserrat's text there exists a respect and need for analysis of an environment, that created by Akbar, seen as a complex, dynamic and cohesive system, where control of nature is a symbol of political control of the territory, especially as evidenced through descriptions of the domestication of animals, hunting and agriculture. Descriptions made during the seventeenth century English and Dutch invasion would be deserving of a different interpretation. Furthermore, it is particularly interesting to research the utilitarian use of sixteenth century descriptions during the invasions of the 19th century.[75]

Notes

1 Gauvin Bailey. *Art on the Jesuit Missions in Asia and Latin America, 1542-1773.* Toronto: U of Toronto P, 2001; *The Jesuits and the Grand Mogul: Renaissance Art at the Imperial Court of India, 1580-1630.* Washington: Smithsonian Institution, 1998; Beach, Milo Cleveland. 'An Early European Source in Mughal Painting.' *Oriental Art* 22.2 (1976): 180–188; *The Grand Mogul: Imperial Painting in India, 1600-1660.* Williamstown: Sterling and Francine Clark Art Institute, 1978; *The Imperial Image, Paintings for the Mughal Court.* Washington DC: Freed-Hardeman College, 1981.

2 For an introduction to A. de Montserrat's text, see: Josep Lluís Alay. 'Introducció,' Antoni de Montserrat, *Ambaixador a la cort del Gran Mogol: viatges d'un jesuïta del segle XVI a l'India, Pakistan, Afganistan i Himàlaia.* (Lleida: Pagès, 2002), 9–51. For further information on the map of Tibet produced by Antoni de Montserrat, see, Sven Hedin. 'Early European Knowledge of Tibet', *Geografiska Annaler* 1 (1919): 290–339.

3 Antoni de Montserrat, *Ambaixador a la cort* ... 55–57

4 Montserrat 58.

5 Montserrat 201.

6 A 'now' different to the medieval literary and pictorial representation through which it was possible to view both the past and the future, see Charles M. Sherover *The Human Experience of Time: The Development of Its Philosophical Meaning.* (Evanston: Northwestern UP, 2001).

7 Montserrat 201, 261.

8 To observe the process of correcting ancient texts during the conquest of America, see: Roa-de-la Carrera, Cristian. 'El Nuevo Mundo como problema de conocimiento: Americo Vespucio y el discurso geografico del siglo XVI.' *Hispanic Review,* 70. 4 (2002): 557–580.

9 For the dispersal of plant species in India after the discovery of America, see Haggen 'The Bahia–Goa Route in the Dispersal of Brazilian Plants to Asia. *American Antiquity* 25.2 (1959): 267–268.

10 Montserrat 131.

11 Montserrat 310.

12 Montserrat 124.

13 Montserrat 287.

14 On European medical theories regarding the tropics see David N Livingstone 'Human Acclimatization: perspectives on a contested field of inquiry in Science, medicine and geography' *History of Science* 25 (1987): 359–394; Dane Kennedy, 'The Perils of the Midday Sun: Climate Anxieties in the Colonial Tropics' *Imperialism and the NaturalWorld,*

ed. John M. Mackenzie (Manchester: Manchester UP, 1990), 118–140; David Arnold, *The Problem of Nature Environment, Culture and European Expansion* (Oxford: Blackwell, 1996); Mark Harrison *Climates and Constitutions. Health, Race, Environment and British Imperialims in India 1600–1850*. (New York: Oxford UP, 2000); David Arnold, ed. *Warm climates and western medicine : the emergence of tropical medicine, 1500–1900* (Amsterdam: Rodopi, 1996).

15 See Álvarez Raquel Peláez. *La conquista de la naturaleza americana* (Madrid: Consejo Superior de Investigaciones Científicas, 1993); Rebok, Sandra. 'Alexander von Humboldt y el modelo de la Historia Natural y Moral' *Hnet* 3 (2001): 1–25.

16 Montserrat 86.

17 Montserrat 200.

18 Montserrat 199.

19 Montserrat 322.

20 Montserrat 197.

21 Dauril Alden. *The Making of an Enterprise: The Society of Jesus in Portugal, Its Empire, and Beyond, 1540-1750*. (Stanford: Stanford UP, 1996); Andrew C. Ross *A Vision Betrayed: The Jesuits in Japan and China, 1542–1742* (Edinburg: Edinburgh UP, 1994).

22 Montserrat 78.

23 Montserrat 146.

24 Montserrat 140.

25 Montserrat 170.

26 Montserrat 70.

27 Montserrat 256.

28 Montserrat 153.

29 Montserrat 166.

30 Montserrat 76.

31 In a note in the margin, the author indicates his intention to write globally about the universe of India, a reference to the second book, which is now lost.

32 Montserrat 263.

33 Irfan Habib, *The Agrarian System of Mughal India* (Bombay: Asia Publishing House, 1963).

34 Wilfrid Blunt, 'The Mughal Painters of Natural History' *Burlington Magazine* 90. 539 (1948): 49–50.

35 Montserrat 266.

36 Montserrat 147.

37 Montserrat 248.

38 Montserrat 250.

39 Montserrat 80.

40 Alfred Crosby, *Ecological Imperialism: The Biological Expansion of Europe, 900–1900* (Cambridge: Cambridge UP, 1994).

[41] Joanne Woolway 'Spenser and the Culture of Place' *Early Modern Literature Studies*, Oslo, 1996. 1 Nov. 2006, <tp://extra.shu.ac.uk/emls/iemls/conf/texts/woolway.html>

[42] See Karen O'Brien, 'Imperial Georgic, 1660–1789', *The Country and the City Revisited: England and the Politics of Culture, 1550–1850*, Gerald Maclean, Donna Landry and Joseph P. Ward: eds. (Cambridge: Cambridge UP, 1999); John Chalker, *The English Georgic: A Study in the Development of a Form* (Baltimore: Johns Hopkins UP, 1969); Dwight L. Durling. *Georgic Tradition in English Poetry* (New York: Columbia UP, 1935); Richard Feingold. *Nature and Society: Later Eighteenth-Century Uses of the Pastoral and Georgic*. (New Brunswick: Rutgers UP, 1978); Alastair Fowler. 'The Beginnings of English Georgic'. *Renaissance Genres: Essays on Theory, History, and Interpretation,* Barbara K. Lewalski, ed. (Cambridge, Mass: Harvard UP, 1986, 105–125; Jane Tylus. 'Spenser, Virgil and the Politics of Poetic Labor.' *ELH* 55.1 (1988): 53–77; Anthony Low. *The Georgic Revolution* (Princeton: Princeton UP, 1985).

[43] Neil Evernden *The Social Creation of Nature* (Baltimore: Johns Hopkins UP, 1992)

[44] José Manuel Naredo *La economía en evolución* (Madrid: Siglo XXI, 1987) 91.

[45] Naredo 80, 91.

[46] Joan Pau Rubiés *Travel and Ethnology in the Renaissance: South India through European Eyes, 1250–1625* (Cambridge: Cambridge UP, 2000).

[47] Sanjay Subrahmanyam, *The Portuguese Empire in Asia 1500–1700: A Political and Economic History* (London and New York: Longman, 1993), 147.

[48] Montserrat 145.

[49] Montserrat 69.

[50] Montserrat 124.

[51] Kapil Raj 'Colonial Encounters and the Forging of New Knowledge and National Identities: Great Britain and India, 1760–1850,' *Nature and Empire: Science and the Colonial Enterprise Osiris* 15 (2000): 119–134.

[52] Montserrat 124.

[53] This idea is repeated in another fragment when describing Akbar's character. 'When he goes to war, he always goes hunting.' Montserrat 322.

[54] Anand S. Pandian. 'Predatory Care: The Imperial Hunt in Mughal and British India.' *The Journal of Historical Sociology*, 14.1 (2001): 90.

[55] Montserrat 323.

[56] E.F. Wellesz, 'An Akbar-Namah Manuscript' *The Burlington Magazine for Connoisseurs* 80. 471 (1942): 135–143.

[57] Ebba Koch, 'Mughal Palace Gardens from Babur to Shah Jahan (1526–1648),' *Muqarnas* 14 (1997): 143–165.

[58] Montserrat 142.

[59] Montserrat 225.

[60] Montserrat 169.

[61] Montserrat 161.

[62] Montserrat 128.

[63] Clarence J. Glacken. *Huellas en la playa de Rodas: naturaleza y cultura en el pensamiento occidental desde la Antigüedad hasta finales del siglo XVIII* (Barcelona, 1996) 350s.

[64] Montserrat. 82 and 156

[65] Montserrat. 69, 71 and 127

[66] Richard Helgerson, *Forms of Nationhood: The Elizabethan Writing of England*. (Chicago: U of Chicago P, 1992).

[67] Trevor J. Barnes and James S. Duncan, eds., *Writing Worlds: Discourse, Text and Metaphor in the Representation of Landscape* (London: Routledge, 1992); Denis Cosgrove and Stephen Daniels, eds.; *The Iconography of Landscape: Essays on the Symbolic Representation, Design, and Use of Past Environments* (Cambridge: Cambridge UP, 1992).

[68] Clarence J. Glacken, *Huellas en la playa de Rodas. Naturaleza y cultura en el pensamiento occidental, desde la Antigüedad al siglo XVIII.* (Barcelona: Ediciones del Serbal, 1996) 653; Stephen Daniels *Fields of vision: Landscape Imagery and National Identity in England and the United State* (Princeton: Princeton UP, 1993); James Duncan and David Ley, eds. *Place, Culture, Representation* (London and New York: Routledge, 1993) 12.

[69] Guillermo Castro. *Naturaleza y Sociedad en la Historia de América Latina*. (Panama: CELA, 1996), 141.

[70] Juan Carlos Solórzano. '*Los antecedentes de la conquista española en América: crecimiento económico en Europa del norte, desarrollo del comercio marítimo portugués y expansionismo militar castellano* (1000-1500).' *Avances de investigación del– CIHAC* 73 (1994): 6.

[71] Jorge Cañizares Esguerra 'New World, New Stars: Patriotic Astrology and the Construction of Indian and Creole Bodies in Colonial Spanish America, 1600-1650,' *American Historical Review* 104 (1999): 33–68 and 'Nation and Nature: Nature Narratives and Identities in Latin America,' forthcoming.

[72] Ravi Rajan, 'Imperial Environmentalism: The Agendas and Ideologies of Natural Resource Management in British Colonial Forestry, 1800–1950,' *Nature and the Orient: The Environmental History of South and Southeast Asia*, ed. Richard Grove et. al. (Delhi: Oxford UP, 1998).

[73] Francisco Roque de Oliveira. *A construção do conhecimento europeu sobre a China, c. 1500 – c. 1630. Impressos e manuscritos que revelaram o mundo chinês à Europa culta*, Doctoral Thesis, Barcelona, 2003 and '*Cartografia antiga da cidade de Macau*, c. 1600–1700. *Confronto entre modelos de representaçao europeus e chineses*' *Scripta Nova* 10.218 (2006): 53.

[74] Maria Antonia Martí Escayol '*Las descripciones geográficas: la introducción de las Filipinas en la ciencia europea*' *España y el Pacífico* ed. Legazpi, Leoncio Cabrero, (Madrid: Sociedad Estatal de Conmemoraciones históricas, 2004) 33–62.

[75] Mark Harrison, *Climate and Constitutions: Health, Race, Environment and British Imperialisms in India 1600–1850* (New York: Oxford UP, 2000).

5. Between 'Adagia' and 'Aporia': Representations of Alterity in François Rabelais' *Gargantua* and Pieter Bruegel's Paintings

Davinder Mohini Ahuja

In order to establish its central thematic concerns of community and Christian love, François Rabelais' *Gargantua* (1534) invokes a parabolic memory replete with classical and Biblical metaphors. By situating his moral allegory within the ideological matrix of Christian humanism and through privileging an unmediated and unified Nature, Rabelais narrates a sovereign plot located in Stoic Time. Stoic Time is here understood as a natural, objective and moral element in the structure of the world that has affinity to the materialist rather than any transcendental image or the Platonic world of ideas.[1] Conversely, however, Rabelais' systemic subversion of the intended moral order through techniques such as parody and licentious speech performs a defacing of normative values and creates a slippage that disseminates meaning. Textual intention becomes alienated and argument, seemingly so uniform earlier, begins to resemble a self-engendered paradox or aporia.

In depicting the indifferent and ahistorical rhythms of Nature, and with its tenets in proverbial wisdom, Pieter Bruegel's iconography is an accruement of adages, parables, and mythology. At one level, the painter's narration of assured faith and persuasion is an attestation of self-hood and judgment. Like Rabelais before him, Bruegel's thematic use of adagia belongs to an episteme that is self-referential and mimetic. Paradoxically, however, while representing his moralistic paradigm, Bruegel often obscures the transcendental thematic through strategies of alterity, or the state or quality of being other,—distancing the implied centre of the 'text' through detachment, opposition or satire. Narrated time is made discontinuous with startling effect and hermeneutic is released into obscurity.

The popularity of proverbs during the sixteenth century shares with Renaissance humanism its historical interest of bringing a detailed understanding of the Classical past to bear on the letters and life of the present and to criticize the present in the light of the past. *Adagiorum Collectanea* (1500), compiled by the Dutch humanist Desiderius Erasmus and which expanded from its first edition in 1500 to the tenth edition in 1536 to include over 4000 proverbs, brought immense popularity to this genre. Central to the genre's intent was the context and occasion for reflection on education and instruction of modern day rulers. Proverbs encapsulate time-honoured truths and ancient wisdom through the use of metaphors or allegory, hyperbole and enigma. Thus adagia, though often using semantic ambiguity or *double entendre*, codifies moral correction. At one level then, as proverbial wisdom, the adage belongs to the absolute and transcendental moral realm: its preconceived essentialist and utopian time stunts narrative growth, with the effect that its narrative possibilities seem foreclosed.

Conceptually and diametrically opposed to adagia lies aporia, which was originally a Greek term meaning puzzle: etymologically, 'a-poros' means lacking a 'poros', a path or a passage. For Plato, 'aporia' is an integral dimension of knowledge. In his Dialogues such as *Meno* (370 BCE) and *Phaedo* (360 BCE), it is used as a particular model of dialectic that minimises uncertain signification and clears conceptual puzzlement in the reconstruction of true knowledge. It is significant that in Plato aporia is grounded in remembrance or anamnesis defined as the thesis that knowledge is wholly a process of recollection of pre-existent and universal fundamental moral truths.[2] The method of aporia in Plato is thus an exercise in logical deduction and reasoning. However, it can assume very different dimensions as in the case of Jacques Derrida for whom aporia suggests a structural infinity, a hypothetically unlimited knowledge of conditions, rules and imperatives of interpretations. The implied openness towards a future resists being circumscribed by the limits of signification. As such, aporia in Derrida is a rhetorical figure of doubt in which the conditions of possibility or 'presence' of an event or concept are, paradoxically, its own conditions of impossibility. Thus the aporiatic 'play of the text' where the grand prophetic narrative is deconstructed is fundamentally opposed to the social, political, and cultural–materialist matrices of moral meaning that constitute adagia. Aporia, is used in this essay generally to mean an interpretive impasse that engages with the experience of non-passage—of being in doubt, or confusion, concerning itself with 'being stuck' in dialectic, as Derrida says.[3]

Situated between adagia and aporia as it were, Renaissance literature and art is characterised by 'a tension between its attraction to a past representing the fullness of original truth and its resistance to that past in the face of puzzling historical contingency.'[4]

In both Rabelais and Bruegel, the text's prescriptive and teleological moral framework is forced into tension by elements that perform an alterity repeatedly. This paper will analyse the similar narrative strategies and the accompanying paradoxical significations that emerge in the works of both Rabelais and Bruegel in order to demonstrate the dialectical exchange between the past and the ephemeral present and will explore the contrariness in their works between moral theme and aporiatic technique, an opposition that subverts and alienates their structures of representation and creates an otherness of time.

Centering around the debate between the material and putative reality on the one hand and the constant reminders of imaginary ideals on the other, as well as the aporiatic processes that find themselves suspended somewhere between these two paradoxical ends, this essay suggests three focal points in its comparative analysis: Body, History and Language, and Utopia, and is divided accordingly.

Gargantua opens with the Prologue and its implicit inter-textual genealogy in the form of the satyr Silenus, half-beast, half divine-profundity that represents schizophrenic duality. Playfully contrasting the exterior and the interior, the comic and the serious as it does, the Prologue instructs the reader to look beneath the surface for a sub-textual meaning different from the surface one. In asking readers not to impose hermeneutic closure on the text's multi-valent discourse, Rabelais sanctions incertitude in what seems to be the novel's first instance of a series of reversals and '*peripetiae.*'

Body

In a sweeping gesture of epic reversal and anarchic carnival, Rabelais' *Gargantua* privileges 'the lower bodily stratum'.[5] Rabelaisian laughter, with its politics of transgression, symbolised through the subversive *Mardi gras* (the carnival before Lenten fasting) as Bakhtin upholds, undermines the prevailing institutions of power and 'sublimates death to announce rebirth.'[6] Rabelais' corporeal poetics are materialistic and refer to his exaltation of the functional open body, the prolific site which serves the drama of birth, coitus, death, growing, ingesting, and excretion. As Renate Lachmann observes, 'This corporeal drama applies not to the private, individual body, but rather to the larger collective one of the folk'[7] where images of community serve, as Bakhtin's politics see it, a locus of fertility and growth. This cyclical regeneration of the open body situated within an unmediated and pure time, and totally integrated with nature, travesties the closure of medieval asceticism and mysticism.

A post-Bakhtinian reading of *Gargantua,* however, reveals a textual dimension fraught with semantic paradox. In a major paradigmatic shift, and by the time we are shown into the Abbey of Thélème close to the end of this book, the scatological Gargantuan body is completely subordinated to mind and spirit. In Thélème, projected as the narrative's Utopian space in which Thelema, the evangelical Will of God reigns, bodily functions become marginalised until they are made invisible. Man's harmony with nature is redefined not in the external bodily emblematic, but through intellection, honour and good conscience.[8] In following 'Do What Thou Wilt', the Individual will replicates God's Will, which in turn, is Everybody's Will. Undifferentiated thus, its' pure harmony belongs to the illusory realm of the Platonic Idea. Divested of its function of direct description, this metaphoric usage dismantles the text's earlier corporeal realism and alienates rational or objective time.

Moreover, although it continues to endorse its faith in community, 'If some man or woman said, 'Let's drink', all drank...'[9] the idea of the community itself, however, now seems mediated through the Abbey's Epicureanism, with its 'civilising practice' of nurturing refinement and taste, and its hierarchies of culture and class 'well born.'[10] These tropological exotica and courtly practices index their withdrawal from popular culture and are qualitatively different from Rabelais' earlier projections of a bucolic green world. Thus, Thélème combines both generic opposites—satire and Utopia. Whether this anti-abbey can be read as an ironical hypallage, or its hyperbolic description be taken at its face value, for the Rabelaisian reader, certitude is teased into chiastic indeterminacy.

Again, themes of power and transgression are situated in the hermeneutical realm of myth. In the mythical narrative of the giants, if on the one hand, 'the magical property for superabundant growth thematically overwhelms and obscures the inevitable decay of matter',[11] then on the other, its exaggerated grotesquery ruptures the narrative's Stoic Time in which it was originally situated. The magic realism that surrounds Gargantua's strange and parodist nativity as he comes out of his mother Gargamelle's ear reads the body simultaneously in terms of realism as hyperbole and an incredulously irrational fiction. Reading the Rabelaisian body as a metaphor for maturation and abundance becomes problematised as 'bi-dimensionality of giant and man fuses to create an enthralling illusion'[12] of transformation.

Another example of how paradox works in Rabelais, the brooch on Gargantua's cap is a puzzling device and is much more than a mere embellishment to the young giant's apparel. It has a motto and an emblem. Earlier readers have remarked on the motto around the figure of the androgyne as Saint Paul's classic exposition of brotherly love or agape: 'Charity seeketh not her own (gains)' (1 Corinthians 13). Although the androgyne, symbol of perfect love, is the emblem of Christian love, the hieroglyph remains impenetrable. As Jerome Schwartz argues, the Pauline motto in praise of self-less Christian love, contrasts sharply with the egocentric conception of *eros* which is expressed in the pseudo-androgyne image where the two heads, unlike the hermaphrodite in Plato's *Symposium*, look at each other.[13] Gargantua's device juxtaposes an androgyne figure symbolising a love which parodically seeks its own, and the Pauline definition of charity which does not. The meaning inherent within the figure of the androgyne is different from the meaning that accrues to it from its implied para-textual context of Plato's *Symposium*. The antithetical nature of the two elements thus forms a dialectic of paradox wherein the performative and the constantive dimensions co-exist simultaneously making the device perplexing.

Like the French author before him, Pieter Bruegel's paintings resonate with the aporiatic and share the Rabelaisian obfuscation between the overt meaning and the hidden. Abraham Ortelius, the humanist cartographer who made the first world atlas, *Theatrus Orbis Terrarum*, and friend of Bruegel in Antwerp, claimed in 1574 that Bruegel's work 'gives something beneath what he paints'.[14] In his portrayal of kermises (annual village festivals held on the feast day of the local patron Saint), outdoor fairs and festive peasant weddings, Bruegel, like Rabelais, foregrounds the common man merrymaking boisterously and seeks a new vernacular realism. The realism of the unconscious demands of the body with their secularising tendency suggests an opposition to medieval hermeticism. The painter's stunning gift for physiognomy culminates in three brilliant compositions of tremendous vitality that he produced during the 1560s: *Wedding Dance in the Open Air* (1566), and two rustic scenes, *The Peasant Dance* (1567), and the *Peasant Wedding* (1567).

Bruegel's *Wedding Dance* contains concrete manifestations of frolicking peasants with their awkward gestures. On the surface, Bruegel's precise register of indigenous material culture and sartorial detail—clothing, headgear, trousers, belts, laces —makes the painter an exponent of rustic and ethnographic curiosity. Exhibited in an image of holiday excess, lust and gluttony and with their 'intoxicating powers of sensual experience'[15] the bodies of the dancing figures form the painting's central thematic concern of indulgence and extravagance. The entropic condition of the undifferentiated body as repetition is contrarily juxtaposed with the peasants' erotic energy and libido. With their outstretched arms and their masked faces, Bruegel's animistic peasants resemble carnival dolls. Again, while the representation of the repetitive 'body' points to a common and formulaic existence, mirroring the universal in its basic truth, the faces that appear masked also hint at the dualistic identity thus suggesting differentiation and bifurcation. This use of the mask generates the *doppelgänger* effect. The allegory of natural profusion, celebrated as fantastic repetition, is dismantled. The mask as a device of defacement dehumanises the figures that seem to move towards an absence of identity, erasure, and a perplexing non-signification. Thus, despite the extraordinary vitality of the bodies, and in what seems like Bruegel's black humour, their empty faces lack human subjectivity. This results in estrangement, even a lack of integration with its rustic context. In other words, although bodily dislocations, and eccentric points of view all emphasise the earthy quality of the figures, yet they appear as self absorbed and heedless. Unlike Rabelais's gentle giants, they are not idealised but pessimistic and satirical portraits of the natural man. The folklorist thesis that approbates 'Peasant Bruegel' as the sympathetic ethnographer who depicted Brabant's popular folk motifs, stands deconstructed.

In another instance, the whole composition of *The Peasant Dance* (1567) vibrates with the rhythm and force of movement. The round and dense human forms are massive. The ruthlessness of the galloping couple, and the rowdy eating and drinking, contrast strangely with the delicate foliage of the trees and the peaceful mood of the landscape. Although what is given is an essentially realistic scene, the definitive presence of the Madonna replica that the revellers totally disregard, underlines that we are in an allegorical rather than a strictly mimetic mode. If, on the one hand, these frolicking peasants may be seen as an antidote to the closure implicit in hermeticism, then on the other, the scene may be read as the highly negative exemplum of belligerent peasants that while showing the dark underside of bacchic revelry, demystifies the 'naturalistic' subject. Bruegel probably intended this uncertainty. Like Rabelais, he seems to neutralise difference by framing it as paradox. The threatening aggression associated with knives and the upward mobility indicated by purses so prominently placed here, are haunting reminders of the radical power reversals of the Peasants Revolt of 1525, when the lowest rural and urban classes effectively seized control of large parts of Germany for several months.

Thus, multiple layers of often complex meaning can be discerned in Bruegel's imagery. As Walter Gibson points out, while *The Wedding Dance* can be seen as a 'dance of Death'[16], similarly, *The Peasant Dance* can be seen to embody the deadly sins, generally Lust and Gluttony. Again, whether the peasants in the paintings should be considered as moral exempla in the late-medieval tradition, or whether they might be evidence of festive practices and the comic, not satiric mode of representation, is to address a polemic that reconstructs the 'interpretive model' the audience brought to this particular visual encounter.

History and Language

In the subtexts and inter-texts that inform it, Rabelais' language performs a dynamic copia. Rabelais' humanism thrives on otherness as it questions, transforms, and reinvents rules of language. The farcical pastiche of Rabelais' language resonates with exaggerations and ludic deformations. The pedagogical debates of the sixteenth century between the old and absurd didactic certainties of medieval scholastic learning on the one hand, and the more mobile space of humanist education on the other, find their most hilarious expression here. Like Erasmus in the *Praise of Folly*, Rabelais (who admired Erasmus immensely), gives a monstrous and fantastic caricature of the bumbling theologians of the Sorbonne in the person of Janotus de Bragmardo. His deliberately obscure language and sophistry suggests a potentially dangerous doctrinal bigotry: he creates a language so larded and insular that nobody understands it. Rabelais, the Renaissance Humanist is vituperative in dismantling the citadel of medieval ignorance. Conversely, and reminiscent of the frank, insulting and fearless truth-speaking of the Ancient Cynics such as Diogenes and Menippus, Rabelais' 'parrheisia'[17] defaces the positive valuation of Christian humanist discourse: 'Friar John of the Hashes…returned to the choir, where the rest of the monks, gaping like so many stuffed pigs, were singing… That's shitten well sung! He cried when he saw them…'[18] His volatile and explosive language carries potency to demolish Picrochole, the warring and pharisaical enemy.

Again, vilified as Goths and Barbarians, and denigrated to the core, Rabelais inscribes the ethnic others, targets of his malediction, denunciation and endless insults on the great gate of the Abbey of Thélème. As he enacts a brutal ethnic violence, Rabelais re-inaugurates the founding gesture on which the 'agon' of cultural prejudices is built. The fundamental prejudice of locating the disparaged other on the opposite side of a 'transcendental' beauty and culture is a dividing practice that does not reconcile with his professed adage of love and charity.

While Rabelais' potent diatribe and 'parrheisis' shows the underside of verbal usage, Bruegel's use of Babel is significant in suggesting how the quest for any absolute meaning is eventually confusing and that not just the narrative about time but narrativity itself is enigmatic and disconcerting. If on the one hand, language usage provides the thesis of being in time, then Babel's confusion suggests a deferral or non-arrival of meaning. In Bruegel, the unresolved polemic between the past and present is best illustrated by paintings such as the enigmatic *The Tower of Babel* (1563) (see Figure 10).[19] While they necessitate meditation on memory and retrospection, the antinomies that constitute its signification—ruins and reconstruction—creates dialectic between human quest for meaning and the corrosive powers of time: thus, the very idea of Babel seems to be constructed on a labyrinth of transitions. As such, the painting may be seen as an allegory of temporality that performs a poetics of historiography.

Babel represents an adage. In the biblical passage in Genesis 11:1–9, God punishes Nimrod's 'hubris' for building the tower of Babel and confounds the people who built a tower whose top may reach unto heaven with confusion of languages (Babel being Hebrew for confusion). As a metaphor then, Babel stands as the nexus point between human aspiration and man's transgression. Bruegel's own visual treatment, therefore, builds upon Babel's indeterminate and paradoxical positioning within western humanistic discourse. If, on the one hand, the monstrous dimensions of *The Tower of Babel* are a pronouncement of Bruegel's humanist tendency and fascination with ideal and utopian enterprise, then on the other, they represent the arrogance of human aspiration and its attendant transgression. By showing both human existence and human experience as subject to the contingent and even tragic dimension of time, Bruegel's symbolic discourse speaks of 'aporias' of temporality.

With its grim reminder that speculation on time is an inconclusive rumination, the simultaneous depiction of past, present and projected future becomes perplexing for the viewer. Rising in the centre is the huge spiraling tower on which the multitude of antlike figures is swarming in the process of construction. Babel's 'ziggurat' form combined with a reference to the ruined Roman Colosseum that the tower replicates, suggests a juxtaposition of two temporal frames—the old and the new. Innovation is opposed to historical sedimentation in this tropical meta-historical narrative. Again, in his reference to the ruined Roman Colosseum, Bruegel uses, as Karl Mansbach maintains, 'this double symbol of ruined imperial might as an emblem for the frustrated aspirations of the Spanish King Philip II',[20] whose plans of imposing Catholic orthodoxy on the people of Flanders met with resistance.

At another level, the symbolic logic of the 'zigurrat' form—geometrically structured and systematically progressive as it appears—may be read as the rational layering of tradition. Built on the normative idea of repetition as progress, the Tower of Babel's mathematical and conservative structure represents 'formal' knowledge testified through its inscription of symmetry. Primarily an aporiatic gesture, the confusion of Babel is the passage to chaos that confounds the civilisational aspirations that its monolithic tower embodies.

Moving on to another brilliant work, *Landscape with the Fall of Icarus* (1555?) is one of the best examples of Bruegel's pictorial strategy of contrasting antithetical motifs and arranging compositions in binary patterns, so as to enable dialectical reflection. A mythological and fictional event with its traditional symbolic rejection of excessive pride and ambition, Icarus' fall is contrasted with the realistic mode of the plowman, the shepherd and the fisherman who all appear as exempla of the common man and humble labour. The quiet, eternal, and stoic motions of the spacious natural world appear oblivious to human events and to the startling phenomenon of the fall.

In relation to the symbolic level of the fall, that is, eternal punishment, the three figures might be said to persevere in their task of gaining eternal reward, salvation. Stoic indifference and preoccupation are seen everywhere as detachment. What is particularly significant, however, is that Icarus appears only as two legs jutting out of the sea. Compositionally speaking, the moralistic and spectacular failure of human ambition in a dim corner of the canvas is dwarfed by the scale of a massive landscape. The visually magnified role of the plowman whose action of plowing as renewal of nature contrasts with Daedalus' aggressive 'altering' of nature which results in his son's death. Whether or not Bruegel read Ovid directly or heard it from Ortelius, his *Fall of Icarus* (see Figure 11) is one of the most involved reverse *ekphrasis*, a visual commentary in art of a famous classical text.

Against the context of the dramatic contrast between land and sea, the presence of a third component—that of the distant ships problematises the existing dialectic. As the ethical transactions of the plowman[21] give way to historical time, the image of the ship with its passage into social transformation and conflict, interpellates the viewer in the alterity of the new emergent order, and into the complex historical contingencies of the time—commerce, a passage into distant lands and colonial expansionism.

What is noteworthy here is that narrated time of each constituent part moves at a different pace—eternal time or essentialist time as represented by the Plowman, fictional event or melodramatic time represented by Icarus, and the ship representing historical contingency. The three temporal planes are discrete from and indifferent to one other. In what looks like a meditation on time, this disconnectedness amongst the separate time schemes suggests an aporiatic rupture in the harmonious landscape.

Utopia

In *Gargantua*, magnificence, opulence and cornucopian abundance make Thélème an unreal and inaccessible space. Open to hermeneutical exegesis in its metaphoric and tropological representations as it may be, the Abbey as Utopia constitutes magical hyperbole. The Rabelaisian magical and improbable narrative promises Christian love and may be read as a paradoxical framework within which to analyse Bruegel's proverbial composition.

Deriving from its association with linguistic and literary materials, the complex and puzzling *Netherlandish Proverbs* (1559) is Bruegel's compendium of proverbial micro-narratives. With its visually overwhelming and dense figural coverage, it belongs with two other encyclopedic works by Bruegel: *Carnival and Lent* (1559) and *Children's Games* (1560). A literary and conservative means of social regulation with their interest in moral instruction, for Christian humanists, proverbs were the secular counterpart of such universalistic enterprises as Christopher Plantin's *Polyglot Bible* (1572). As with Rabelais' humanism, they demonstrate a pre-eminently optimistic faith in man's inherent goodness. Again, Erasmus' own adages are a synthesis of Christianity and Classical thought to guide the conduct of life. Inspired by Erasmus' *Praise of Folly* that had reached unprecedented heights of popularity in the Netherlands between 1550 and 1568,[22] and like the ingenious accumulation of popular and learned wisdom in the Eleventh Chapter of *Gargantua*, which is one continuous chain of proverbs, Bruegel's own collection of proverbs is vast.

The iconography in *Netherlandish Proverbs* that contains anywhere between 85–126 proverbs, is to be understood as a composite picture of 'the World upside down',[23] seen through many individual acts of folly. Margaret Sullivan identifies several proverbs in Bruegel's painting[24]—the young woman putting the blue cape around her old husband is deceiving i.e. cuckolding him. Conversely, the image also serves as an example of male anxiety and gynephobia. Casting roses before swine is a variant of the biblical casting pearls before swine. To shave a fool from Lucian means to fool someone. Erasmus gives Aristophanes as the source for 'eels are captured when the waters are muddied', making the point about tyrants who profit when the state is in turmoil. The example of the well-dressed man standing in front of the ruined castle wall throwing money into the water also appears in Erasmus' *Adages*. 'To throw seeds in the water' captures the idea of wastefulness and profligacy. Everyone is intent on his or her foolish or evil business. The inverted globe that hangs at the entrance of this village of fools is an allegorical allusion to the perversity and madness of the World. The world upside down with its popular motifs is based upon the principle of hierarchical inversion and represents a threatening or desired reality whose social mobility posits social revolution. However, the didacticism of proverbs conflated with the subversion of the world upside down creates a paradox and obfuscates authorial intention. The disciplining process of the social imaginary or false consciousness of ideological recollection is inherently problematic. It is at odds with the natural drive of human inclination to folly here depicted as natural desire. Suspended between negation and affirmation as these micro-narratives are, generally speaking, the idea of resistance as a condition of its own contrariety informs the entire work ostensibly given to moralising. That the social field offers resistance to proverbial wisdom may then be seen as a reverse gesture where provocative action works towards a destabilisation of force relations. Through *Netherlandish Proverbs* and its multiple nodes of immorality and by projecting a static and defunct future cut off from the present what Bruegel does, is to give his viewers a schizophrenic discourse and interpenetration between presence and absence.

The polymathic web of dystopia seen within the perspective of adagia ends with the shadow of a lone sailboat. The boat sails away from the scene towards a distant city beyond the waters perhaps suggesting repudiation of the world on its passage to salvation. At one level thus, Bruegel's narrative follows a horizontal movement of linear chronological time. This progression is based on moral judgment and historicality and apprehends causal logic that links present with future. The transition from objective reality of the physical world articulated as folly to passage into the noumenal realm serves as a strategic reminder of the ends of judgment, knowledge, and truth. As such, the movement from the world of action to a transcendent or teleological conception of salvation as the function of History is circumscribed within the grid of judgment and logic. Such an understanding of time imposes a potentially totalitarian ethical category on an already existing world. This direction also articulates the notion of fixity underlying adagia. Within its structural metanarrative, and underneath the fictional acts grasped together, is a reflective judgment of an interpretive community within a spatial and mnemonic coherence. This generates a conceptually unified practice showing itself to the viewer as a 'utopian face' or 'sacred island'—an allegorical opening to the future.

However, while Bruegel's imitation or representation collects many self-sufficient, auto-referential, and individual tableaus into an integrated narrative whole in order to create a material unity of its signs within an ethical category, the very subject of the painting is based on negation. Structured as a positive subject (salvation) that is always negating itself (folly), the idealised face of eternity or redemption contains its own destruction. The allegorical distance between the sign (the reality of actions as folly) and referent (the ideal or utopian as redemption), dismantles the logocentric grounding of the 'sacred'. The ideal future is made discontinuous with the present continuous performance of folly here so prominently depicted. Not just that. If one looks closely at the painting, there is the sense that the supposedly condemnable actions of folly do not appear condemned at all. Rendered in warm earthy tones with lines formed into round endearing shapes, the theatrical mimesis of a 'foolish', 'fallacious', and 'fallen' community in the present mode appears a far more attractive proposition than the lonely boatman on path to future salvation. Again, through a deliberate focus on the performance of worldly actions alone in his composition, and contrasting the experience of a material reality with 'action' of the mind, Bruegel reclaims importance of the human time. His privileging of the present, and simultaneously of alterity, makes his intention enigmatic such that ethical binaries become blurred and reflexivity about any future seems marginalised. Bruegel thus foregrounds temporal aporias of human existence and suggests that there is an aporia in the construal of time as past, present, and future into a whole.

One of the great strengths of Stoicism, Gilles Deleuze[25] reminds us, lies in having shown that 'every sign is a sign of the present, from the point of view of the passive synthesis in which past and future are precisely only dimensions of the present itself.' Typically, in yet one more gesture, difference becomes collapsed once again, between sign and the referent, between time conceived in the past and time represented in the impossible present, and between 'adagia' and 'aporia'. Rabelais and Bruegel, the great Renaissance Humanist thinkers taught us that the gap between the fallible man and the desirable man is conflated as aporia between the question of man's inventive narrative imagination and the subject who is made responsible by the expectation of the other.

Notes

1 For my understanding of the concept of Stoic Time, I am indebted to Panayiotis Tzamalikos's 'Origen and the Stoic View of Time,' *Journal of the History of Ideas*, 52. 4 (1991). Tzamalikos also demonstrates how to the Stoics, time always remained a 'something' located between being and non-being, in a state of existence and non-existence and thus an aporia.

2 I owe my understanding of Plato's concepts of aporia and anamnesis to two sources in particular: Maurice H. Cohen's 'The Aporias in Plato's Early Dialogues,' *Journal of the History of Ideas,* 23.2 (1962): 163–174 and Dominic Scott's 'Platonic Anamnesis Revisited,' *The Classical Quarterly* n.s. 37.2 (1987): 346–366.

3 Jacques Derrida, *Aporias* trans.Thomas Dutoit (Stanford: Stanford UP, 1993).

4 Francois Rigolot, 'Father Figures: Genealogy and Narrative Structure in Rabelais,' *Modern Philology*, 91.4 (1994): 482.

5 Mikhail Bakhtin, *Rabelais and His World* trans. Helene Iswolsky (Cambridge: MIT P, 1968): 368.

6 Bakhtin 88.

7 Renate Lachmann, Raoul Eshelman and Marc Davis, 'Bakhtin and Carnival: Culture as Counter-Culture,' *Cultural Critique:* 11 (1988–89): 124.

8 According to Marian Rothstein, 'Androgyne, Agape, and the Abbey of Thélème,' *French Forum*, 26. 1 (2001): 5; good conscience is synderisis. Rothstein explains 'synderesis' as the tendency to be drawn to what is good, inherent in human nature.

9 Francois Rabelais, *Gargantua and Pantagruel* trans. J.M.Cohen (London: Penguin Books, 1955): 159.

10 Rabelais 158.

11 Kitzie McKinney, 'Diversions ofTransformation in Pantagruel's Medlar Myth,' *The French Review* 49.4 (March 1986): 550.

12 Andre Winandy, 'Rabelais' Barrel,' *Yale French Studies* 50 Intoxication and Literature (1974): 14.

[13] Jerome Schwartz, 'Gargantua's Device and the Abbey of Thélème : A study in Rabelais' Iconography,' *Yale French Studies*, 47 (1972): 236.

[14] Quoted in Perez Zagorin, 'Looking for Pieter Bruegel,' *Journal of the History of Ideas* 64.1 (2003): 73–96. Bruegel is believed to have shared the unorthodox opinions of the Antwerp group of distinguished scholars, artists, and authors such as the celebrated geographer Abraham Ortelius (1527–1598), the great printer and publisher Christophe Plantin (1520–89), and the Dutch writer and engraver Dirck Coornhert (1522–90), all described as religious libertines. Among these men, some belonged to the religious sect known as the Family or House of Love.

[15] Ethan Matt Kavaler, *Pieter Bruegel: Parables of Order and Enterprise* (Cambridge: Cambridge UP, 1999): 147.

[16] Walter Gibson, *Pieter Bruegel and the Art of Laughter* (Berkeley: U of California P, 2006) 7. Other influential readings on Bruegel's peasants include Svetlana Alpers's 'Bruegel's Festive Peasants,' *Simiolus* 6 (1972–73): 163–76, Margaret D. Carroll's 'Peasant Festivity and Political Identity in the Sixteenth Century', *Art History* 10 (1987): 289–314 and Margaret A. Sullivan's *Bruegel's Peasants: Art and Audience in the Northern Renaissance* (New York: Cambridge UP, 1994).

[17] Antonia Szaberi, 'Rabelais *Parrhesiastes*: The Rhetoric of Insult and Rabelais's Cynical Mask,' *MLN* 120 Supplement (2005): S84–S123.

[18] *Rabelais* 27.

[19] The version of *The Tower of Babel* under discussion is the painting in the Kunsthistorisches Museum, Vienna and is different from *The 'Little' Tower of Babel* c.1563 which is housed in the Museum Boymans-van Beuningen, Rotterdam.

[20] Karl Mansbach, 'Pieter Bruegel's Towers of Babel', *Zeitschrift f ü r Kunstgeschichte,* 45 Bd., H.1. (1982) 47.

[21] Ethan Matt Kavaler, *Parables of Order and Enterprise* (Cambridge: Cambridge UP, 1999).

[22] With their condemnations of social mobility and the aspirations of the poor, proverbs reveal a thoroughly conservative outlook. These were evidently an effective means of social regulation at a time of social unrest. As noted by critics such as Zagorin, Kavaler and Margaret Sullivan, the proverb illuminated by Erasmus (who must have been current in Bruegel's humanist circle) and exemplified by Luther became at this time a major means of moral indoctrination of the lower classes by a newly entrenched, but still insecure bourgeoisie in a period of continuous social conflict.

[23] David Kunzle, 'Bruegel's Proverb Painting and the World Upside Down', *The Art Bulletin* 59.2 (1977): 197.

[24] Margaret Sullivan, 'Bruegel's Proverbs: Art and Audience in the Northern Renaissance,' *The Art Bulletin* 73.3 (September 1991): 460.

[25] Gilles Deleuze, *Difference and Repetition* trans. P. Patton (New York: Columbia UP, 1994) 143.

The Eighteenth and Nineteenth Centuries

The Eighteenth and Nineteenth Centuries

If Renaissance art and literature focuses on the drama of human existence in time, captured in portraiture and mythological-religious themes, the neo-classical age continues this tradition but adds to it a new interest in the natural world for its own sake. Instead of religious fervour, intellectual bravura or the so-called focus on man, we may note a shift towards a secular, bourgeois outlook characterised by reasonableness. This outlook manifested itself in the rise of landscape painting and the depiction of bourgeois interiors, especially in the Netherlands. At the same time, the age enshrined classicist conventions. Consequently, even the representation of landscape tended to be divided between nostalgic evocation of bucolic simplicity and an intimately realistic mode looking forward to the brave new world of the Enlightenment and Romanticism. Underlying the nostalgia is a classicist model of serene, idealised nature exemplifying, as in Alexander Pope, the truth of *discordia concors.* The same nostalgia, however, is transposed from the past to a realisable future of revolutionary transformation. These simultaneously backward-looking and forward-looking impulses invite a bifocal view of the age.

The fulcrum of division was the concept of 'nature'. On the one hand, neo-classicist elegance and correctness were founded on *la belle nature*, an idealised, benevolent and rational pattern underlying empirical variety and contrariety, serving as an aesthetic norm.

On the other hand, it was this same irreducible variety and contrariety that acquired a normative status, encouraging the artist towards an increasingly individualised engagement with actuality. Dr Johnson's praise of Shakespeare demonstrates this divided and indecisive aesthetic, whereby he uses neo-classicist criteria only to leave them behind in endorsement of varied contradictoriness. Similarly, if his criticism of metaphysical poetry because of its allegedly forced and irresponsible heterogeneity betrays a neo-classicist bias, it indicates at the same time the trajectory of an alternative aesthetic which prompted T.S. Eliot much later to identify the supposed flaws as the hallmark of poetry.

Idealised serene 'nature' fitted into the culture of politeness is often associated with the Shaftesbury circle. Nature in this view was an end-product, the actualisation of a potential made possible by the human artifice of civilisation. In contrast to this, nature had also been identified with that which is anterior to and untouched by human intervention. Anticipated by Montaigne and others, this view is to be found, once again, in Johnson's account of the Hebrides and the Western Islands. From Thomson's *Seasons* through Akenside to Wordsworth's nature poetry, we experience this oscillation and transition: by the latter half of the eighteenth century, nature is identified with the untamed potential of revolutionary transformation.

Actually, from the very outset, the neo-classical age was troubled by a tension between canons of refined elegance or lingering baroque-mannerist preciosity and the forces of democratisation. Unlike the poets in the court of Emperor Augustus, the epigonic Augustans subscribed to an aesthetic that could not find its proper aristocratic context any more. Historians of the eighteenth century have noted the peculiar juxtaposition of patrician and plebian perspectives or polite and popular canons. We must not forget that if it was an epoch of neo-classicism, it was equally, if not more, one of modern science and the Royal Society. The stability that the age cherished was more conceptual than actual, since it is in this period that all the traditional institutions were transformed by the financial revolution. Thus even if we narrow down our attention to landscape painting, we mark the divided response, the very dialectic of the age torn between nostalgia and hope, idealisation and realism. Of course, it is this two-way pull that holds the key to the age, for the eighteenth century is also an age of revolution, of the intellectual foundations of the French Revolution in particular. The rise and consolidation of print culture laid the economic and technological basis for the art of cartoon and illustration: literature and the visual arts were brought together in actual physical terms.

The two essays in this section 'Between Retrospect and Prospect...' and 'Picturing Power...' admirably exemplify the divided model of the long eighteenth century. Highlighting the irreverent energy of cartoon, caricature and popular literature in revolutionary France, the latter essay 'Picturing Power' is explicitly concerned with political upheaval and social transformation, holding satiric acerbity and revolutionary hope in balance. This was satire not directed at the emergence of the new order, as much

Tory satire was, but at the *ancien régime*. The end of a world is the beginning of another, inviting the bifocal view of reality outlined above. The essay on Claude tries to bring out his transitional location for he belongs to an earlier phase of contradiction between idealised nature and nature as the opposite of all that is tamed and controlled by man. His landscape beckons us out into the luminous distance of the Enlightenment even as it is steeped in Virgilian melancholy.

6. Between Retrospect and Prospect: The Landscape Painting of Claude Lorrain

Shirshendu Chakrabarti

Critics have generally associated the work of Claude Lorrain (1600–82) with what Kenneth Clark calls the tradition of ideal landscape, nostalgically recovering the Arcadian golden age celebrated in classical myth and bucolic poetry.[1] This is not a landscape committed to the irreducibly local and specific, as in Constable's intimate knowledge of the Stour valley. It is by contrast one which tends towards the general, making manifest a pre-ordained harmony and universality which sinks all empirical differences. This classicist tendency continued to hold sway, eloquently defended as late as 1759 by Imlac in Johnson's *Rasselas*[2] and above all shaping the influential aesthetic doctrine behind the *Discourses* (1769–91) of Joshua Reynolds. In conformity to the neo-classical aesthetic norm of *la belle nature*, nature in ideal landscape is the product of inclusion and exclusion rendering this underlying harmony visible: features are selected from nature rather in the way poetic diction is created out of the elements of ordinary speech. This 'nature' actualises its inherent potential for order and serenity by being 'civilised' from the state of untamed wildness that we habitually associate with the concept today.

But Claude is above all the representative of a divided age, caught between reminiscence and discovery, between classical values and the scientific revolution. This opposition between neo-classicist appeal to the past and the scientific vision of the future, between old and new forms of knowledge is a distinctive feature of the seventeenth and eighteenth

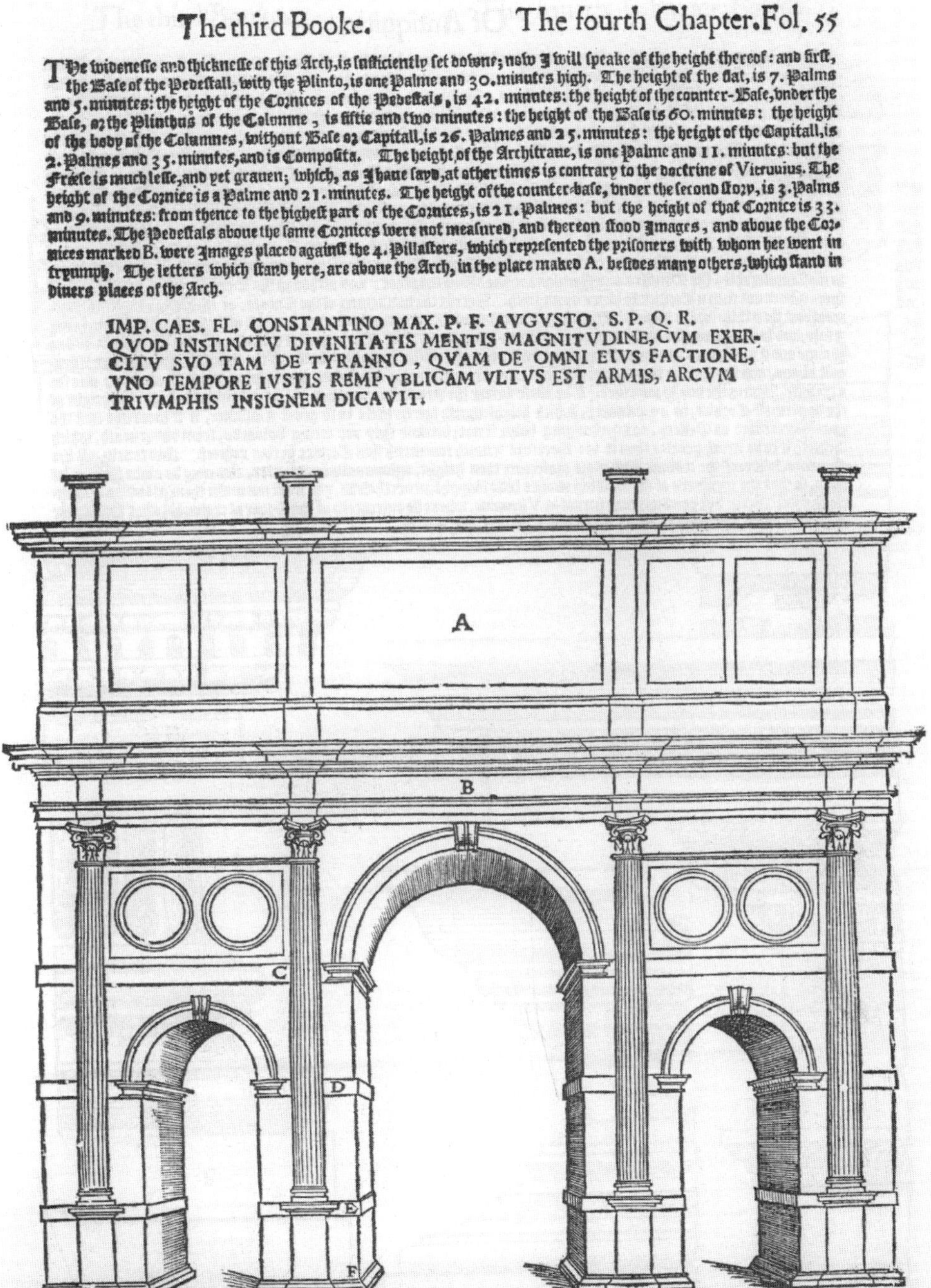

The third Booke. The fourth Chapter. Fol. 55

The wideneſſe and thickneſſe of this Arch, is ſufficiently ſet downe; now I will ſpeake of the height thereof: and firſt, the Baſe of the Pedeſtall, with the Plinto, is one Palme and 30. minutes high. The height of the flat, is 7. Palms and 5. minutes: the height of the Cornices of the Pedeſtals, is 42. minutes: the height of the counter-Baſe, vnder the Baſe, or the Plinthus of the Columne, is fiftie and two minutes: the height of the Baſe is 60. minutes: the height of the body of the Columnes, without Baſe or Capitall, is 26. Palmes and 25. minutes: the height of the Capitall, is 2. Palmes and 35. minutes, and is Compoſita. The height of the Architraue, is one Palme and 11. minutes: but the Freeſe is much leſſe, and yet grauen; which, as I haue ſayd, at other times is contrary to the doctrine of Vitruuius. The height of the Cornice is a Palme and 21. minutes. The height of the counter-baſe, vnder the ſecond ſtory, is 3. Palms and 9. minutes: from thence to the higheſt part of the Cornices, is 21. Palmes: but the height of that Cornice is 33. minutes. The Pedeſtals aboue the ſame Cornices were not meaſured, and thereon ſtood Images, and aboue the Cornices marked B. were Images placed againſt the 4. Pillaſters, which repreſented the priſoners with whom hee went in tryumph. The letters which ſtand here, are aboue the Arch, in the place maked A. beſides many others, which ſtand in diuers places of the Arch.

IMP. CAES. FL. CONSTANTINO MAX. P. F. AVGVSTO. S. P. Q. R.
QVOD INSTINCTV DIVINITATIS MENTIS MAGNITVDINE, CVM EXER-
CITV SVO TAM DE TYRANNO, QVAM DE OMNI EIVS FACTIONE,
VNO TEMPORE IVSTIS REMPVBLICAM VLTVS EST ARMIS, ARCVM
TRIVMPHIS INSIGNEM DICAVIT.

Figure 1. Sebastiano Serlio, the Arch of Constantine, from *The Five Books of Architecture*, 1611.

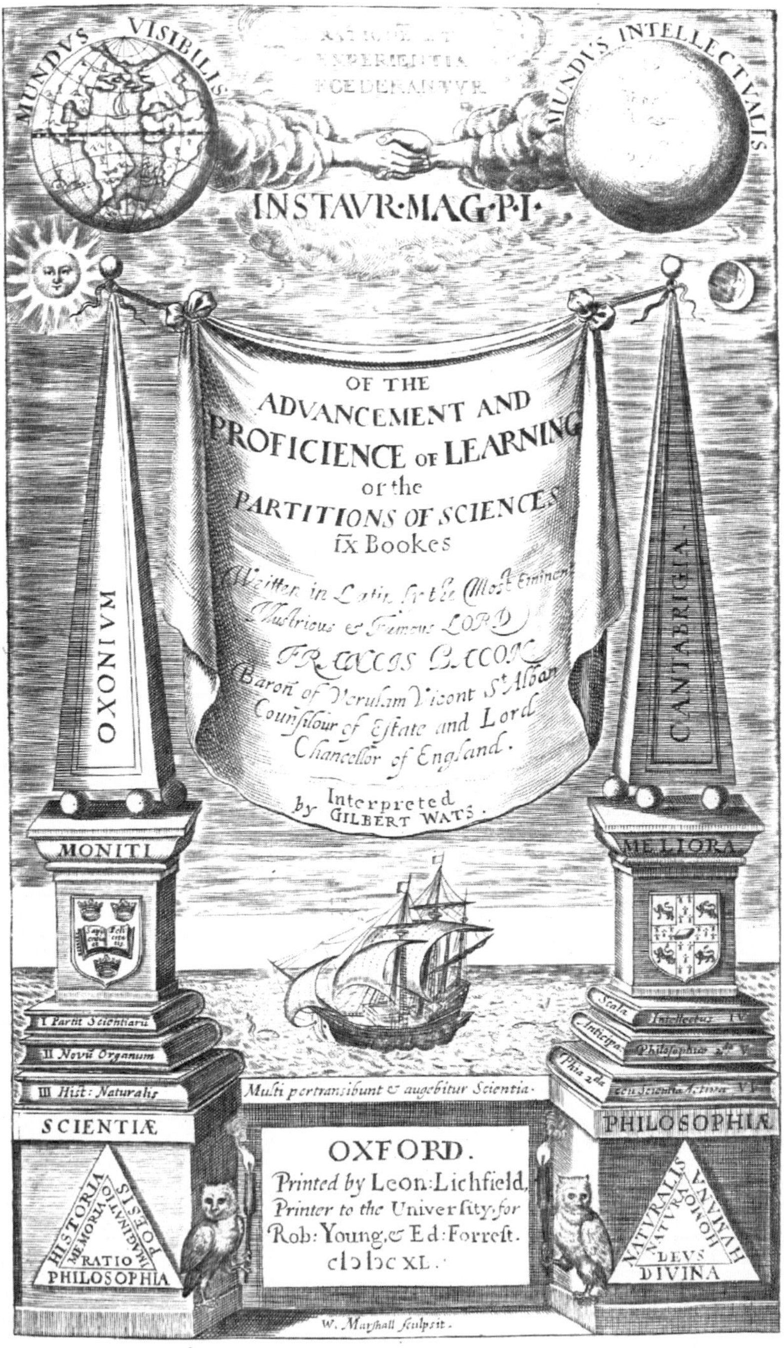

Figure 2. William Marshall, Frontispiece to Francis Bacon, *Of the Advancement and Proficience of Learning*, 1640.

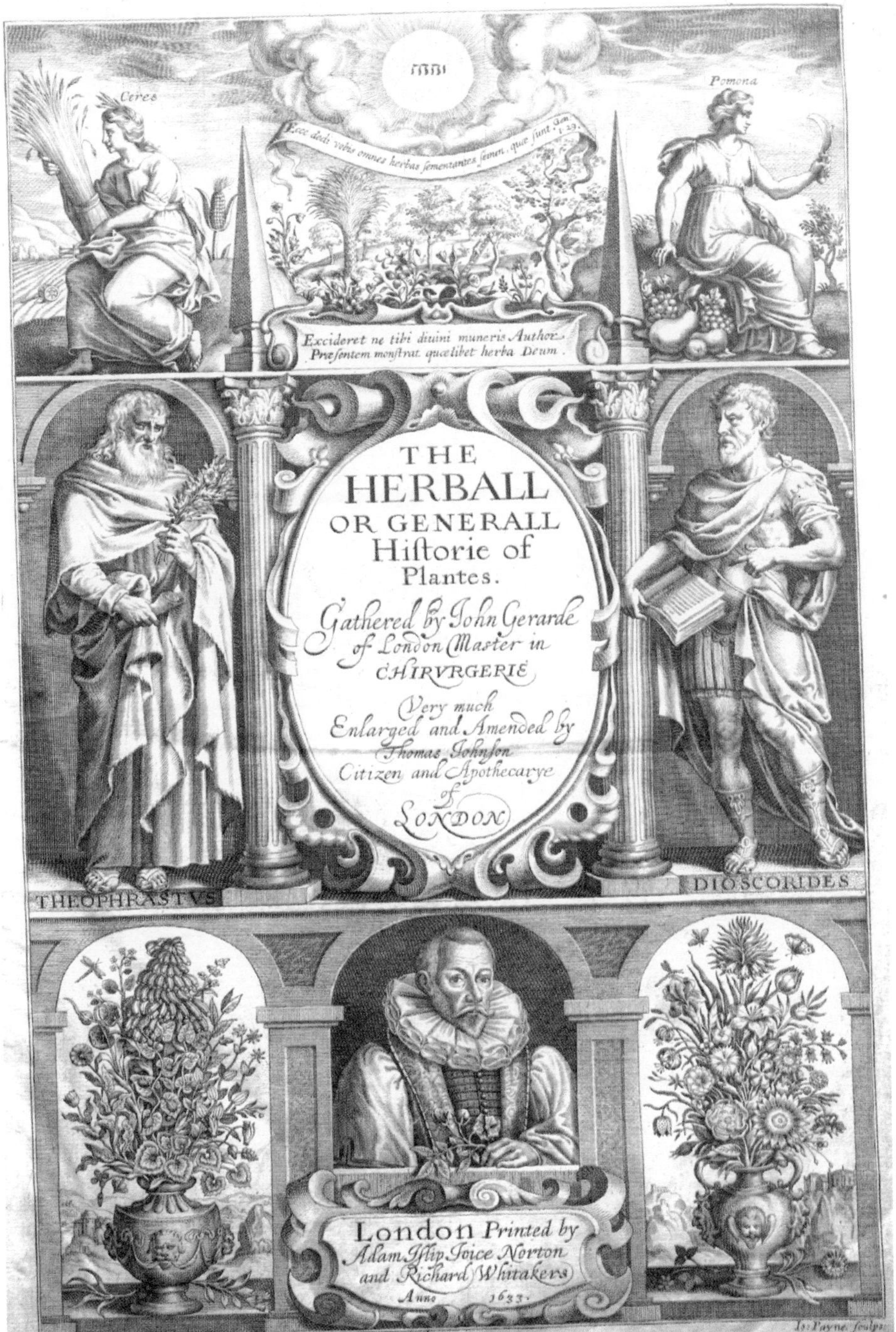

Figure 3. Frontispiece to John Gerard, *The Herball or Generall Historie of Plantes*, 1633.

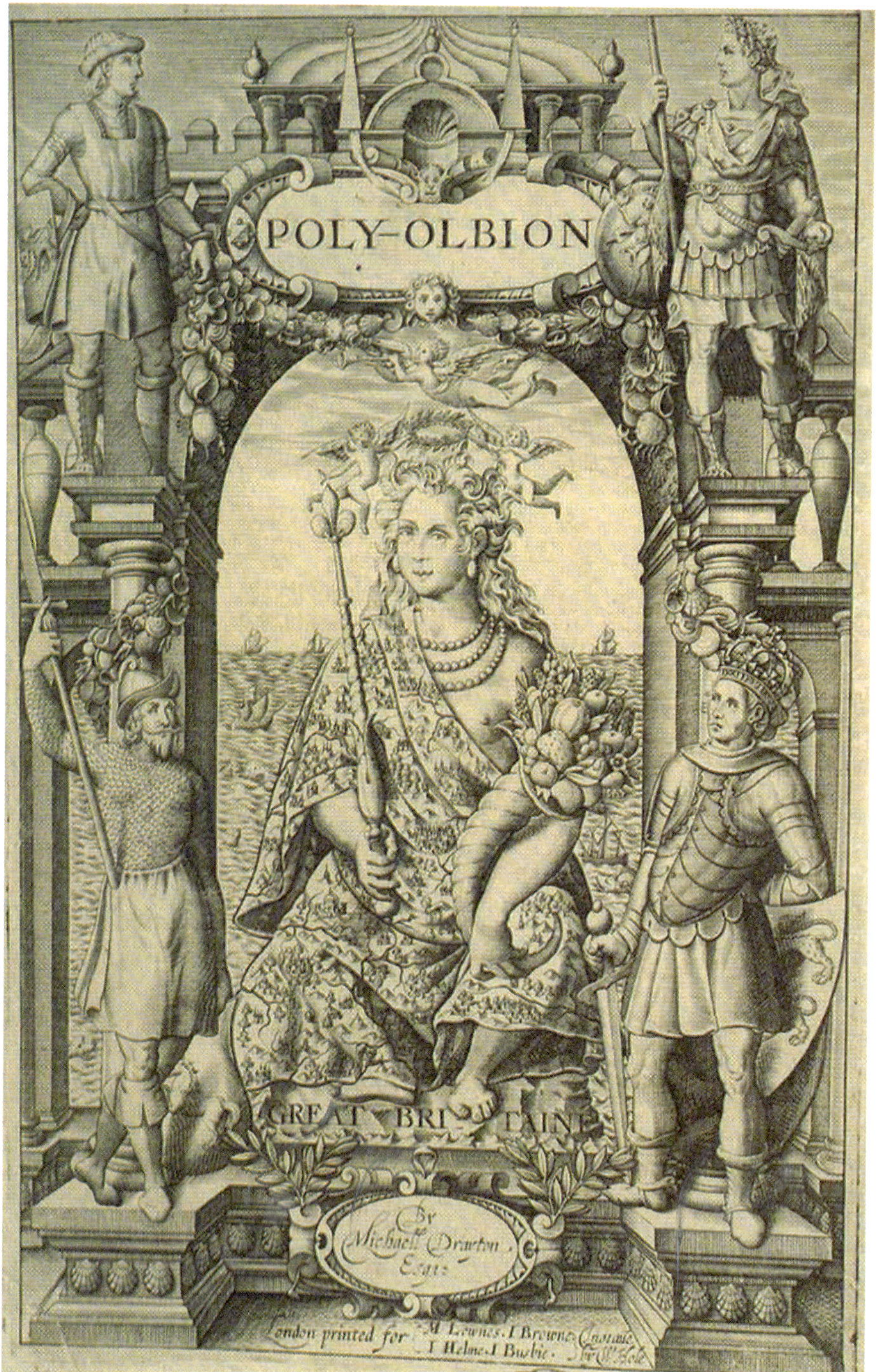

Figure 4. William Hole, Frontispiece to Michael Drayton: *Poly Olbion*, 1622.

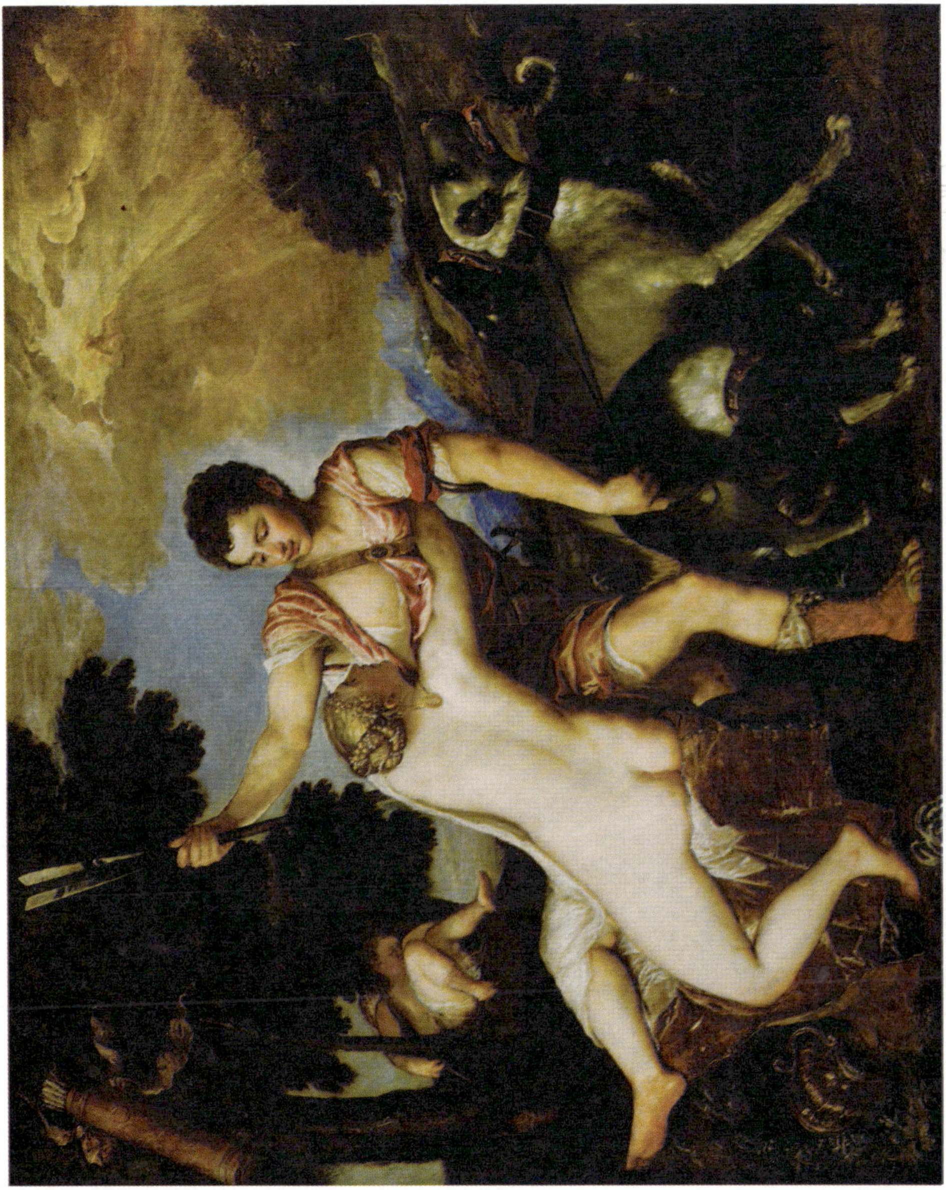

Figure 5. Titian, *Venus and Adonis*.

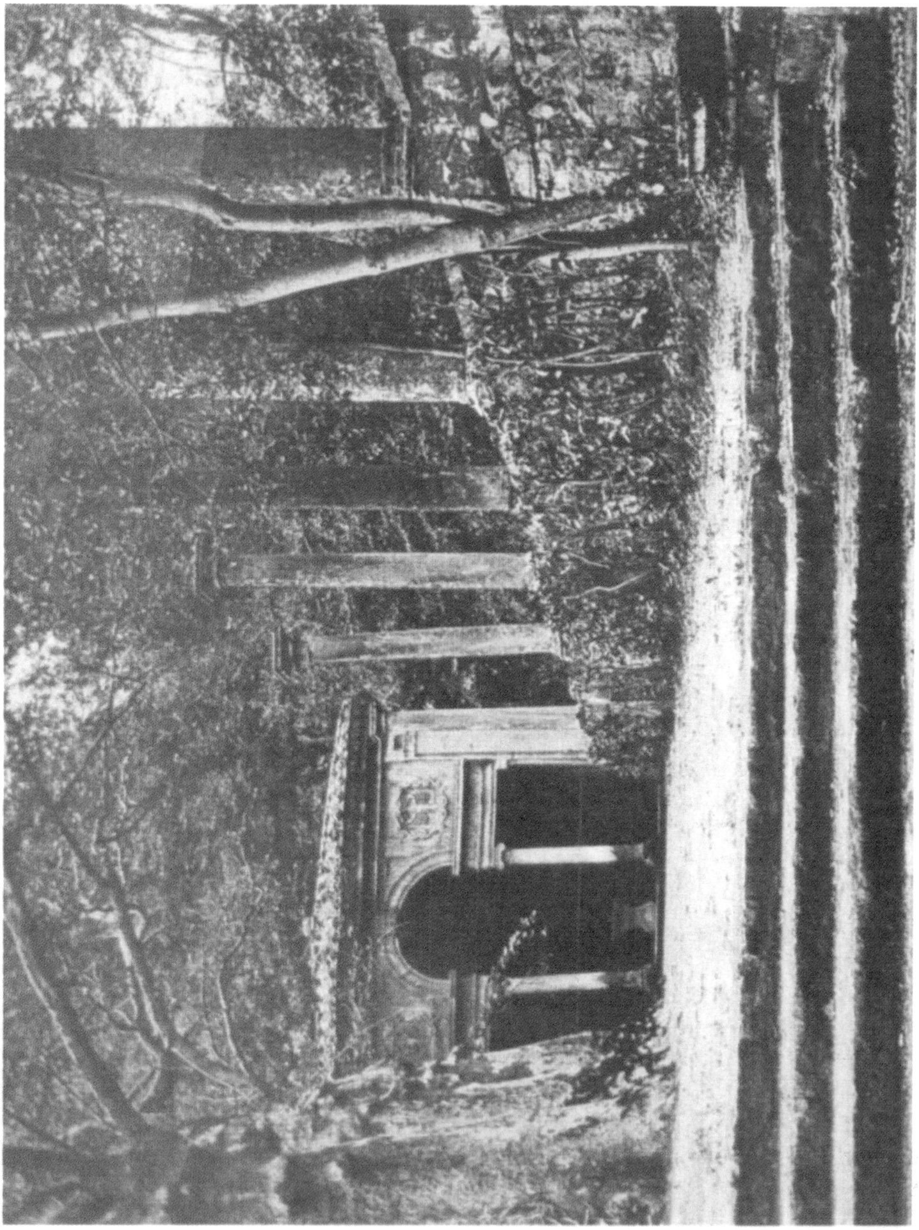

Figure 6. The Villa Lante, Bagnaia. The Loggia of the Muses, one of a pair at the top of the garden, adjoins a colonnaded conversation area with classical benches for enlightening conversation *all'antica*.

In Charles Latham. *The Gardens of Italy*. Vol. 2. London: Country Life, 1905.

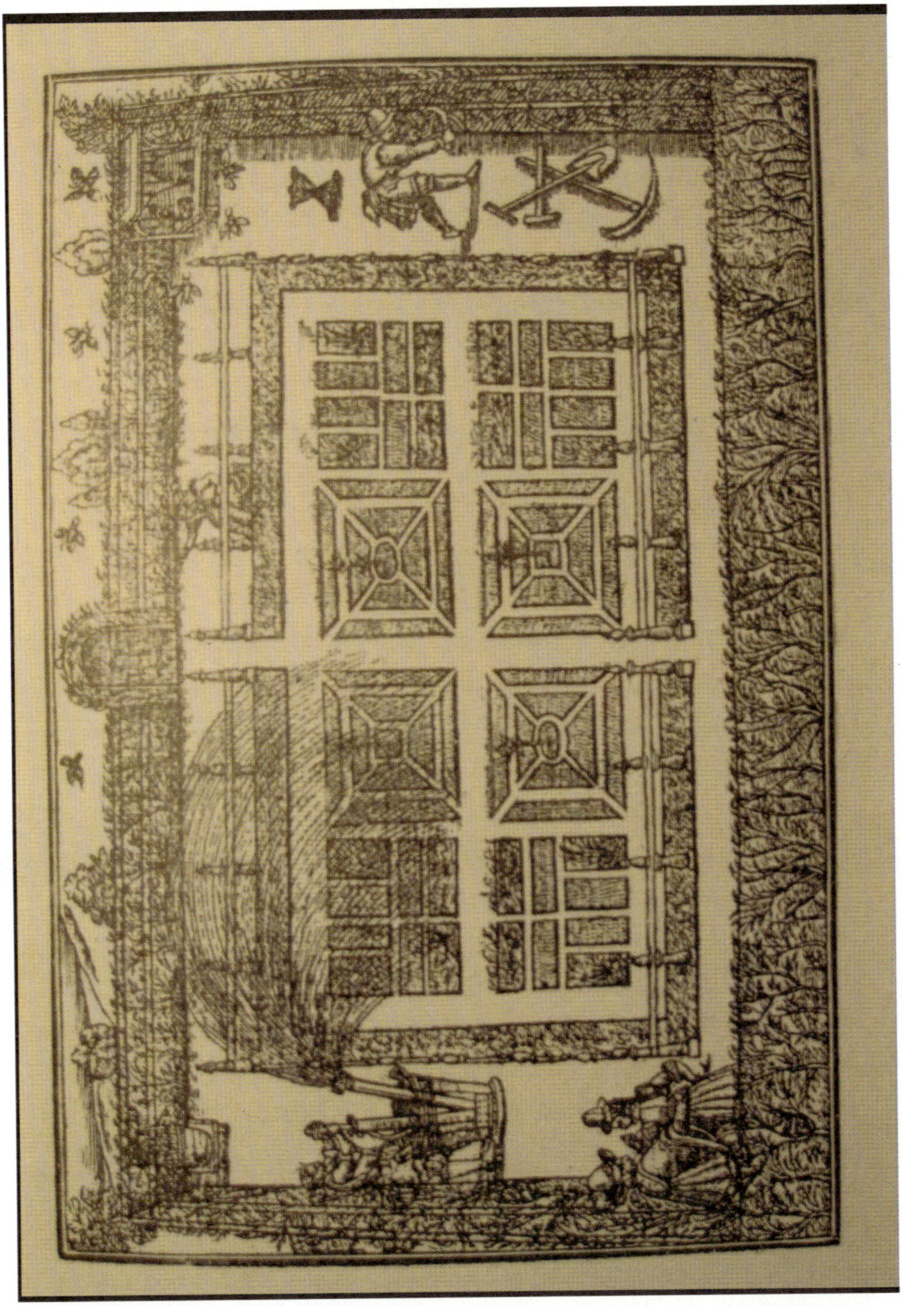

Figure 7. Tudor Garden from Thomas Hill's *The Gardener's Labyrinth*. Wood cut. In Reginal Blomfield and F. Inigo Thomas. *The Formal Garden in England* London: Macmillan, 1897. Page 39.

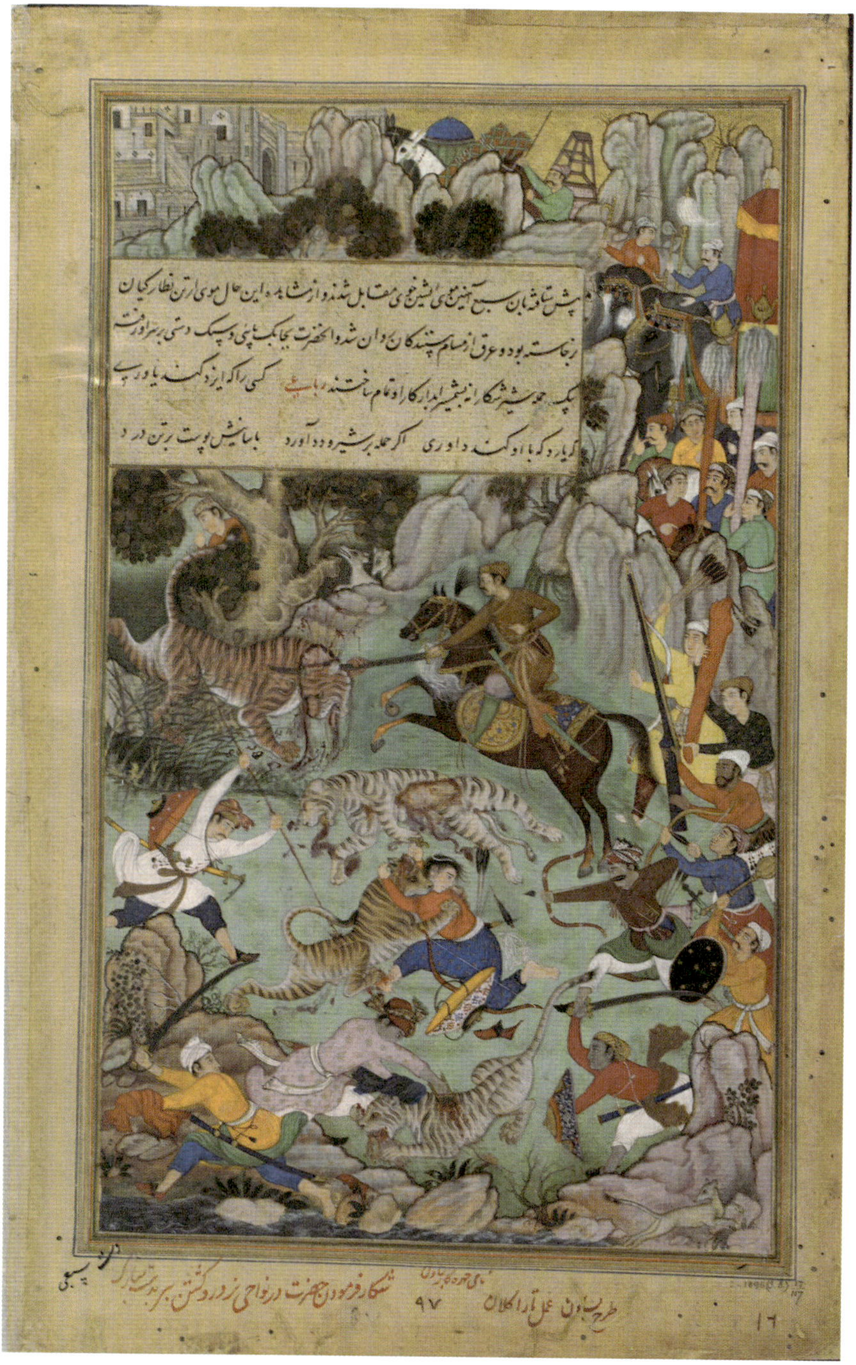

Figure 8. Basawan, *Akbar slays a tigress that attacked the Royal Entourage.*

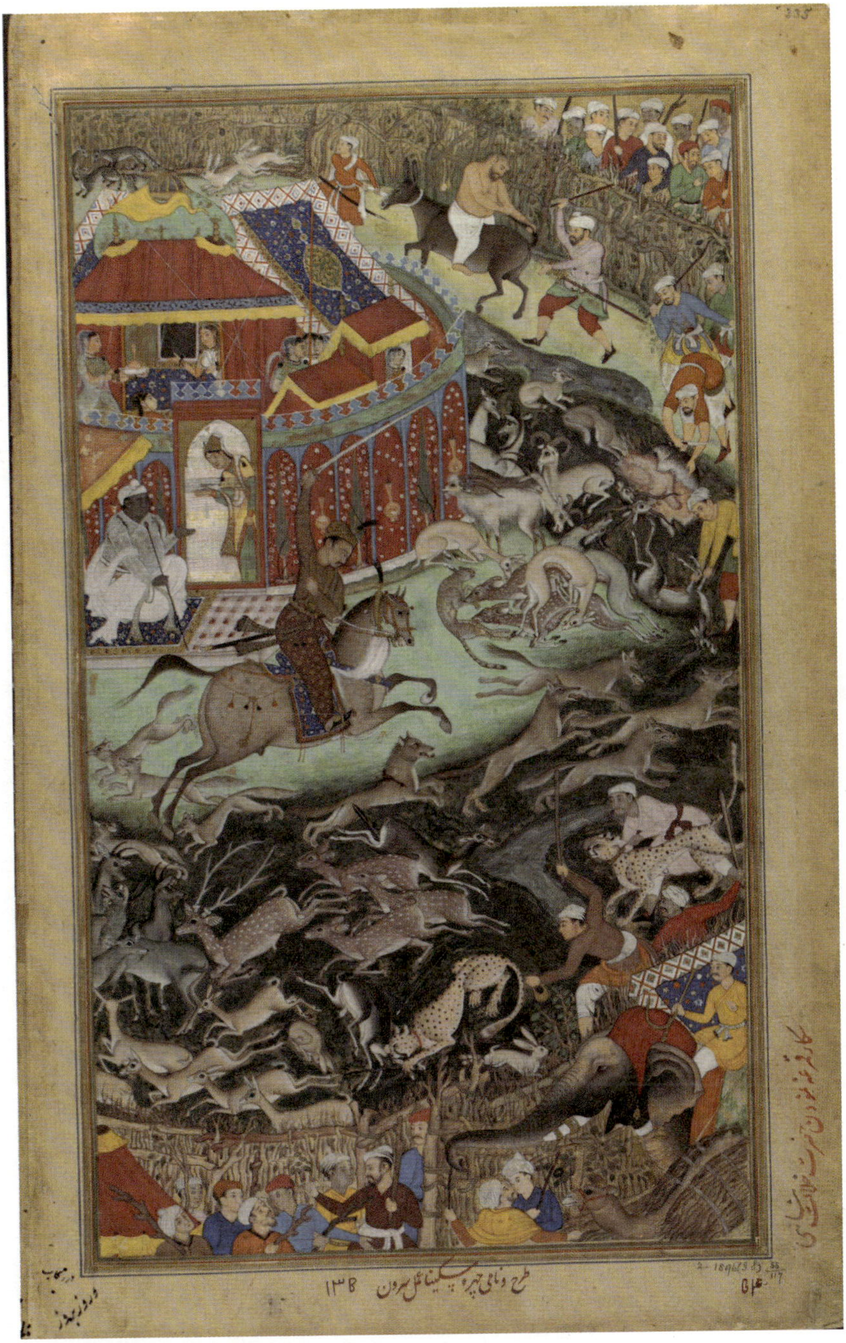

Figure 9. Muskin, *Akbar Hunts near Lahore and Hamid Bakari is Punished by having his head shaved and being mounted on an ass.*

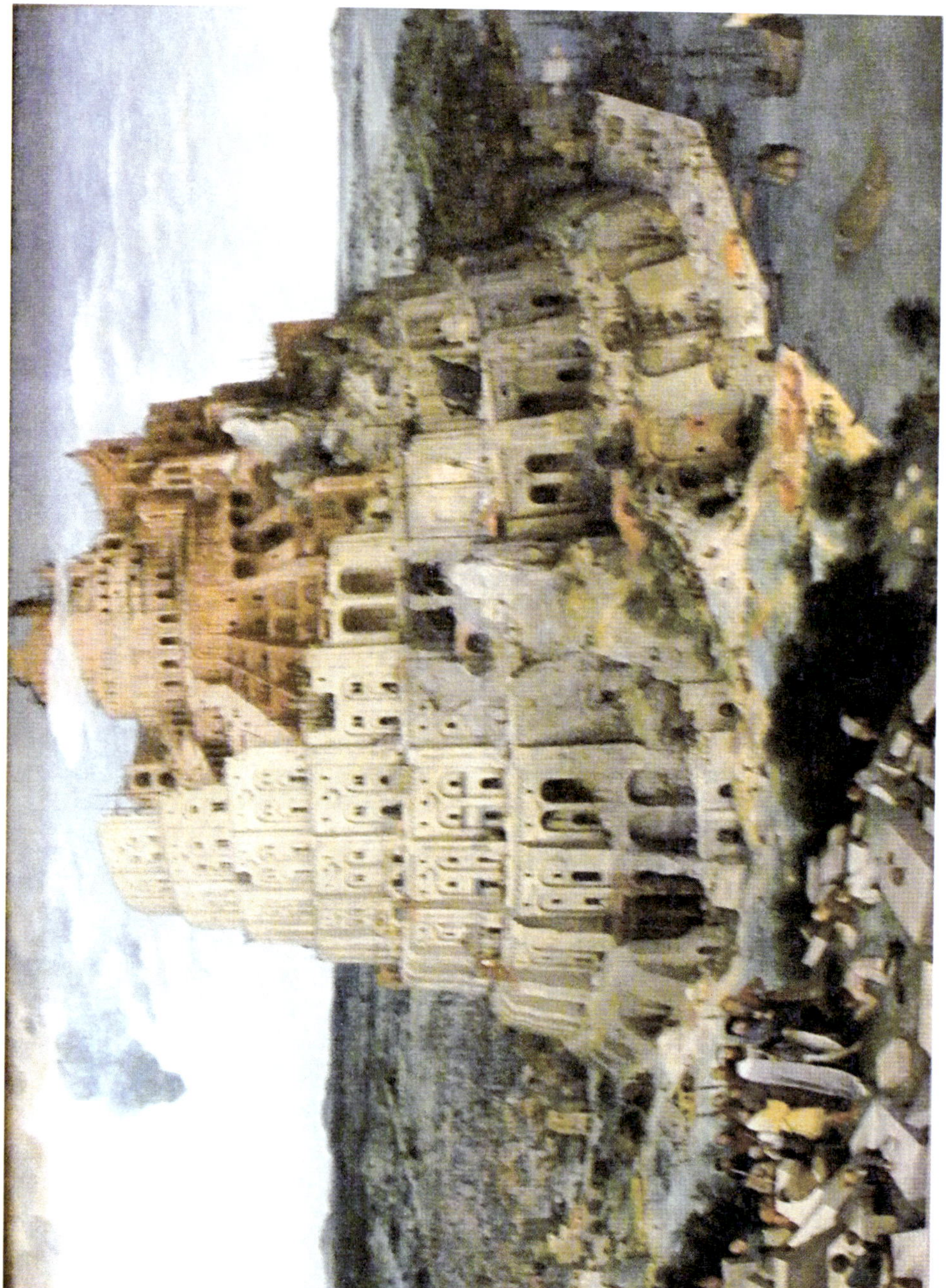

Figure 10. Peter Breugel, the Elder, *The Tower of Babel*.

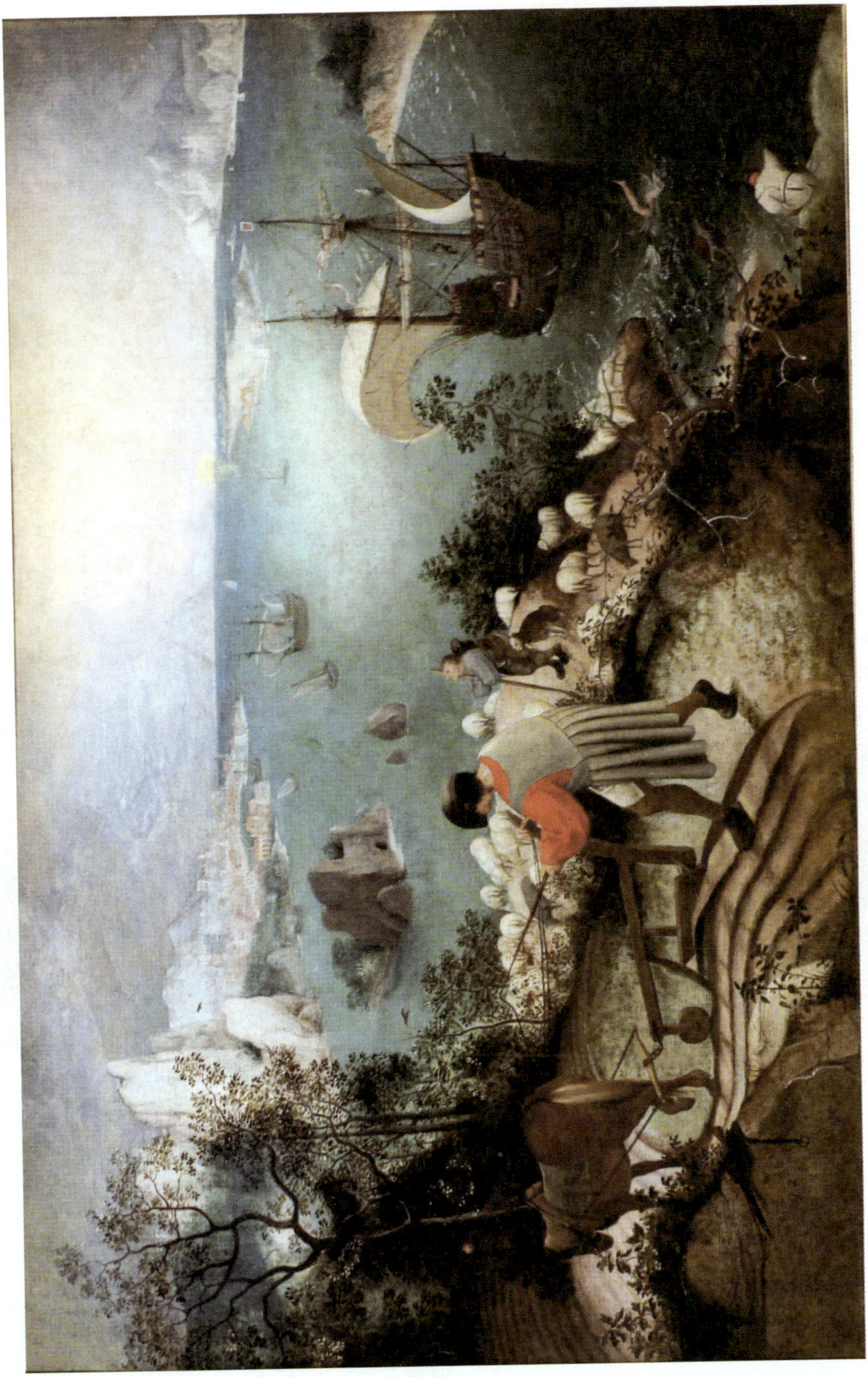

Figure 11. Peter Breugel, the Elder, *The Fall of Icarus*.

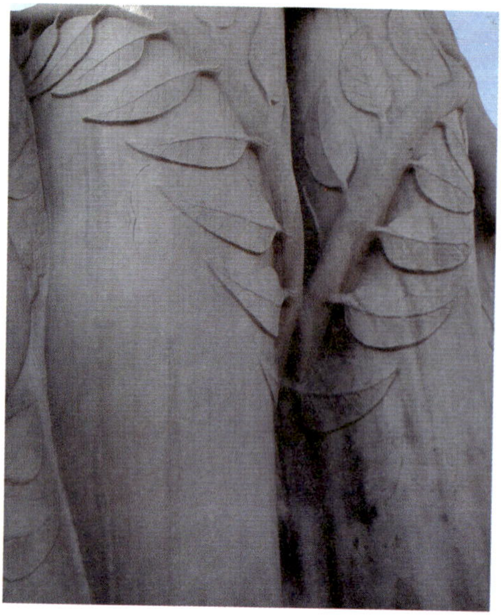

Figure 12. Gommateshwara.

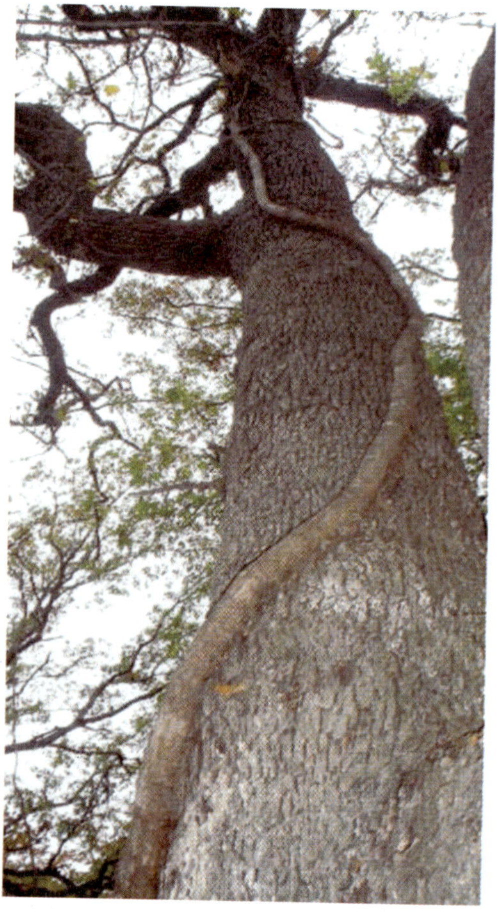

Figure 12a. A vine climbing a tree. Photograph by Vincent Villafranca.

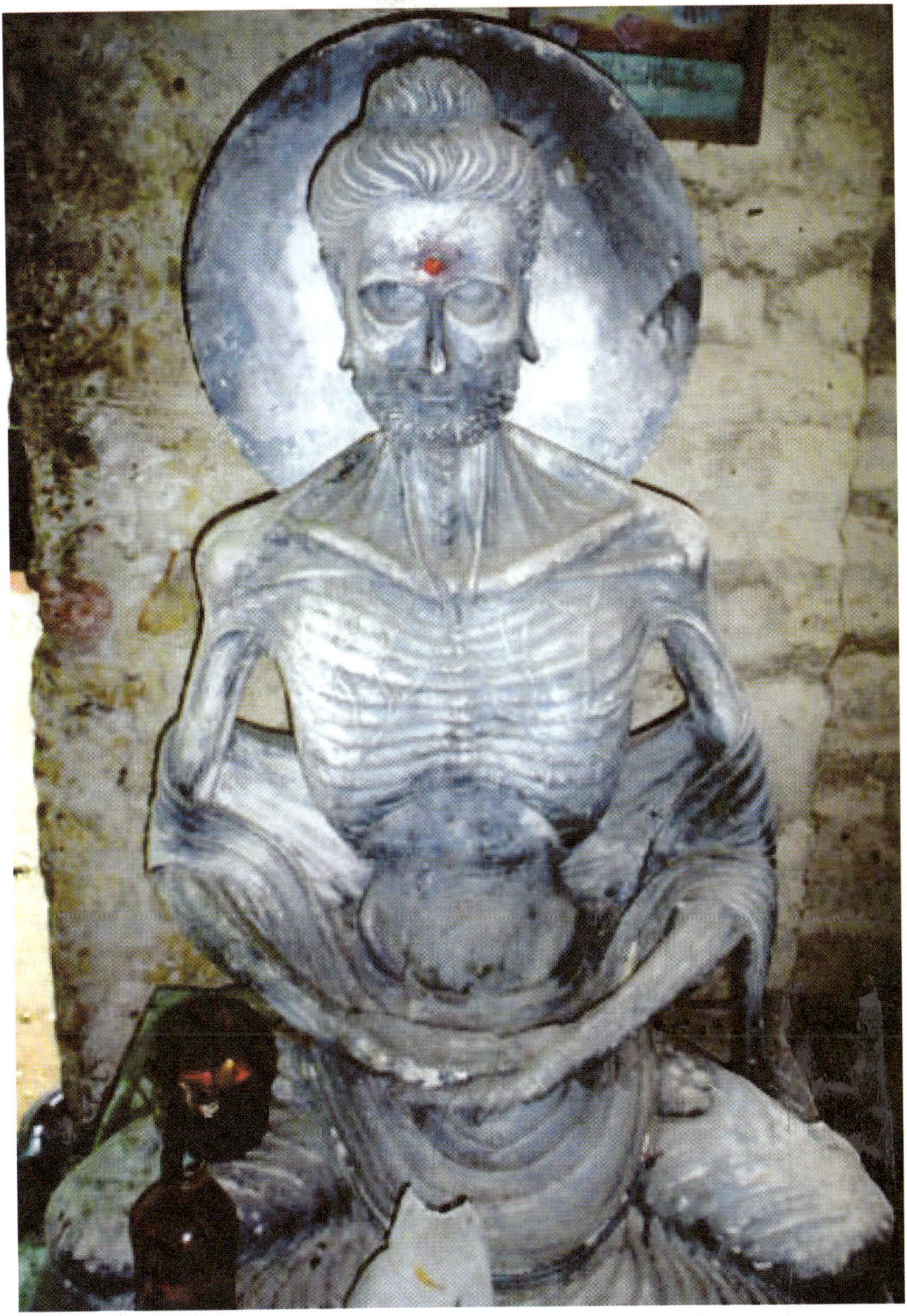

Figure 13. *The Fasting Buddha*, Mahabalipuram.
Photograph by Vincent Villafranca.

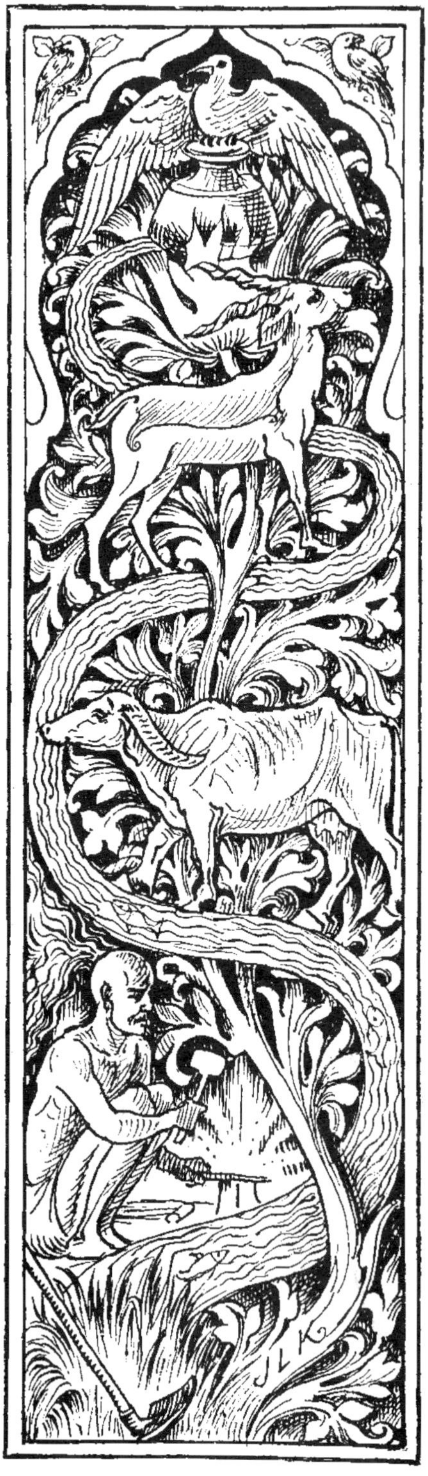

Figure 14. Illustration to 'The Sparrow and the Crow' by John Lockwood Kipling from *Tales of the Punjab*, by Flora Annie Steel.

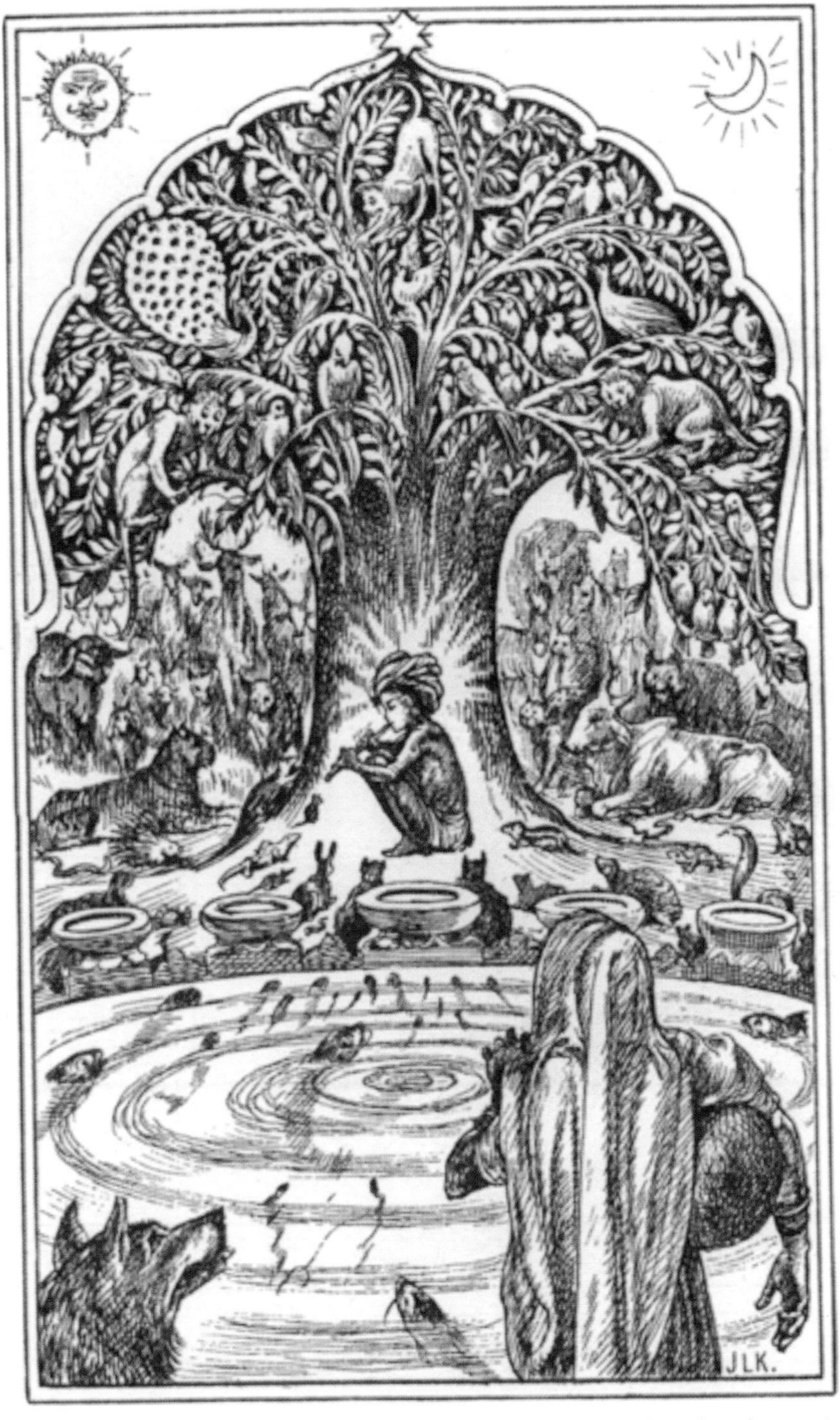

Figure 15. Illustration to 'Little Anklebone' by John Lockwood Kipling from *Tales of the Punjab*, by Flora Annie Steel.

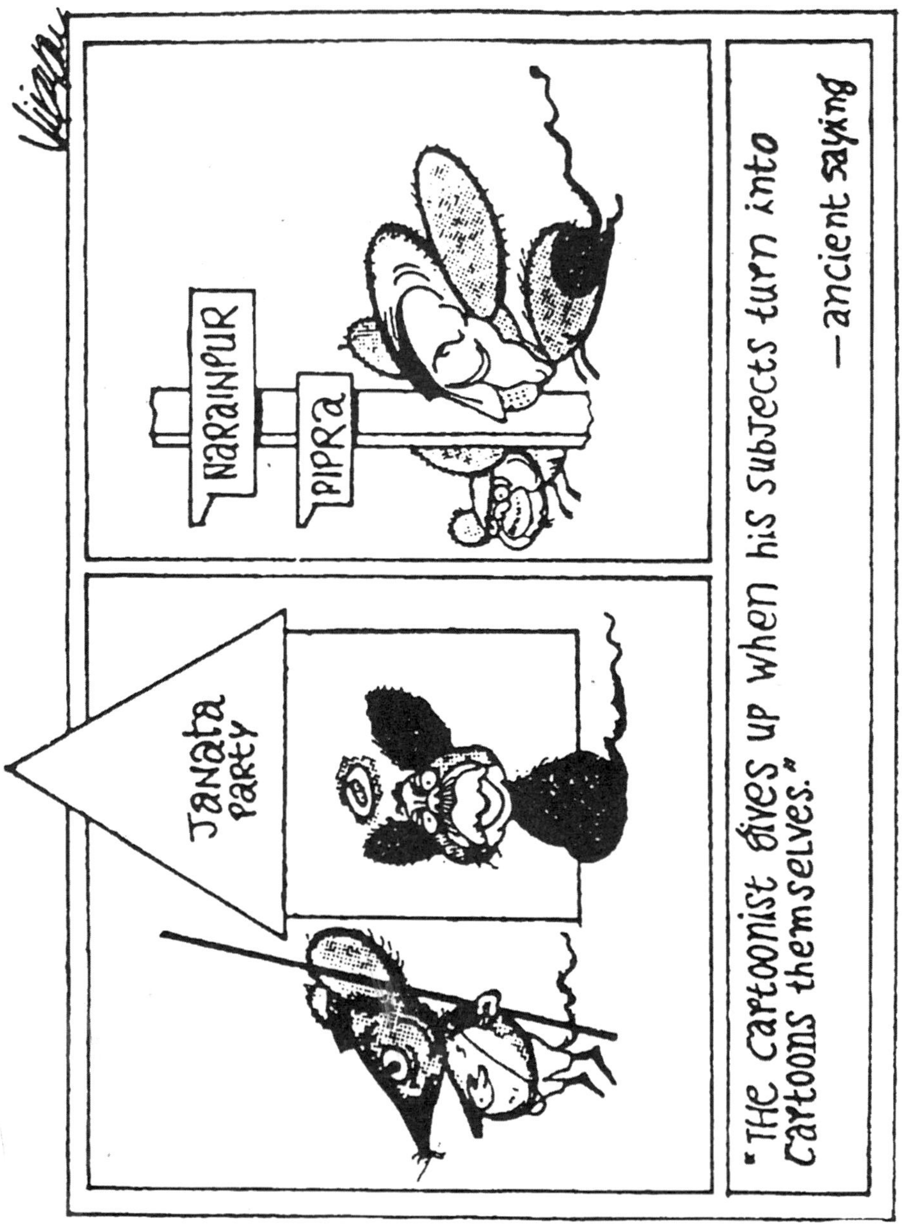

Figure 16. Cartoon — O.V. Vijayan

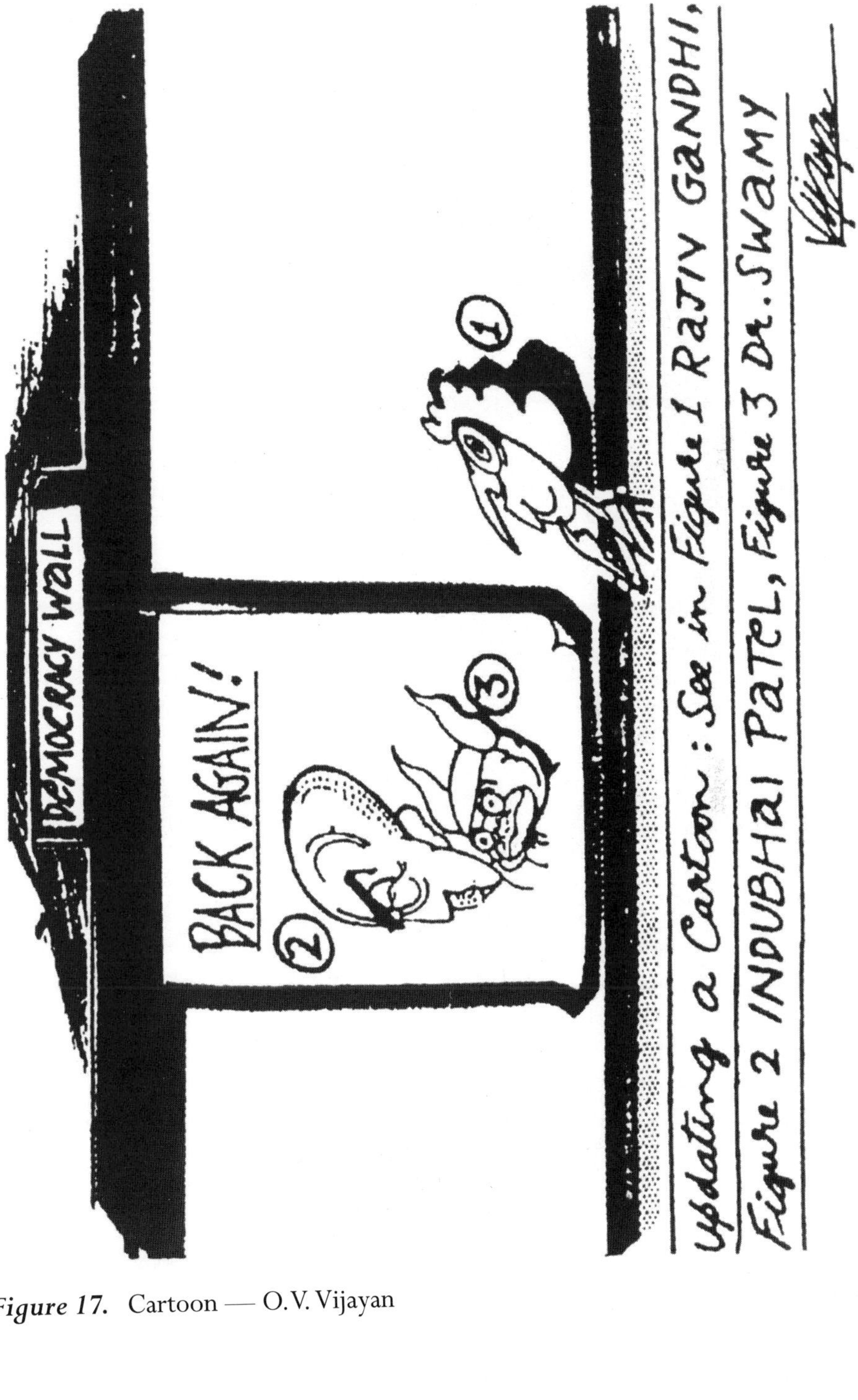

Figure 17. Cartoon — O.V. Vijayan

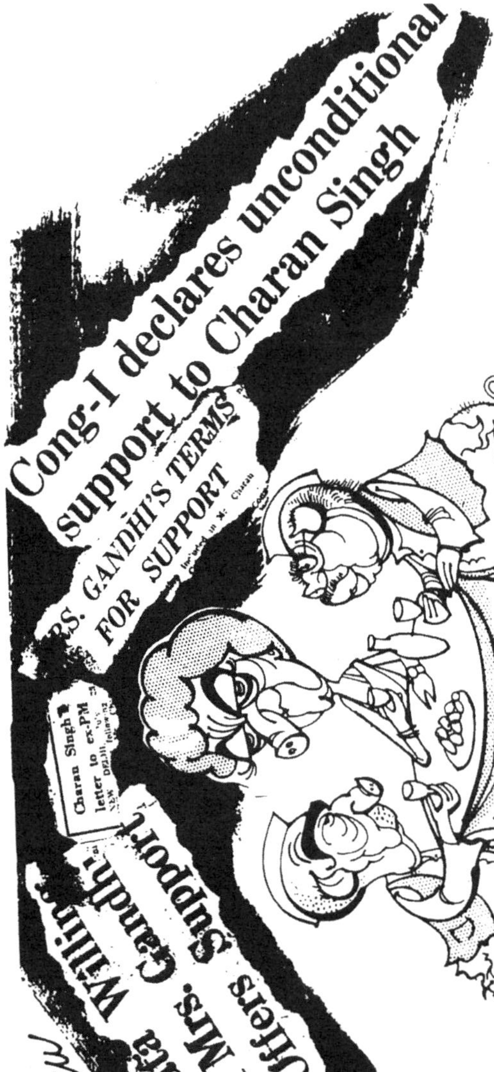

Figure 18. Cartoon — O.V. Vijayan

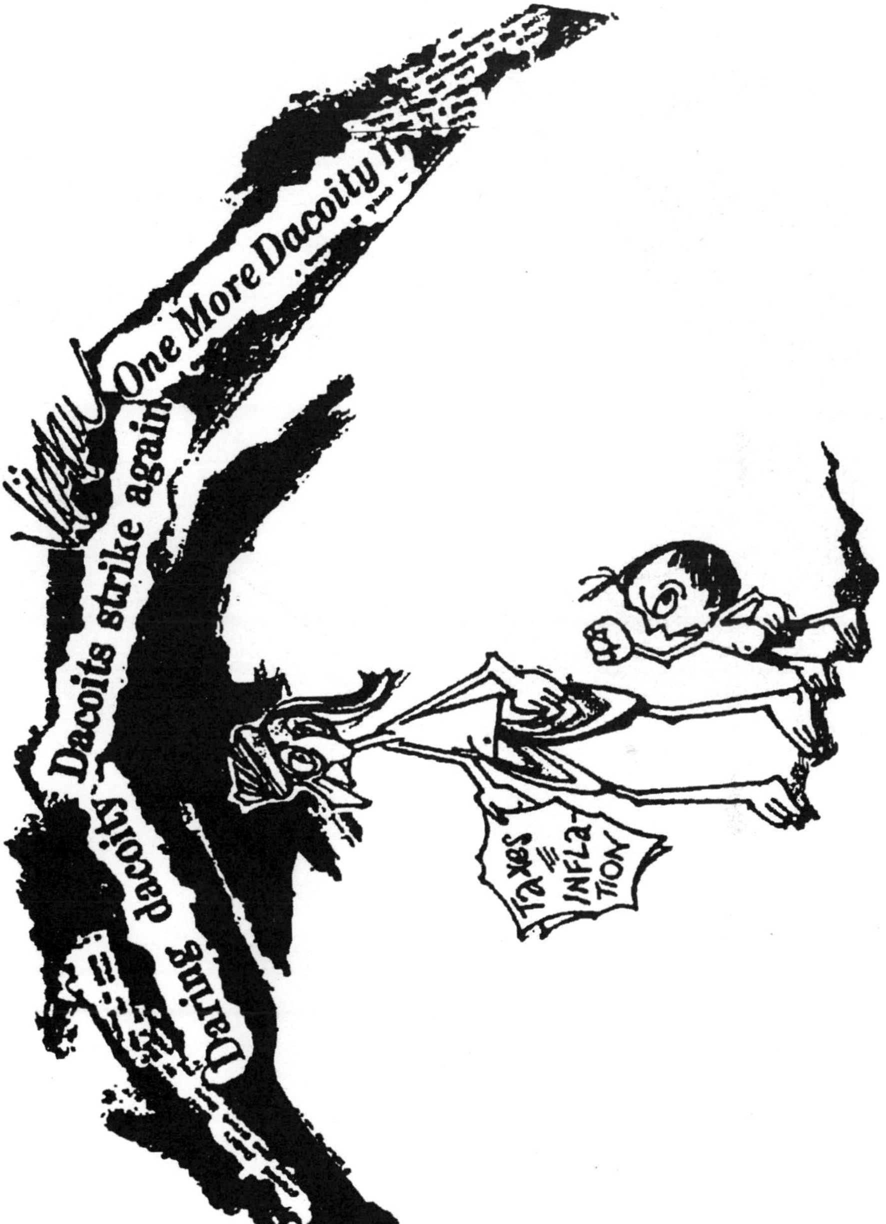

Figure 19. Cartoon — O.V. Vijayan

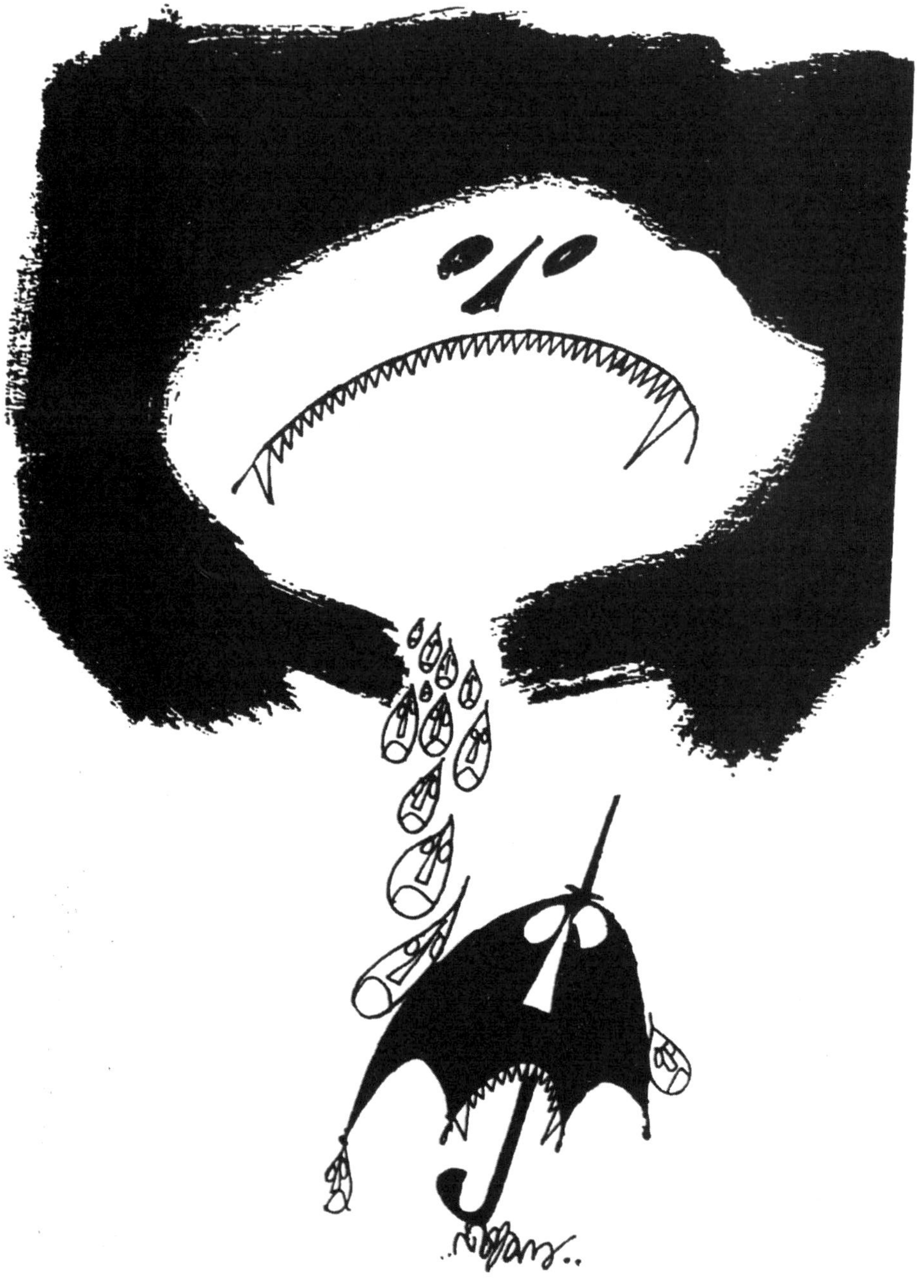

Figure 20. Cartoon — O.V. Vijayan

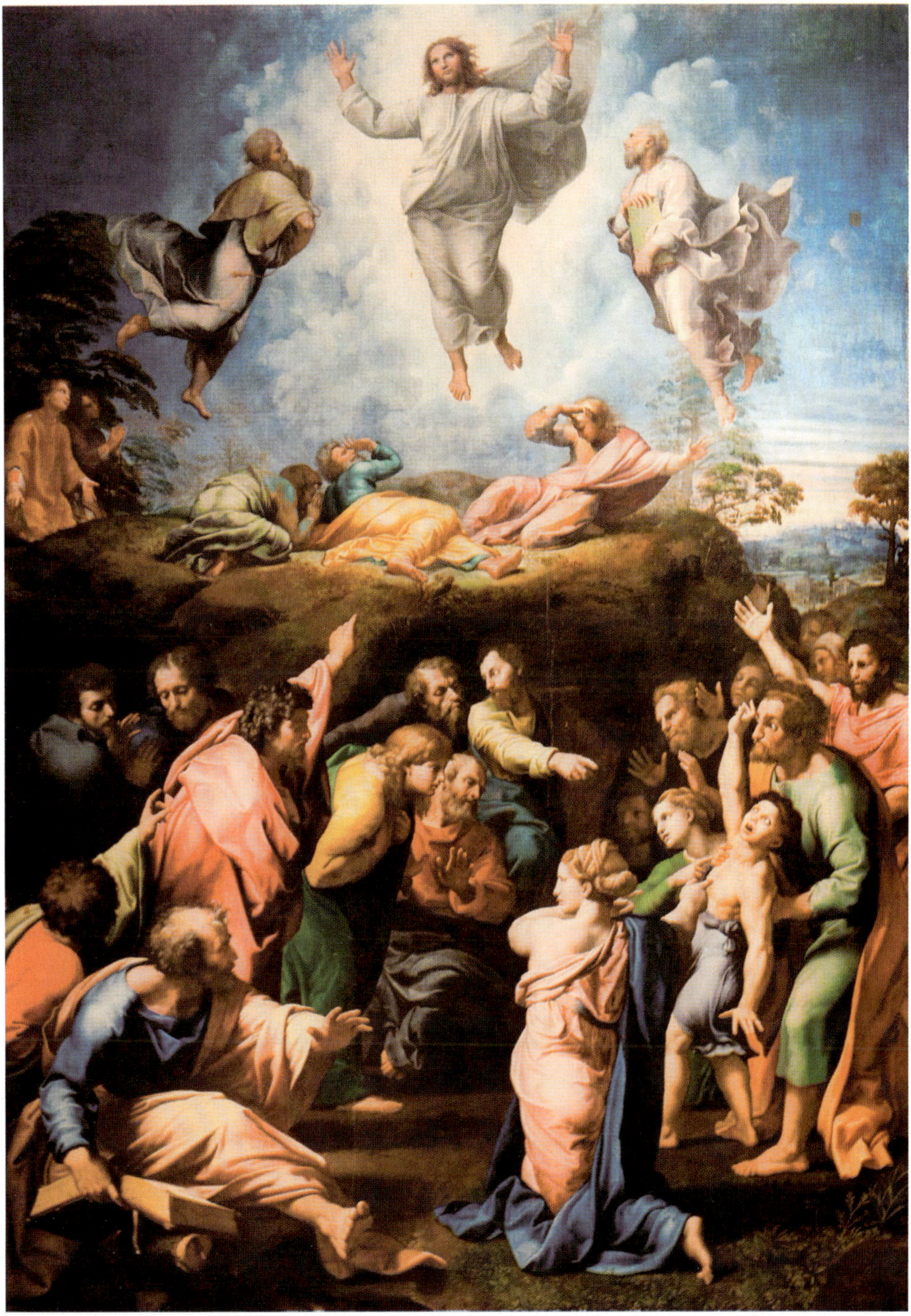

Figure 21. Raphael, *The Transfiguration*.

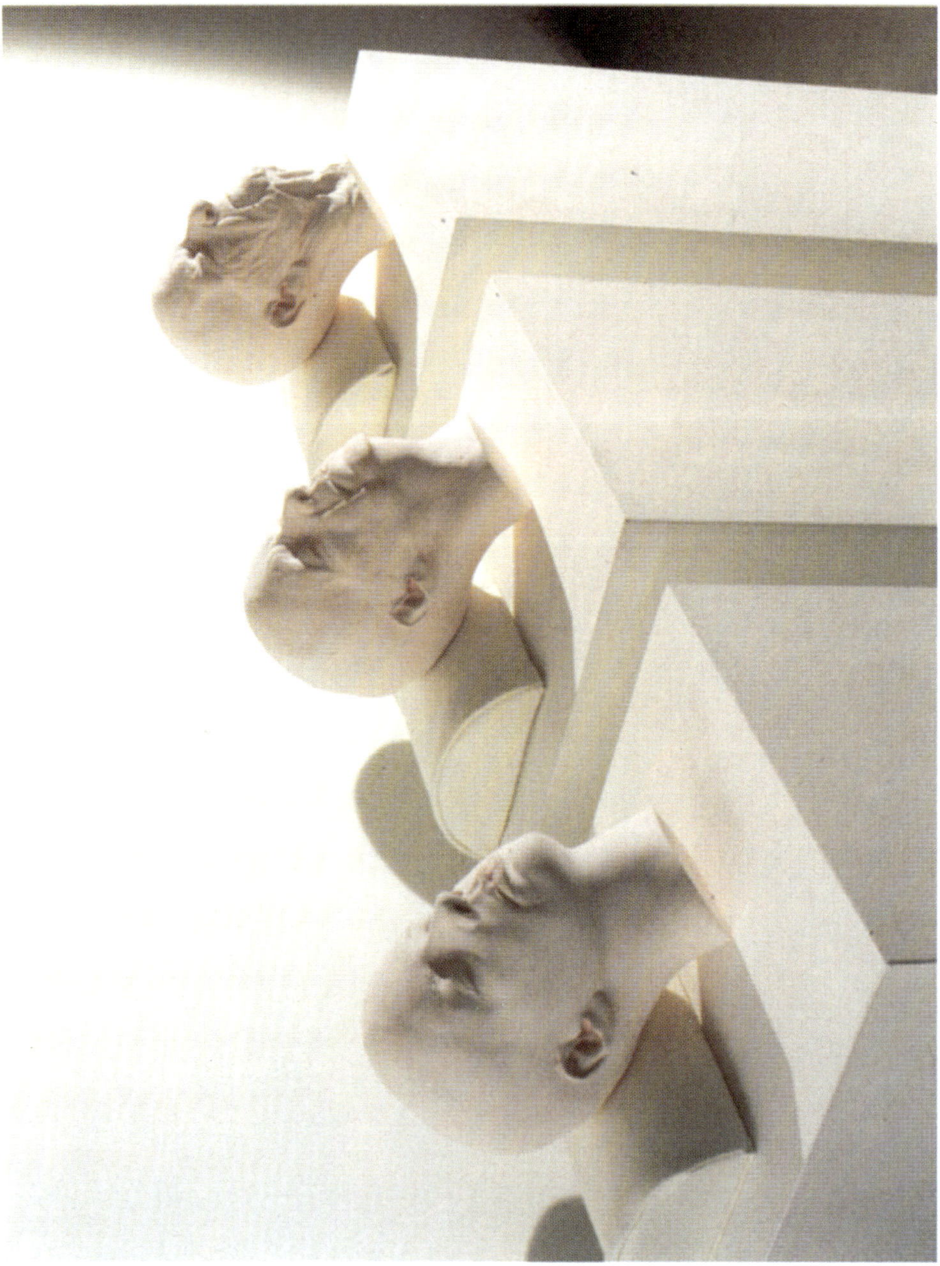

Figure 22. *Forensic Projections (28, 58, 88)* Rachel Lachowicz 1992.

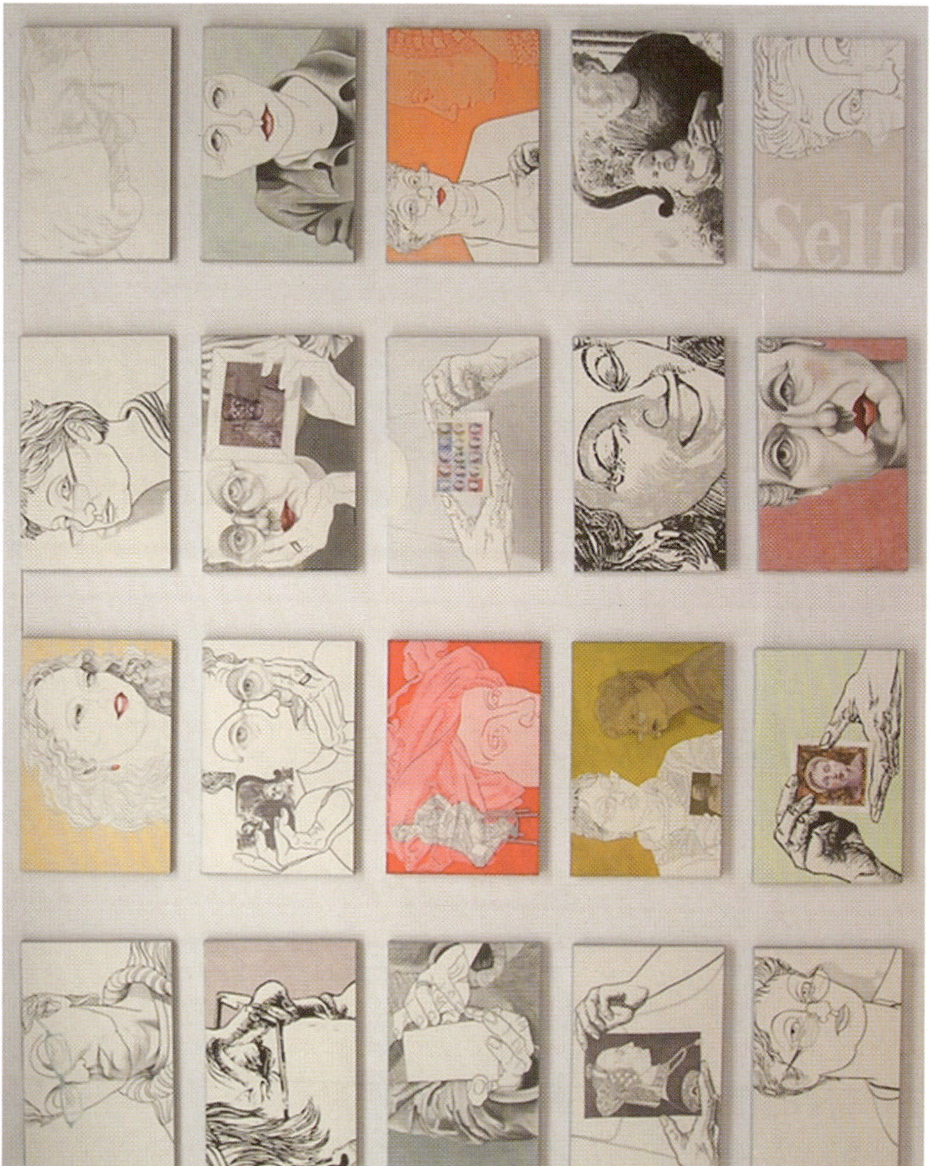

Figure 23. Loris Button, *Facing Time—Self portraits, 2005-2006.*

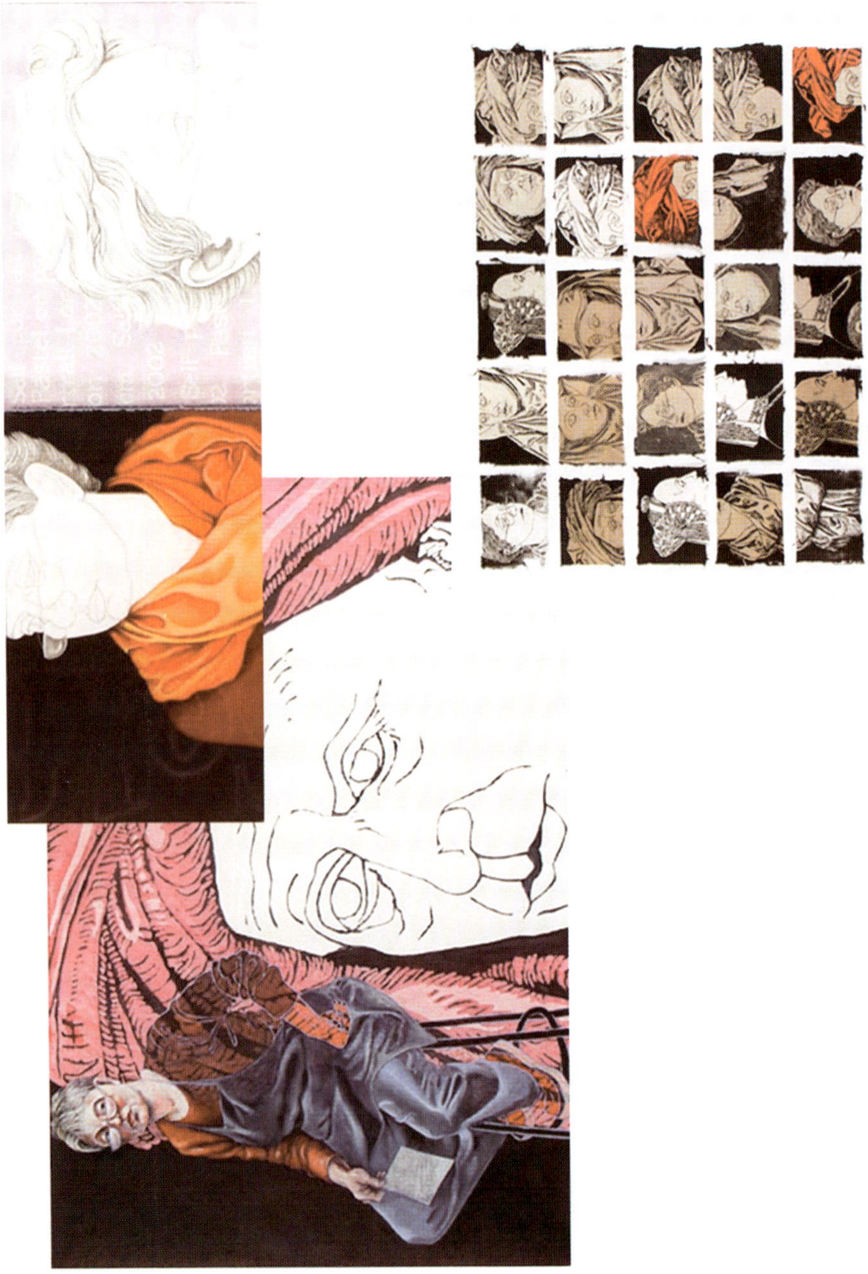

Figure 24. Loris Button, *Self portraits, 2002, 2003, 2004.*

centuries in Europe. Virgil's *Aeneid* provides the primary literary model of this convergence of the end of an order and the beginning of another and significantly enough, the later Claude heavily relied on the epic. Socially the division stemmed from a gradual polarisation of the patrician and the plebeian classes through the two centuries resulting in the split between the polite and the popular. No doubt, the attempt to recover classical canons of order, regularity and serenity contributed to the larger scientific search for plainness and precision against the tortured irregularity of the baroque. But the canons of *politesse* could not find their proper courtly context, that Virgil had found in Augustan Rome, because the aristocracy was in decline and the forces of democratisation had become irresistible. Thus, in the quarrel between the ancients and the moderns, history was on the side of the latter. Similarly, the transition from ideal Arcadian landscape to the realistic portrayal of nature was inspired by a fundamentally scientific interest in the external world for its own sake.

Hence it is not surprising that Claude's generalised landscape reveals intimate and precise knowledge of the Italian campagna and above all of the melting, fusing light with its *contrejour* effects, silhouettes and dark masses. The repose and order of Claude's scenes are tinged with a Virgilian lacrimae rerum, a wistful reminiscence of lost innocence. Claude achieves this unified mood by the warm and soft light that he inherited from Giorgione and Titian, and by the tonal frugality modulated through the receding planes of his canvas. At the same time, there is a note of optimism in the way in which Claude carries us in imagination into the open air where the sky is the source of light governing all aspects of nature. Once again Italy is a particularly happy choice since it combines a visible classical past with the institutions of modernity. Italy was the cradle of the Renaissance because of the classical heritage (that could be recovered easily) as well as the unprecedented economic and political transformation that came to the country early.

Claude's indebtedness to the visual pastoral (the *fête champêtre* theme) is evident in the way the serene rural scene, not unrelated to the politics of retirement, offers a retreat and refreshing solace to the shepherds, travellers, pilgrims and indeed viewers. The key motifs include a clump of shady trees, a pool or stream of water often reflecting the sky and green pasture where the flocks graze and the human figures rest. It is a landscape in which human figures live in close harmony with nature, living on its fruits. Since the pastoral world antedates the agricultural, Claude's landscape excludes physical labour, otherwise indispensable to the man-nature relationship and indeed to any realistic portrayal. Instead of toil we have in Claude an idealised landscape of leisurely activity, at times bordering upon lassitude. Of course, the mythical harmony is necessarily qualified by the somewhat indefinable elegiac feeling and sense of transience that characterise much neo-classical art.

At the same time, it is with Claude that a decisive break is made with landscape serving as background to religious, heroic and historical event. Although mythological and legendary events frequently constitute the human drama in his landscapes, for the first time we can sense the real meaning, as it were, almost unaided by knowledge of these events, in the poetically unified mood, in the very delineation of nature. Landscape thus becomes the central subject and while the stories remain important, they function now in the background as the past, an archaic world of primitive simplicity. It is worth reminding ourselves that many of the paintings have two or more titles and these were often added later, some when they were bought by English aristocrats in the sales after the French revolution.[3] Imbued with a classical sense of the past and transience, the stories harmonise with the age's backward-looking impulse, the specimens, often in ruins, of classical architecture suggesting the rise and fall of civilisations. The landscape, by subtle contrast to the mythological–religious element, primarily uses light to create a sense of beginning and adventure which draws us out of the enclosed refuge of tranquillity into the much-admired luminous distance. Mediated through and broken by foliage and mound, reflected in water, the light always carries us behind and beyond the dark masses on the sides. In other words, the impulse for reminiscence of lost simplicity is matched by the hope of recovering it in the future. If Claudian man is banished from mythical innocence it is not into fallen nature, for it is redeemed nature which holds centre stage capturing in the luminous distance the brave new world of the Enlightenment. Thus nostalgic movement into the past yields a vision of the future: retrospect and prospect are subtly interrelated through the median consciousness of Claude unravelling the mythical origins of the Enlightenment.

If we examine Claude's relationship to topographical poetry or the literature of Epicurean retirement in the seventeenth century—the country house or garden poem and the essays on idealised rustic life—the larger transitional character of the age becomes evident. In poems like Denham's *Cooper's Hill* (1642), Edmund Waller's 'A Poem on St. James's Park As Lately Improved by His Majesty' (1661), Pope's *Windsor Forest* (1713), Dyer's *Grongar Hill* (1726) and of course Thomson's *The Seasons* (1726–30), landscape becomes an occasion for generalised description and reflection, moral, literary and political. This 'harmoniously confused' landscape constructed on the principle of *discordia concors* is a subtle amalgam of backward-looking aristocratic *otium* and the *negotium* of emergent bourgeois culture. If the Enlightenment project of the perfectibility of man is founded to some extent on Locke's premise that there are no innate ideas in the mind, then the educating and enriching role of nature is its logical conclusion. In fact, in his dialogue, *The Moralists: A Philosophical Rhapsody*, Locke's pupil, Shaftesbury, sets forth an impassionate defence of this role of nature. Pope advocates the moral and educating influence of nature with similar enthusiasm in *The Guardian*, No.173: 'There is something in the amiable simplicity of unadorned Nature that spreads over the mind a more noble sort of tranquillity, and a loftier sensation of pleasure.'[4] Around the same time, Addison echoes the sentiment in *The Spectator*, No.477, continuing the tradition of the garden or country house as the topos of reflection and refined pleasure: 'You must know, sir, that I look upon the pleasure which we take in a garden, as one of the most innocent delights in human life…It is naturally apt to fill the mind with calmness and tranquillity…and suggests innumerable subjects for meditation.'[5] This relationship between Nature and the mind of man is developed with greater clarity by Mark Akenside in *The Pleasures of the Imagination* (1744). A legatee of Shaftesbury and Hutcheson, Akenside attempted to move away from the dominant model of the Horatian epistle mastered by Pope towards a more Virgilian one. Somewhat in the manner of Claude, this retrospective turn enabled him to open up the prospect of Romanticism and its preoccupation with the enhancing and harmonising influence of Nature on the imaginative genesis of poetry.

In highlighting this influence of nature, Claude and the topographical poets pre-supposed a nature that was not in convulsion: landscape becomes the topos of the rational control of passions. Unlike Turner, Claude has no interest in turbulent nature. The ideal of peaceful, rustic simplicity is directly related to the classicist aesthetic of adequacy and frugality, the avoidance of excess that continues to be a cultural goal—that of reasonableness as opposed to totalising rationalism—till the early eighteenth century. Pope's 'Epistle IV. To Richard Boyle, Earl of Burlington: Of the Use of Riches' is a celebrated and anthologised satire of the tawdry display of newly-acquired wealth in gardening and architecture. The criticism is not unrelated to the opposition in *Gulliver's Travels* between Lord Munodi and his estate on the one hand and the devastation caused by Laputan science on the other. But the last section of Pope's poem acknowledges the economic benefits of wasteful lavishness, thereby juxtaposing the politics of nostalgia and the value of commerce and progress. From hindsight this juxtaposition could be seen as an interlocked combat between pre-capitalist man and the *homo oeconomicus*. The two perspectives, opposed to each other, are conflated by the political ideology of Bolingbroke and his circle.

But Claude in any case cannot be fitted into the neo-classicist harness for, while Pope or Thomson set store by garden or park scenery—Thomson in fact revised *The Seasons* on the basis of Hagley Park—he is resolutely for the open countryside. In this sense his legacy truly bears fruit much later through Turner and Constable in Impressionism. Perhaps his irreducibly transitional character is acknowledged in the term 'baroque classicism' sometimes applied to his work; indeed Claude's landscape is founded upon the inclusive contradictories of enclosed stillness and mobility. Marcel Roethlisberger has demonstrated the constant presence of time in Claude's landscape; the resting or dancing figures are almost always in transit.[6] Even as the spectator's eye makes out the human scene in the shaded foreground of apparent timelessness, illuminated often by broken, hidden or reflected light, the *coulisse* draws the eye away out of the mutual absorption of form and content, out of the pastoral into a world of time involving travel, transport and commerce.

The social implications of baroque classicism suggest the emerging world of the Enlightenment in which the search for serenity and the new forms of knowledge had not yet fallen apart. Claude's world is one where science and rational enquiry grew under royal and patrician patronage, as in the institution of the Royal Society. Science and reason had been promoted as an alternative to the supposed irrationalism of the Puritan revolution and had been therefore endowed with the patrician values of harmony, peace and *politesse*. As we progress in the eighteenth century, we encounter, however, what J.H. Plumb has described as the social transference of the Enlightenment, whereby the upper class empire-builders fall back upon the study of the classics (especially in the famous public schools like Eton and Harrow) while the impulse to new knowledge acquires a demotic base. Consequently, the polarisation of patrician and plebeian is reflected in that between polite and popular: serenity and energy are no longer unified.

For Claude, this unity has not yet been ruptured and is rather a vital reality animating his vision. In choosing his topos for ideal harmony, he thus did not have to take recourse to the garden or the park; he chose the open air in the open countryside. It is not surprising that in the seventeenth century Claude was primarily admired for his marvellous naturalness, his verisimilitude and of course his mastery of light and distance. The natural simplicity was found marvellous because hitherto landscape, even when it aspired beyond the merely decorative and unrealistic, lay suppressed under allegorical/symbolical baggage, under fantasy bordering upon the phantasmagoric. The elongated rocks, outcrop and jutting crags so often encountered in pre-Claudian landscape suggest a Gothic fear of treacherous and inimical fallen nature which man must reject along with the devil and the flesh in order to attain redemption.

But in the landscape painting of Salvatore Rosa, Claude's contemporary, we have a representation of the savage (as natural) as an alternative to the serene. Since they were aware of each other's work, perhaps Claude acquired from Rosa the ability to suggest a fear of the unknown and ungovernable. The mythological stories of savagery and violence that he depicts with an almost eerie calm bear testimony to Claude's intermediary location between the so-called soft and hard schools of primitivism. Somewhat like Shakespeare, he at once juxtaposes the serenity and the brutality of the mythical world. Claire Pace has drawn our attention to the double influence of Virgil and Ovid according to which the fear of the unknown in Claude is an Ovidian inheritance rather than Virgilian. Ovid often subverts the pastoral, providing an idyllic setting to violence, where wood and water no longer offer solace and refuge but suggest danger. In the Rape of Europa paintings, the familiar theme of embarkation/disembarkation in Claude's coastal scenes is charged with imminent drama. As Claire Pace has argued, instead of Titian's voluptuous energy we have here a seemingly festive, innocent scene with the sea as an ominous presence, suggesting in addition the individual's loneliness.[7] A similar foreboding of imminent tragedy underlies the idyllic peace of *Landscape with Acis and Galatea*. With the mountain jutting into the sea we have the same ambiguity of water, at once the source of life and death. The gathering clouds suggest the tragic fate and the caves and water in a mysterious setting suggest the elemental forces underlying peace. In all these Ovidian examples, we have a different version of ultimately the basic theme of adventure, enlightenment and the new forms of knowledge; only the discovery of the unknown is fraught with trauma and destruction.

In Claude's underlying scheme of composition the dark *coulisse* on one side with its shadow extended across the first plane of the foreground plays the crucial role of a *charnière*. It draws us into the shaded and sequestered retreat, into mythical serenity and at the same time draws us out, sometimes along a bend in the river and sometimes through modulated succession of parallel planes towards the luminous distance. In *Landscape with Merchants* (*c.* 1630), an early painting of Claude, we have the basic elements of his distinctive style. There is the usual scene of rest in transit, the daily activity of the merchants harmonising with the diurnal rhythm of Claude's light. There is also a ferry (transit) in the middle distance—boats on the river and ships on the sea are a constant reminder of travel and commerce. Nothing is introduced for effect because the landscape is unburdened of emblem and allegory into its newly-found freedom of the ordinary. The *coulisse* on the left is constituted of typical Italian foliage sifting the light, catching it almost insubstantially on the further and higher branches and beckoning us to the illuminated world. The reflected light in the river draws the eye along its bend into that same world. The source or further reaches of the river, like the source of the light, is always hidden, mediated and reflected. In other words, the human subject's level perception of the world in which he moves and lives acts like a filter parallel to the other filter of idyllic repose. Thus indeed, in linking reflected, mediated light with actual light, seclusion with openness, Claude relates the ideal with the actual.

Architecture in Claude's landscape combines the vertical form of classical columns and Italian towers with the diagonal of trees—sometimes the entire *coulisse* with its dark mass is diagonally inclined—to forestall the insipid monotony of receding horizontal planes. But there is always a poetic mystery, a suggestion of enchantment that the Romantics admired, a feeling or mood that is anterior to the intellectual design. The obvious contrast is with the sure and severe classicism of Poussin's landscapes dominated by geometry and Cartesian reason and what Clark terms 'uncompromising frontality'. In Claude's *Italian Coastal Landscape* (1642), schematic pattern is shaped and controlled by atmosphere, which is also the aerial perspective that gives a recessional continuity to soften the more rigid movement of the coulisses. The bent tree trunk supporting a tent on the right reinforces the diagonal of the tree on the left. In the foreground are figures inhabiting the pastoral world and the actual at the same time (in this sense the figures are like and unlike those of Giorgione). Their position links them through the bridge to the ruined columns which they have left behind in the past and are now poised delicately on the verge of the open sea and reflected light. This light along with the ships presents a different order of time from the shaded darkness on the left. *Landscape with the Rest on the Flight into Egypt* (1666) uses a similar scheme linking the human figures on the right to the ruined classical columns. The whole painting is suffused with a Giorgionesque quality—it is as if Claude consciously acknowledges a clear debt to the Venetian tradition. At the same time, the trees on the left and right compose a circular opening reinforced by the arches in the middle distance sinuously linked to the arches of the bridge in the half-dark foreground. In other words,

Claude first draws us into reminiscence of the Venetian *fête champêtre* and then beckons us out of it into the open.

The bridge often figures more prominently not only as a motif of transit but also as one of the modes wherewith the foreground, middle ground and the luminous distance are arranged within the horizontally succeeding planes. In *Landscape with Shepherds* (1645), we have the usual *coulisse* and the vertical architectural forms. As the eye moves towards the hidden light touching the treetops, the bridge introduces a rhythmic counterpoint along the bend of the river. We notice in particular the arches which become full circles by reflection in water. Not only do the ideal and actual thus blend but the arches also serve as subordinate *coulisses* drawing the eye through them into the open prospect or distant mountains. Like the *coulisse*, the arch obstructs in order to release us from obstruction, in order to make us see or imagine what lies behind the screen. The bridge is often substituted in his paintings by a ford (transit again) or a weir where the change in the water level imparts a controlled movement to the scene. This can be seen in *Landscape with Dancing Figures* (1648). The dancing figures appear to be a self-sufficient group, dancing, chatting and watching the dancers. Yet the eye of the beholder cannot be contained within this enclosed celebration of the marriage of Isaac and Rebecca. The towers, columns, mountains and the water with the weir and the arches of the bridge in the distance almost seduce us once again through the circular opening into the wide expanse of nature. As John White has put it, if Poussin is the painter of near and middle distance, then the flowing, light-blended infinite space is distinctively Claude's.[8] All the elements of his art are unified by the mutually invigorating relationship of sheltered repose and yearning for the luminous distance.

Notes

1 Kenneth Clark, *Landscape into Art* (London: John Murray, 1976), Chapter *IV*, 109–45

2 See Chapter X.

3 I owe this information to Professor Stuart Sillars of the University of Bergen. My paper has benefited much from his comments and suggestions.

4 Tuesday 29 September, 1713.

5 Saturday 6 September, 1712.

6 Marcel G. Roethlisberger, 'The Dimension of Time in the Art of Claude Lorrain' *Artibus et Historiae* 10.20 (1989): 73–92.

7 Claire Pace, 'The Golden Age...The First and Last Days of Mankind: Claude Lorrain and Classical Pastoral, with Special Emphasis on Themes from Ovid's *Metamorphoses*,' *Artibus et Historiae* 23.46 (2002): 127–56.

8 John White, 'The Landscapes of Claude', *Burlington Magazine* 92. 563 (1956): 42–47.

7. Picturing Power: Politics of the Image in Revolutionary France

Megha Anwer

Each society must 'produce' its own space. This process, however, goes beyond the mere appropriation of physical locations. 'Space' includes also the less tangible, seemingly abstract arena of representation—the realm in which society manufactures its 'ways of seeing': of seeing the world, and seeing itself vis-à-vis that world.[1] This essay examines pre-revolutionary and revolutionary France in relation to this notion. The transformation of French society from the monarchical *ancien régime* into a modern[2] republican nation state (the *patrie*) entailed also a shift in France's self-conception—not just in political terms but also in its spatio-visual representation of itself. This essay first traces the shifts in 'attitude' of the revolutionaries towards the body of the French royals, and then goes on to examine those physico-spatial motifs and icons through which revolutionary France chose to symbolise itself.

From Marvellous to Monstrous: Re-presenting the Courtly Body

Prior to the revolution, visual representations of the king, Louis XVI, typically sought to portray him as the sole repository of sovereignty and the 'incarnation of absolutism' (*Body Politic* 8)[3]—or so one would imagine. Archival material, however, refutes any such easy assumption of a uniformly idyllic, non-critical visualisation of the monarch. Long before July 1789, the sanctitude ascribed to the king's person had been blasphemed and ruptured through repeated onslaughts against him, invariably articulated as diatribes against his masculinity and sexual–moral identity. The sexual escapades, or rather their absence in the king's life and, in reverse, the abundance of rumours surrounding Queen Marie Antoinette's heterosexual as well as lesbian dalliances became the subject of proliferating semi-pornographic, caricatural sketches and engravings.

Initially, the King's inability to sexually consummate his marriage evoked much medical interest. Soon, however, the matter came to be seen as a symptom of the corruption and flaccidity in the political state of France. Sexual incapacity was thus re-presented as political impotency and ineptness. If the king did not have the 'force to deflower his wife' (*Body Politic* 43) neither did he have the force or moral authority to head a nation. Secondly, the queen's cuckolding of the king, one might suggest, offered alluring lessons to the masses: if the queen, sexually dissatisfied with the king, could choose alternative lovers why couldn't the people, displeased with his politics, do the same—that is, choose better rulers: themselves for instance.

In some of these sketches, we see the bare-breasted queen inviting and initiating sexual activity from the king—she sits, in one, with her legs spread wide, awaiting penetration; in the second, she masturbates the king who sits in her lap. Her agency in both contrasts with the 'limpness' of the king. The king's 'dullness', also an eighteenth century word for stupidity, offers the queen abundant opportunities to exercise her agency—sexual and general—this time with other men. In another plate, the queen forms the cuckold sign behind the king's head. This static plate (static not just because it is a frieze, but also because the king's impotency ensures that no sexual activity will take place) offers us overt signs for all the sexual action that takes place outside this plate between Marie Antoinette and her paramours—action in which the king's lack or absence will not just be metaphorical, but also literal.

The queen's successful deception and subversion of the king's authority was not, however, a subject of celebration in popular culture. On the contrary Marie Antoinette's power made her the object of immense misogynistic satire and ridicule. Pierre Saint-Amand[4] in a fascinating essay illustrates the long history of what he calls the 'Marie Antoinette syndrome'—the fear of powerful women. A woman who could dominate the king himself needed to be restrained in every possible way—through humiliation, decapitation,[5] or, if need be, through both. The queen's body, so far the source of her power over and against the king, now appears as the very site upon which the revolutionaries will 'tame' her.

Thus, the Federate pact of July 1790 takes on a new visual appearance. The queen's body, in this plate, paralleling the disappearance of the body of the king, gets reduced to her genitals. Her face, torso and legs have been altogether dispensed with, and only the emblem of her power, her vagina, is retained and decorated as a dis-em-bodied abstraction. Furthermore, the 'imperial vagina' is flanked on both sides by a battalion of penises. These pluralised erect phalluses are the exact antithesis of the king's inert member. If the king's limpness signified his lack of control over the queen's body, the erect and canon-like penises of the new French Federation are ever ready to assault and penetrate the queen. Someone needs to control the lascivious queen—since the king can't, the new '*cunt-federation*' takes over.

This 'desacralisation' of the royal body culminates in the ultimate ritual of dismemberment: decapitation. However, as Saint-Amand points out, the guillotining of the king and the queen, respectively, denoted very different parables. If the king's beheading ushered in a new political regime, the queen's assassination was more a necessary 'moral' act, than a political one. She was punished more for her excesses as a woman of easy virtue, than for her political status as queen. Herbert, a journalist who reported on the queen's execution, recounted the 'orgasmic bliss' (Saint-Amand, 'Terrorising Marie Antoinette' 387) that enveloped the masses on seeing the 'feathered tart' receive just punishment. It was precisely for her sexual crimes rather than her political tyranny that she needed to be beheaded. Jacques Louis David's sketch of Marie Antoinette on her way to the guillotine captures this gendered dimension in her execution. The trappings and markings of the queen—the crown, gown and general opulence and regalia—are entirely absent from her person. If David hadn't particularised her as the queen, there would be little means of recognising her as one. The implication is clear— she need not have been the queen at all. Like Charlotte Corday (murderer of Marat) or Olympe de Gouges (author of the *Declaration of Rights of Woman*), both of whom were also sent to the guillotine, she represents *any* transgressive woman.

The carnivalesque debunking of the kingly/queenly bodies was matched by a similar visual reconstitution of the figure of the aristocrat into the great beast 'Iscariot'. If the king was reconfigured as a decrepit despot, his ally, the aristocrat, emerged as the monster unleashed by the despot to safeguard their mutually shared domain. Iscariot is armed from head to foot with the weapons of tyranny—his head, like Medusa's, is crowned with green snakes, he carries a dagger and sword, and his hands and feet are shaped like the tiger's claws (*Body Politic* 157, 158). It is important to note that besides visual burlesque and caricature, the revolutionaries also deployed religious and Biblical iconography and allusions to demonise their enemies. Not only is Iscariot an incomplete anagram of the word 'aristocrat', the coinage invokes also a reference to Judas Iscariot—the ultimate traitor.

The sexual turpitude of the queen too gained an added dimension of horror and revulsion through association with the figure of Iscariot. If on the one hand 'Iscariot' evoked Judas, on the other he represented the extension of the queen's (sexual) monstrosity. Therefore in several other depictions he is referred to as the 'female monster' of 'Austrian origin', or as the 'degenerate product' of the union between the queen and an aristocrat. The realm of popular politics flooded with proliferating illustrations of Marie Antoinette as a monster—in one she is depicted as Harpy and in another as Hydra. Hydra, the multi-headed monster, primarily signified the aristocracy. Yet, by furnishing it with breasts its links with Marie Antoinette were made explicit.

The body politic that David's *Oath at the Tennis Court* portrays stands in sharp emblematic contrast to the feminised Hydra (*Body Politic*). If Hydra has been captured in the moment of its destruction—the spears of the people are piercing its breast/heart—David's *Oath* delineates the moment of *birth* of a new entity: the People's Republic. Similarly, if the multiple heads of the Hydra are the corrupt and degenerate aristocrats responsible for destroying France, then the heads taking the oath in David's painting belong to the righteous democrats. And finally if the Hydra-monster is a feminine creature, the new body politic in the *Oath*, is exclusively and unambiguously male—women are entirely excluded from this grand political spectacle and ritual. The canvas is covered with masculine figures, all embracing one another, and dedicating themselves to *their father* land. The inference is obvious—women's bodies can be recruited into the domain of representation to define the evil that plagues the nation. However, the feminine shall find no place in the defining and elevated moments, or when new, liberal politics, in all their promise and hallowed import, are being formulated.

Evidently, then, the castigation and demonisation of the court and its constituents through laughter and caricature was not deemed enough. The revolutionaries would leave no stone unturned in their attempt to disparage the figures of authority. Where laughter failed to demystify, grotesque and horrific images were sure to succeed. In addition, the liberals (as demonstrated in the discussion of David's painting) visually conceptualised themselves in direct opposition to their enemies. And yet, like so many purportedly 'democratic' and 'progressive' movements, the French Revolution too dipped into the ever-fertile pool of misogynistic images and narratives to propagate their 'radical' agenda. Emancipatory gender politics would have to wait another century (at least) before it could be considered at par with the discourse of class and nation.

The aesthetics of sketching and caricature must momentarily hold our attention before we proceed to the next section. Albert Boime[6] calls caricature the 'language of revolution'. He suggests, rather evocatively, that the process of creating a sketch or caricature can be read as a metaphor for the French Revolution. If caricature distorts its subject of representation, the Revolution also works through 'desacralising' (often through distortion) its enemies. Again, as an artistic mode sketching, like the Revolution, is predicated on minimalising excess and opulence. Similarly, like a revolution, the sketch too is the outcome of a momentary and spontaneous upsurge—political upsurge in one case, and an imaginative/creative outburst or upheaval in the other. Finally, both the revolution and the sketch are unfinished products—unfinalised entities in the process of 'becoming'. We will never know what the ultimate outcome of the sketch or the revolution is going to be, and that is what adds to the enigma and fascination of both. Edmund Burke too compared the 'horror' of a revolutionary nation to the 'crudeness' of an unfinished work of art; simultaneously *contrasting* the 'stability' of a monarchical regime to the formal 'beauty' of a finished work. Burke's 'profound' insight, dare one suggest, however reveals a measure of not just political but also artistic unimaginativeness. How curious that a man who could produce an entire treatise on the subject of sublimity should have failed to recognise a real example of the sublime confronting him in its most basic, elemental form—as just a few lines orchestrated to create a swirl of radical and original significations.

Who Shall Lead the People? The Battle of the Icons

The revolutionaries had wanted to distance themselves from the feminine, rococo art of the *ancien régime* with its excessive use of colour, artifice and metaphors. The earliest republicans believed that 'an enlightened [masculine] nation had no need of icons and symbols' ('Imaging the Revolution,' 11). Their circumstances, however, created a paradoxical situation. The revolution was still relatively new and had to be made accessible to the masses. The obvious means to achieve this was by making the abstract ideals of the revolution—liberty, equality, and fraternity—come alive through the 'vivid and appealing language of signs'.[7] Moreover, the '*transfer of sacrality*'[8] (Ozouf *Festivals and the French Revolution*) from the monarch to the people wouldn't be complete without the revolutionaries creating their own 'sacred' symbols. As Durkheim[9] argues, no society can achieve a sense of solidarity without manufacturing symbols around which it can organise itself. Thus, no matter how irreligious a society may be, it would need to fashion its 'gods'. Clearly, the revolutionaries understood this practical prerequisite for success: the use of images, no matter how problematic, was inescapable. As a compromise they decided to opt for images that were 'transparent',[10] direct and virile, as opposed to the simulated and feminine images used by the French elite. A second paradox lies here —a revolution which organised the new body politic around its male members (once again refer to David's *Oath*), and which strove strenuously to employ 'virile' images to do so, ended up choosing the feminine emblem of Liberty as its most defining symbol of self-representation.

A few examples of the use of the figure of Liberty before one undertakes an analysis of the reasons for this choice: Pierre Thomas LeClerc's drawing, *La Liberté* (1793) depicts a young woman in forward motion, connoting the onward movement of the Revolution. The club she carries (like Hercules) suggests that the work of the revolution is not over. In fact this drawing arrests Liberty in the very moment of her work—the destruction of the hydra of despotism trampled beneath her feet. Nonetheless, the harmony and joy that she brings to the people is emblematised in the serene expression of her face, the beauty of her flowing robes and the laurel leaves she carries to honour the revolutionaries. In another anonymous engraving (1790), Liberty's posture is even more typically feminised than in the previous drawing. She stands passively with the symbols of the revolution—the liberty cap and the tablets of the Declaration of the Rights of Man and Citizen. Her body is petite and 'devoid of muscularity and tension' (Juneja, *Imaging the Revolution*, 19). Liberty, here, is as feminine as feminine gets.

Why then did the masculinist politics of the revolution choose this figure? One argument offered is that even though the queen epitomised the moral degeneration of France, it was really the king who represented political tyranny. Therefore a feminine figuration of liberty would stand as a perfect antithetical corollary to the patriarchal monarch. Maurice Agulhon[11] adds that familiarity with Catholicism made a Marian figure more accessible to the French. Furthermore, this stable, nurturing, feminine figure stood as a direct counter-point to not just the king but the often unstable and disappointing male revolutionaries (like Lafayette and Mirabeau) themselves. The feminine ideal was seen as uncontaminated by the grimy world of politics.[12]

Monica Juneja forwards another interesting reading—the male form, she suggests, escapes universality and anonymity and always functions as a contexualised particular. Women, on the other hand, are seen as embodying a transcendental, abstract quality, as residing 'beyond public structures and therefore [able to] lend themselves more easily to the representation of abstract notions' ('Imaging the Revolution' 13). Moreover, by personifying Liberty in female form, the revolutionaries converted this political value into an object of male acquisition, a reward that all revolutionaries could desire, strive for and possess. The feminisation of Liberty, therefore, is also a transformation of this political notion into a sexualised lure for men to conquer.

Despite this 'lure' of Liberty, for a while at least the Jacobins led by Robespierre discarded the figure of Liberty for a more volatile, aggressive and masculine icon, Hercules. This decision was prompted by the outbreak of war in 1793. The conspiracies and attacks, from within and outside France, led to the period of 'Terror'. The government now needed a more martial emblem to represent and justify its actions. Thus, the comparatively moderate figure of Liberty gave way to the Herculean Colossus, signifying the awe-inspiring and terrifying might of the nation state.

Hercules was primarily meant to denote the power of the French people, as opposed to Liberty which conveyed only the 'sagacity of the representatives' of the people (Hunt, 'Hercules and the Radical Image in Revolutionary France'). The representatives had achieved Liberty for that 'Herculean' entity, the People, by killing the king. Now it was up to the people to safeguard it. Ostensibly, the work of the leaders was over—the people had taken over—and therefore the symbol of Liberty had served its purpose and could be marginalised. All focus had now shifted to the People, and the icon that represented them—Hercules.

It might seem that the leaders of the revolution were paying homage to the might of the People by handing to them the responsibility of furthering/defending the revolution. However, a closer scrutiny of the association of the People with Hercules shows the limits of this seemingly magnanimous gesture (magnanimity in any case retains authority and moral superiority with the donor). Firstly, one of the most striking characteristics of Hercules is that he is not a particularly bright or 'enlightened' giant. His achievements depend less on brain than brawn. Thus even in handing over power to the People, their representatives are cleverly retaining the realm of ideas and intellect for themselves. The leaders acknowledge the strength of the People by recognising their 'Herculean' virtues. In the same breath, however, they are also expressing scepticism about the intelligence of the People, and their capacity for unaided self-governance. It turns out that the image of Hercules is less than fully empowering. This hero of the revolution, ironically, is given no share in the planning of the revolution; he can only implement the plans crafted by the leaders. Secondly, Hercules may stand as the emblem of the People, yet the People were eternally dependant on their representatives to *explain the significance* of this classical icon. Ironically, without the 'theoretical' mediation of their leaders, the masses wouldn't even recognise their own image in Hercules.

All said and done, though, the classical myth of Hercules fitted the Republic's self-conception more exactly than the figure of Liberty. Like Hercules, the French state saw itself on the crossroads between vice and virtue, and like him the people of France had to fight the monsters of despotism and tyranny, thereby choosing the road to Liberty. Regnault's painting *Liberty or Death* encapsulates this element of choice that lay before Hercules and symbolically before revolutionary France. The winged Hercules, typifying the revolution, is flanked on either side by personifications of Liberty and Death. We know that he must choose between the two, but the confident and grandiose flight of Hercules declares to the viewer that the choice has already been made—he has chosen Liberty and therefore now prospers and spreads his wings.

The guiltlessly exposed genitals of Hercules bring us back to the gendered construction of the new republic—the 'People' whom Hercules represents and addresses in this painting are exclusively and definitionally male. The revolutionary cult of brotherhood *(fraternité)* is also manifest in the images of men embracing one another in David's *Oath*. In killing the king, their metaphoric father, the revolutionaries emerged as what Lynn Hunt[14] terms a 'band of brothers' (Hunt, 'Band of Brothers'), playing out the Freudian concept of the 'family romance' in which children reject their parents and replace them with more desirable ones. While the construction of the king as a 'bad father' enabled the revolutionaries to deal with the guilt of parricide/regicide, they stopped short of carrying forward the 'family romance' to its logical conclusion. Having disposed of the father, they did not replace him with a new father figure. Instead they preferred to operate as a cult of young men, which resurrected, if at all, only dead revolutionaries to patriarch status. This contrasts with American history where Washington emerged as the 'father of the nation'. Robespierre or Marat in their lifetime never represented themselves as 'fathers'. They were always the 'friends' or 'brothers' of the people. Marat, for instance, became connected with political fatherhood only after his death.

The republic was thus conceptually constituted by robust, masculine patriots, who seemed to have come into being without a lineage, and, if they died in battle, perhaps even without heirs. The fathers mattered little. David's *Oath of Horatii* demonstrates as much. In this painting, the father, reconciled to the idea of giving up his sons to the nation hands them their weapons of war. The brothers standing together in embrace shift the balance of power to their side. Power and authority in the new state lies not just with men, but specifically men who are brothers, not fathers.

The question begs to be asked: in the midst of this frenzied euphoria about youthful brothers-in-arms, where and how did women figure? The 1789 etching by Johann Peters, *The New Bastille Square*, offers a telling account—even though the mother looms large and is placed in the foreground as compared to the dwarfed king, her role in the Republic is contained within the parameters of the 'nurturer' of future soldiers and republicans for the nation. As a matter of fact, one of her sons is already dressed as a soldier. The fetishisation of women as mothers lead to several depictions of women with their breasts exposed. An anonymous engraving *Republican Mother Nursing Her Infant* (1793) lays down an even more precise role for women—motherhood as such is not enough. They must be a particular kind of mother—one who nurses her own children. This engraving seems to feed into the Rousseauvian paranoia, which Republican France shared, regarding wet-nursing. All good women of the republic, this engraving commands, must nurse their own children.

After the fall of Robespierre, when the figure of Hercules had proved inadequate and ephemeral—he had come to be too closely related to 'The Terror'—it was this symbol of the nursing mother that the Thermidorians chose as most representative of their ideals—peace, patience and nurture (as opposed to the bloodthirst of the Terror). This, and the even more pacified feminine allegory of Liberty (now depicted as seated rather than standing or marching) helped France emerge out of the shadows of regicide and the months of the guillotine. It is exceedingly ironical that the revolutionaries eventually found it necessary to coalesce around the bodies of women—both at the start and at the end of the revolution. If the body of a woman (the queen) initiated the revolution, as 'provocation' so to speak, then the body of another woman (the mother) helped the revolutionaries recover from the horror of the Frankensteinian monster they had unleashed in the form of the Terror. The feminine thus re-enters revolutionary representation—as a pacifying presence.

Ultimately, therefore, the tussle between images undergoes radical transformation. If icons were earlier competing to best represent the ideal and idea of the revolution, by the end of the century, the icons were chosen not for their closeness to the revolution but rather their (relative) distance from it. This may be best understood by that iconic symbol of 'modern' France, the Eiffel Tower—An image that is large and phallactically erect on a scale surpassing any human colossus that David could have imagined, and yet one that, politically, speaks the least to the People of France, much less to those revolutionaries across the world to whom the Revolution in France has continued to stand as inspiration for over two centuries.

Notes

1 Interestingly this spatial metaphor feeds into the understanding of culture offered by Jonathan Dollimore and Alan Sinfield as "the whole system of significations by which a society or a section of it understands itself and its relations with the world". These "significations" (which constitute culture) one might suggest, come into being and operate precisely within this literal and representational space that Henri Lefevbre proposes. Dollimore, Jonathan, and Alan Sinfield, eds. *Political Shakespeare: Essays In Cultural Materialism* (Ithaca and London: Cornell UP, 1985).

2 I use the word "modern" because the French Revolution initiated the discourses of law, nationhood and political propaganda in a manner that had no precedent in history.

3 Antoine de Baecque, *The Body Politic: Corporeal Metaphor in Revolutionary France, 1770-1800* trans. Charlotte Mandell (Stanford: Stanford UP, 1993).

4 Pierre Saint-Amand, 'Terrorising Marie Antoinette,' *Critical Inquiry* 20.3 (1994): 379-400.

5 Hélène Cixous in 'Castration and Decapitation' refers to the deployment of the fear of decapitation as a weapon used by men to keep subversive women in control. Women, she argues, can escape being completely subsumed by the symbolic because they lack 'lack.' What for men is a signifier of women's inferiority, the lack of the penis, becomes for Cixous an empowering absence. However men cannot allow women to have an upper hand in anything, and if they must suffer from castration anxiety, then it becomes necessary to fill women with terror about loss of a body part too – hence the deployment of the fear of decapitation. All women who ask questions and dare to laugh, or more precisely "laugh at," thus refusing to listen (respectfully) to the commands of the law of the father – the 180 wives of the Chinese king, the Sphinx and Medusa – must all be dealt with in the same way: off with their heads! Helene Cixous, 'Castration and Decapitation' trans. Annette Kuhn, *Signs* 7.1 (1981): 41-55.

6 Boime, Albert. 'Sketch and Caricature as Metaphor for the French Revolution'. *Zeitschrift für Kunstgeschichte*, 55 Bd., H.2. (1992): 256–67.

7 Edouard Pommier quoted by Monica Juneja, 'Imaging the Revolution: Gender and Iconography in the French Revolution Political Prints' *Studies in History* 12.I (1996): 1-65.

8 Mona Ozouf, *Festivals and the French Revolution* trans. Alan Sheridan (Cambridge: Harvard UP, 1988).

9 Emile Durkheim, *The Elementary Forms of Religious Life* trans. Joseph Ward Swain (New York: Free P, 1967).

10 Rousseau in *The Discourse on the Arts and Sciences* (1750) advocated the ideal of transparency and "natural language". J. J. Rousseau, *The Discourse on the Arts and Sciences* trans. Ian Johnston. 1750, 22 Sept. 2006 http://records.viu.ca/~johnston/rousseau/firstdiscourse.html.

[11] As discussed in Lynn Hunt, 'Hercules and the Radical Image in the French Revolution,' *Representations* 2 (1983): 95–117. The reference is to 98–99.

[12] This was of course far from the truth. Women like Marie Antoinette, Charlotte Corday, Olympe de Gouges, not to mention several revolutionary women who had marched to Versailles and dragged the king back to Paris, are blatant refutations of any such 'idealisations' of women as apolitical.

[13] Monica Juneja, 'Imaging the Revolution' 13.

[14] Lynn Hunt, 'Band of Brothers', *The French Revolution: The Essential Readings* ed. Ronald Schechter (Oxford: Blackwell Publishers, 2001).

The Indian Subcontinent

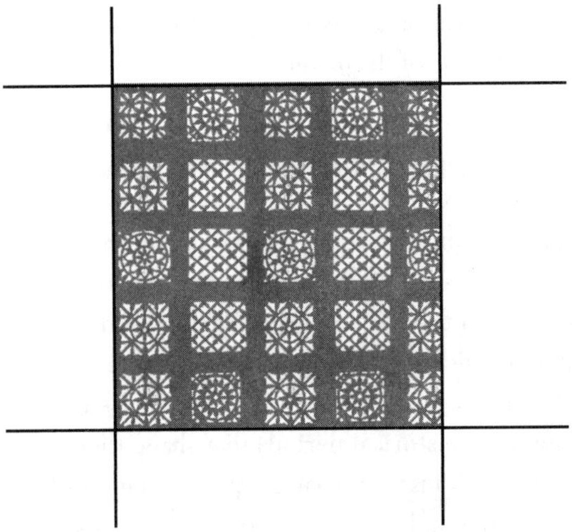

The Indian Subcontinent

A generation or so ago, attempts to imagine India could be briskly dismissed in this way.

> For many Europeans, India evoked a picture of Maharajas, snake-charmers, and the rope trick.... In the imagination of Europe, India had always been the fabulous land of untold wealth and mystical happenings, with more than just a normal share of wise men. From the gold-digging ants to the philosophers who lived naked in the forests, these were all part of the picture which the ancient Greeks had of the Indians and this image persisted throughout many centuries. It might be more charitable not to destroy it, but to preserve it would mean the perpetuation of a myth.[1]

Myths and their legacies can be astonishingly durable, however, as postcolonialism found when it began to dismantle images of India as being complicit with the colonial will to power. As a more recent survey notes, a work of art may comment upon a historical process, but it is also a product of a specific aesthetic method. Thus it repays scrutiny on both counts.

> Existing post-colonial criticism prompts only a partial analysis because it is concerned to investigate the mentality underlying works of art, much less often addressing the technicalities of their production. To ignore production, or to subsume it under mentality, is to repeat an ancient fallacy: it is to mistake representation for perception. These two

> are not the same. Between an artist's perception of an object and its representation lies a physical action, the making of the picture.[2]

Images converse with each other, and with the political and cultural imperatives that shape them. A study of attempts to imagine India must be sensitive to both these lines of conversation and relationship.

While nature and time continue to be the critical filters through which a wide range of artistic representations are studied, there are two areas of significant change in this section. One has to do with the way in which Time is handled. The works of art studied here do not—to put it mildly—share a historical frame of reference with regard to their production. They range from the third century to the present AD. Yet they share a need to comment upon the historical periods that shape them, even though these are as widely different as early Buddhism in what is now Pakistan, the British Empire, and India during the nineteen-eighties and after. Their commentary is analysed typically through a consideration of diverse methods of artistic representation, and through the responses that these methods have evoked over time.

The other shift has to do with the range of art forms examined in this section. These include sculpture, black-and-white illustrations, poster and film images, photographs and cartoons. Form is addressed when its requirements and constraints shape content but it cannot be regarded as the distinguishing feature of this section. That slot belongs to the ongoing conversation in which nature and time are shown to comment upon each other, and—in the process—to revise the way in which the subcontinent looks at itself and at other territories and peoples.

The chief occupational delight in this section is also its chief occupational hazard. There is an unusually broad range of cultural contexts to which the reader is required—by the work of art and by the critical industry that waits upon it—to be responsive. Unlike the Renaissance or the eighteenth and nineteenth centuries, South Asia is presented here as a continuing cultural space despite wild discontinuities of time. This may seem to make geography the lazy escape-route from the ruptures of history, particularly when we look at, say, the statues of Buddha and Gommateshwara from third-century Lahore and tenth-century Deogarh respectively. On the face of it one might say that critical dialogue might be perilous when neither religious practice nor aesthetic theory is consistently verifiable. Nonetheless, Vincent Villafranca's essay offers a close reading of the theme of renunciation in selected pieces of sculpture, to suggest the terms on which such dialogue may begin. Villafranca—a professional sculptor—sets himself the task of following convolutions in stone and in photographic image, to suggest how this reading can be undertaken. Again, a context such as the high noon of Empire—retrievable though that might seem—becomes complicated by the fact that it is impossible to reliably establish Lockwood Kipling's knowledge of the aesthetic theory and tradition of the Lahori artisans he recruited. Christel Devadawson' s essay however uses the image of Mowgli as a critical prism through which JLK's black-and-white line drawings of Empire can be understood, particularly when contrasted with Disney's more recent reworking of the image. With regard to Kaye and Watson, their voluminous collection of photographs, *The People of India*, illustrates the administrative and anthropological necessities to which they subscribed with greater certainty than it does the principles on which they organised their camera-work. Sonali Patnaik—a photographer herself—studies these images to open up the worlds of experience behind them that have traditionally been collapsed into the grand narrative of Empire. Finally, O. V. Vijayan's cartoons and short fiction highlight different kinds of gaps and blank spaces that cannot easily and surely be traced to a common source. Yet Divya Dwivedi studies not so much the common ground between the two forms as the lines of philosophical inquiry that open out from the text and images. Is it sound scholarship to collapse such multiple concerns into a single category labelled 'The Indian Subcontinent'?

We believe the answer is, 'Yes', because in this section, South Asia emerges as a cultural and critical space that gains in coherence and sensitivity when examined in this way. There is a strong sense of political and cultural community as all the essays speculate —although in very different ways—on various relationships between the world (or state) and the individual. The statues of the Buddha and Gommateshwara are shown to derive their strength from their ability to give up their hold on their own monolithic might, as creepers and tendrils curl around them and make them more human. Through the different apologias for Empire constructed by Lockwood Kipling, Kaye and Watson, there comes an insistence that people will not be contained within apparently one-dimensional representations. Mowgli's defiance of adulthood, or the defiance of the law shown by alleged criminals photographed by Kaye and Watson, bring images to life compulsively and disobediently. Vijayan reminds us that caricature helps regulate the political jungle in which there might soon be no people at all, just ungovernable cartoons.

Critical community is less obvious but nonetheless present. The opening essay on Buddhist and Hindu renunciation acknowledges the magisterial reach of Mircea Eliade's *The Encyclopaedia of Religion*, and for detailed work—among others —S. Doshi's *Homage to Shravana Belgola*. Populist points of entry into these fields include Christmas Humphreys on Buddhism and Nirad Chaudhuri on Hinduism. Representations of Empire in general may be studied with Ronald Inden's *Imagining India*. More specific studies include Partha Mitter's *Much Maligned Monsters: History of European Reactions to Indian Art* and Tapati Guha-Thakurta's *The Making of a 'New' Indian Art: Artists, Aesthetics and Nationalism in Bengal, c. 1850–1920*. They set out—from perspectives that differ in viewpoint and detail—the ways in which South Asia and nineteenth-century Europe shape each other in terms of their responses to each other's aesthetic theory and practice. Apart from Vijayan's slice of lifewriting (cited in the essay), sources that might be consulted include R. K. Laxman's

Past Forward, and *The Tunnel of Time*. With I .S. Pillai's *'Don't spare me Shankar,'* they conjure up a tragicomic critique of nationalism suggesting that here, as elsewhere, the underlying realities of art and politics across the subcontinent are fundamentally the same.

Notes

[1] Romila Thapar, *A History of India* (London: Penguin, 1969) 15.

[2] Giles Tillotson, *The Artificial Empire: The Indian Landscapes of William Hodges* (London: 2000) 103.

8. Representations of Nature and Time in South Asian Sculputre: Lord Gommateshwara and the Fasting Buddha

Vincent Villafranca

Nature and time are two themes that have an established tradition in the visual depictions of ascetics in South Asia. In this paper I will be looking at how nature and time have been dealt with in two examples of South Asian ascetic sculpture, the Jain figure Lord Gommateshwara, at Shravana Belgola, and the emaciated figure of the Buddhist tradition referred to as the Fasting Buddha at the Lahore Museum in Pakistan. It is my thesis that the two sculptures solidly project the idea that concern with time's grasp is to be transcended, and unification with nature is essential when one is devoted to true renunciation of worldly and materialistic values. Nature and time are themes that are visually intertwined and connected in these sculptures. In this paper, I will examine the visual representations of nature and time in the two sculptures, and also English translations of extant sacred texts and contemporary writings that deal with the ideas expressed in these works. These two sculptures, Lord Gommateshwara and the Fasting Buddha are indicative of the long-standing human concern with the themes of time and nature. They bring these two sculptures together despite geographical and chronological distance.

Representations of nature are used as a visual tool to depict the passing of time. These two images, Lord Gommateshwara and the Fasting Buddha, express time as a force to be conquered. By conquering time, the subjects are themselves conquered, as their bodies are returned to where they originated, that being nature. Lord Gommateshwara, in his standing repose, is lost in deep meditation to the point that vegetal creepers overtake his stationary limbs and animals take up residence near his feet, whereas the Fasting Buddha exists in quiet repose as his seated physical form is slowly turned into a pile of dust. These visual devices of natural growth and decay are strong indicators of the passage of time. Depictions of such phenomenon give us insight into the concerns of those who lived centuries ago.

In the physical sense, traditional sculpture inherently transcends time. Depending on the materials, a sculpture can exist considerably further into the future than the artisan, or artisans, that brought it into the tangible world. Sandstone, granite, bronze and wood are just some of the media used by craftspeople to represent both sacred and secular content. Existing artifacts have endured into the present by defying natural forces such as erosion and oxidation and act as windows to the past. Often, the original intentions of the artisans of the past still convey a certain level of meaning to us, the modern spectators.

Despite the years of labour devoted to producing stone carvings, artisans generally capture a small representation of time. Representations of Lord Gommateshwara are an exception to this. Lord Gommateshwara, also known as Lord Bahubali, is lost in deep meditation as he becomes part of his natural surroundings. Despite his rigid and erect posture, his depictions successfully show the passage of time. The creeping vegetation and elongated arms are effective visual devices in conveying this passage of time. The viewer can easily read this due to the evident representation of plant behaviour and the depicted effects of gravity on the renunciant's arms.[1] The Fasting Buddha also clearly conveys the passage of time. As Buddha sits in his quiet repose, he is lost in the realm of austere asceticism as he blocks out all possible distraction that the material world so generously offers. His lack of concern with matters of the tangible world has affected his body to the point that it can no longer perform the simple task of properly accommodating his robe. These two sculptures have journeyed through the centuries carrying with them their ideas of nature and time.

The Jain saint, Gommateshwara, as seen here at Shravana Belgola, is a masterpiece of devotional craftsmanship. Dated to AD 981, it conveys the tenet of Jainism concerning the transcendence of human existence rather than concern with an ultimate divinity.[2] Approximately eighteen metres high, this statue of Gommateshwara, carved out of grey granite is considered the largest free-standing monolithic statue in the world.[3] His name means 'Lord of the Hillock' as he occupies one of the hills at Shravana Belgola. This site has been revered for centuries due to the numerous Jain saints and devotees who ended their days amongst the sacred hills located there.[4] Commissioned in the tenth century by a Ganga Dynasty general Chamundaraya, this Jain sculpture of monumental proportion maintains a strong devotion to the present day.[5] Due to his individual spiritual achievement,

Gommateshwara holds a distinguished position among Jain images.[6] The presence of the vines immediately distinguishes Gommateshwara from representations of the twenty-four Jinas that are depicted sculpturally in the Jain art tradition.

In addition to the outward message projected by this beautiful rendering, there is an extant text which gives the reader some history of the image. Gommateshwara, according to an English translation of the *Adipurana* (an early ninth century AD Sanskrit account), was the second son of the great Jina Risabanatha, the first enlightened Jain sage, or Tirtamkara, of this age.[7] Risabanatha attempted to teach his ascetic philosophy to his ninety-nine sons when he instructed them that empires are transient, and kingdoms are ephemeral. He instructed them to seek the 'un-withering flower of compassion' that is the great fruit of liberation from the tangible world.[8] After hearing their father's elegant discourse concerning the world, the sons left for the forest to take up a life of asceticism passing their nights at bases of trees and allowing their bodies to be clothed with falling snow and nothing else.[9] The translation of the *Adipurana* states that, 'their limbs were withered by great acts of abstinence…and their bodies became emaciated due to the heat generated by religious austerities.'[10] The only two sons who did not heed their father's instruction were the two eldest sons, Bharata and Gommateshwara.[11] The *Adipurana* text assists the modern viewer by clarifying the meaning of some of the narrative elements exhibited in the representations of Gommateshwara.[12]

Gommateshwara is a good representation of communion with nature. As the passage from the *Adipurana* states, after he defeated his brother Bharata for the control of the kingdom, Gommateshwara rejected his rightful position as emperor. Instead, he chose to be, 'embraced by the vine of initiation, (with) all his clothing cast aside he was like a tree denuded of its leaves. His feet were covered by the expanded hoods of young hissing cobras.'[13] These textual references to vines and tendrils are gracefully sculpted into the grey granite. Gommateshwara's posture is a testament to his perfect self-control.[14] Gommateshwara is similar to an ancient tree, standing in the forest and allowing other living organism to take refuge upon him and parasitise his body (see Figures 12, 12a). Nature's agents take up residence in and around this figure as he becomes a pillar of self control and fierce austerities.[15] As his ascetic brothers passed their nights at the bases of forest trees, so were the nights of the cobras and deer passed at the base of Gommateshwara as he transformed into a part of the sacred forest architecture.

This eleventh century stone rendering of Gommateshwara is located at a temple complex in Deogarh. Gommateshwara is accented by snakes slithering up his inactive legs, while large lizards comfortably sit on his motionless thighs. As the scholar Maruti Nandan Prasad Tiwari eloquently put it, 'The Gommateshwara representations show snakes issuing out of ant-hills which developed near his feet and creepers entwined around his body, suggesting the long period of time in which he was absorbed in penance and meditation.'[16]

Representations of Gommateshwara are also found in late medieval illuminated manuscripts describing the events of the *Adipurana*. Gommateshwara's prolonged communion with nature is depicted by having the creepers rise above and around his head. The image on the right demonstrates this oneness with the environment by placing a large assortment of birds nesting in and around Gommateshwara's hair.[17] These two-dimensional examples are further evidence that the themes of nature and time are solidly intertwined in the depictions of the austere path taken by Lord Gommateshwara.

The Fasting Buddha is another South Asian sculpture that powerfully depicts the union of time and nature. Through the rendered physical decay and suggested natural growth, the modern spectator can easily read that this work is a testament to a life of renunciation and asceticism. Located in the Lahore Museum in Pakistan, this schist Gandharan sculpture dates from third to the fourth century AD. Over the centuries, many copies have been made of the famous Fasting Buddha sculpture. The one pictured in Figure 13 was rendered by Mahabalipuram sculptor T. Baskaran. The birth of Buddhist thought began with the life of Siddhartha Gautama in the mid-sixth century BC. The birth of Buddhist thought began with the life of Siddhartha Gautama in the mid-sixth century BC. As Buddhism expanded, schisms occurred and councils were held as different sects came about. This belief system left us with a plethora of powerful images.[18] The reverence toward the austerities of the Buddha was centuries old by the time the Gandharan artisans sculpted this image. On the base of the sculpture is a depiction of the veneration given to the begging bowl of Buddha by monastics of the third to fourth century AD.[19]

Interestingly, this fasting depiction of Buddha in deep meditation is quite different from the more common renderings where Buddha is not emaciated. This way of depicting the Buddha was rare. The Fasting Buddha immediately gives the viewer a sense of elapsed time through the depicted decay of the human body. The grown-out beard on the ascetic sculpture also lends itself to promoting the concept of the passing of time. The symmetrical design of this form orients the viewer toward the face and chest cavity. The corporeal detail invites the viewer to visually study this work. This fragmented version of the Fasting Buddha is an even better example of elapsed time due to the visible wear and damage to the materials. To those unfamiliar with the tenets of renunciation and asceticism, fear and distress may be experienced upon first sight. However, even the uninitiated spectator can see the beauty in the sculpture if they allow some time for reflection and invite a visual connection to be established with this withered figure. A literary reference to the illuminating effect of beholding and gazing at a renunciant's face can be found in Herman Hesse's 1922 novel *Siddhartha*. In the final passage of the book, Govinda stares into the face of his enlightened friend Siddhartha and does not see the face of his friend. Instead, Govinda sees images of nature in the form of various animals, representations of emotions, babies being born, and the elderly dying. A multitude of images of 'that which is transitory' took the place of Siddhartha's face as Govinda's moment of elucidation occurred.[20] Interestingly, Hesse's next paragraph refers to Govinda as, 'No longer knowing whether time existed, whether this display had lasted a second or a hundred years.'[21] In this case, the act of beholding produced an intoxicating effect as Siddhartha's friend lost touch with time and with the tangible world.

The garment of the Fasting Buddha is another element that relates the passage of time. His robe is depicted as having slipped down over his shoulders and lying haplessly over his forearms and knees. This method of depicting the robe gives the viewer a sense that his shrinking body has reached the point to where it can no longer maintain the simple task of filling a garment. By studying the sculpture, it can be assumed that the flesh withered, the robe fell and the Buddha never noticed as he maintained his course on the path of 'not doing'. The folds and pleats of the cloth take on an organic appearance as the smoothness commonly associated with sculpted cloth is lost.[22]

The veins on the Fasting Buddha play a dual role. The veins demonstrate the emaciation process that has taken place through time of rigorous fasting. The biographies of the Buddha state that as the Buddha fasted, he became so thin that he could touch his spine by pressing on his stomach. This description of the emaciating effect of fasting addresses the physical transformation that took place as the Buddha explored this path of complete renunciation. However, the veins and the sinew of the Fasting Buddha also mimic the behaviour of the plant world in the form of creeping vines that overtake and consume their host. This image shows a close up view of the chest area of the Fasting Buddha. The viewer can easily get the impression that vines and tendrils have flourished over the stalwart and determined figure. This view corresponds strongly with the intertwining motifs of the creepers on the representations of Gommateshwara.

In conclusion, I have shown that depictions of Lord Gommateshwara and the Fasting Buddha have continued to convey their messages to contemporary viewers. I have argued that these two sculptures solidly project the idea that concern with time's grasp is to be transcended and unification with nature is essential when one is devoted to true renunciation of worldly and materialistic values. I have shown that there are some correspondences in these powerful South Asian sculptures. Some early inhabitants of the subcontinent realised that nature and time were appropriate themes to address artistically. These two religions of Jainism and Buddhism, which promote peace and harmony with nature, have transcended time through their lineages of devotees and through sculptural representations. As the artisans and devotees rendered their thoughts and philosophies in the form of sculpture, they shared their message with some of their fellow human beings, of their time and of the present.

Notes

1 M. Nandan Prasad Tiwari, 'A Note on Some Bahubali Images from North India,' *East and West* 23.3–4 (1973): 347. The author looks at northern Indian images of the Jain saint. Lord Bahubali is also known as Gommatesvara in the south at such places as Shravana Belgola.

[2] George Michell, *In The Image of Man* (London: Weidenfeld and Nicolson, 1982) 13–14. Buddhism and Jainism both came about in the 6th century. These two spiritual traditions offered ethical philosophies that could be applied to living rather than offering deities to be worshipped.

[3] N. Sastri, *Sravanabelgola*, Mysore, 1981, 10–15. According to the Department of Archaeology of the government of Karnataka, the Bahubali at Sravanabelgola is considered to be the largest monolithic statue in the world. The statue is 58 feet in height and carved out of grey granite. It is sculpted in the round, unlike the Buddhas of Bamiyan or Ramses II in Egypt which are carved in high relief.

[4] Saryu Doshi, *Homage to Shravana Belgola* (Bombay: Marg Publications, 1981) 78–79.

[5] Doshi 70.

[6] Doshi 37. According to Doshi, to the Jains Gommateshwara represents the first *moksha-gami* soul of this cosmic cycle.

[7] Phyllis Granoff, *The Clever Adulteress and Other Stories, A Treasury of Jain Literature* (Delhi: Motilal Banarsidass Publishers, 1990). This book offers English translations of certain Jain text. The translations are by Ralph Strohl. Tirtamkara is also spelled 'tirthamkara.' Many other spellings have been used for Rasabanatha, including Rishabha in the Doshi book, *Homage to Shravana Belgola*. Doshi mentions that he is also known as Adinatha.

[8] Granoff 214-215. The translation goes on to say that the *siddhis* or *siddhas*, the virtues of spiritual accomplishment from yoga came to rest in them. The allegorical use of 'fire' to refer to their austerity is beautifully put into words in the line, 'for when the body, like a crucible, is heated with asceticism, the soul, like gold, becomes pure.'

[9] Granoff 214-217. The ninety-seven brothers were convinced by their father's discourse and became 'wandering religious mendicants.' They took up with the mistress of asceticism and pursued the mistress of liberation.

[10] Granoff 219-220.

[11] Granoff 214-220. Bharata was in position to inherit the kingdom. He was convinced that the true way to fulfillment was through power. Bahubali was also convinced that his father's way was not the proper way. The two would eventually come to see that Rsabhanatha was right in preaching that the temporal world is not what one should focus on.

[12] This observation concerning the relationship between text and art was made by Dr Lisa Owen of the University of North Texas. She states that the viewer can understand a visual without textual sources. This is especially the case if one is of a community which has a strong oral-tradition concerning their items and works of devotion, such as the Jain community.

[13] Granoff 237. After defeating his brother Bharata, Bahubali decides to take up asceticism. Being one of ninety-nine brothers, Bahubali and Bharata were the only two brothers left that had not retreated to the forest after realising the ephemeral nature of kingdom.

[14] Tiwari, 'Images of Bahubali in Deogarh,' *Jain Journal* 20.2 (1985): 54. The author says, 'The great penance of Bahubali inspired both the Svetambara and the Digambara Jainas to worship him since it is uniquely evocative of the ethos of the continuous self-sacrifice preached by the Jinas.

[15] Tiwari, 'A Note on Some Bahubali Images from North India,' *East andWest* 23.3–4 (1973): 347. The author looks at northern Indian images of the Jain saint. Bahubali is known as Gommatesvara in the south.

[16] Tiwari, 'Images of Bahubali in Deogarh, *Jain Journal* 20.2 (1985): 54. This passage nicely sums up the concept of Bahubali's relationship to time. He has transcended the need to be concerned with time and the need to care for his body. The author used the word 'tapas' for penance.

[17] Doshi, *Homage to Shravana Belgola,* (Bombay, 1981), 38–41. The manuscript image on the left is from the collection of Kusum and Rajeya Swali. The image on the right depicting birds in Bahubali's hair is located at The National Museum, in New Delhi. It is from the manuscript of the Devasano Pado Kalpasutra and the Kalakacharyakatha, dated late fifteenth century. It relates the story in the *Adipurana*.

[18] Mircea Eliade, *The Encyclopedia of Religion* (New York: Simon and Schuster, 1995) 120. Eliade is the editor of this text, however, the section on Buddhism that I took this information from was written by Luis Gomez.

[19] The veneration of the 'begging bowl' is a feature of this Gandharan sculpture that I was told about during a personal conversation with Dr Lisa Owen of the University of North Texas.

[20] Hermann Hesse, *Siddhartha* (New York, 1951) 149–150. Govinda's moment of elucidation is beautifully described by Hesse.

[21] Hesse 151.

[22] This observation was derived from a conversation with Dr Lisa Owen, South Asian Art Specialist, of the Art History Department at the University of North Texas on November

9. Black-and-White or Shades of Grey? Lockwood Kipling's Illustrations of India

Christel R. Devadawson

In the last quarter of the nineteenth century, imperial rule in India faced a curious problem. Little England seemed to have won, and people in the mother country began to find Empire a boring subject. Henry Maine bemoaned the way in which a debate on India, when announced, emptied the House of Commons.

> India is in a sense near to us; all that is superficial and commonplace in it is well known. It has none of the interest of a country barely unveiled to geographers, of the valley of the Oxus, or the basin of Lake Tanganyika. It is mixed up with the ordinary business of life, with the business of government, with debates in Parliament not too well attended, with the Stock Exchange, the cotton market and the annual relief of regiments.[1]

Disenchantment was a threat to Empire. A bored people were unlikely to vote increased funds to govern India, or send out people to govern it. Even if recruits were trained in administration, they were likely to remain incompetent because they were ignorant of the land they governed. When he looked back on this period, Richard Temple, a senior civil servant, spoke of the need for recruits to develop an interest in the peoples of India. He linked good governance to knowledge.

> ...[If] you are to succeed in governing men, knowledge of their languages or of the administration and the law of the country is not quite enough. It is also necessary to know the culture of the people with whom one is dealing... We do wish, firstly, to interest [recruits] in anthropology and secondly, by that means to lead them on to the study of it throughout life, to the benefit of themselves and of those amongst whom they work.[2]

More significantly, during this period, Temple collaborated on a project to popularise Empire among two groups of people who were critical to its success. The first group comprised the existing governing class in India. Temple attempted to interest them in the scholarly activity of collecting folktales of anthropological value. The second group comprised young English people, growing up both in England and India, from whom the future governing class would be recruited. Temple set up the machinery—appendices, catalogues and scholarly apparatus— to make the folktales of value to adult researchers. He co-opted two others to work on the anthology. Flora Annie Steel was responsible for the text. Lockwood Kipling worked on the accompanying line drawings and calligraphic images. He signs as JLK, and I will refer to him in this way.

JLK's illustrations of this 1894 anthology, *Tales of the Punjab* suggest what he derived from his predecessors and what he brought to book-illustration. Most obviously, he comes across as one who applies Ruskin's lessons on artistic composition to the task of illustrating Empire.[3] For example, JLK creates Ruskinesque borders to accompany the incremental folktales. This is a careful choice in terms of form and content. Formally, these borders are a direct application of Ruskin's rules of colour and composition. The components of each composition are held in careful harmony, with regard to their graded significance to the central narrative and their incidental importance to each other. Each component is given breathing space to develop a story of its own, if necessary, away from the central narrative. Ruskin's magisterial laws on colour and composition use the example of great trees to set out the principles of artistic authority. He summarises them in this way.

1. Support from one living root.
2. Radiation, or tendency of force from some one given point, either in the root or in some stated connection with it.
3. Liberty of each bough to seek its own livelihood and happiness according to its needs, by irregularities of action both in its play and its work...
4. Imperative requirement of each bough to stop within certain limits, expressive of its kindly fellowship and fraternity with the boughs in its neighbourhood; and to work with them... to bring out the general perfectness of the great curve ...

As regards content, these folktales are classified as incremental narratives in which each item of the story is repeated with a single addition of a fresh item at a time. Such folktales work along the lines of the nursery rhyme, 'The House that Jack Built'. A character gives rise to a (usually) comic situation. This is repeated to introduce another character in a sequence that seems inevitable and interminable. The principle on which such a Ruskinesque border works may be seen in the illustration to 'The Sparrow and the Crow,' which will have to be summarised before JLK's work can be explained.[4] In terms of folktale classification, the story is a variant on the paradigm of the Impossible Quest. A sparrow cooks *khichrî* (an appetising dish of rice boiled with lentils) that a crow wishes to share. To put off the crow, the sparrow asks it to have a bath before it eats. This proves a luckless quest. The crow asks the pond to oblige, but the pond says it cannot help unless a deer digs a watercourse with its antlers. The deer insists that the crow arrange for milk from a cow to reduce the hardship of giving up its antlers. The cow demands grass, and the grass demands that it be mown with a sickle. The sickle has to be fashioned by a blacksmith, who requires a fire to smelt the iron. As the crow begins to blow the bellows for the blacksmith's fire, it falls into the flames. The sparrow is thus the only victorious partaker of the meal (see Figure 14).

JLK's illustration captures the hierarchy and significance of the narrative. Each entity is placed in terms of its importance in this tale of the quest that is impossible to fulfil. Simultaneously, however, each has an appointed place of its own, so that there is no overlap or blurring. Each entity is thus represented in the fullness of its own imaginative life. At the head is the sparrow, seated jubilantly atop the sealed cooking-pot, to which it is the sole claimant. The deer is not the stylised red deer familiar to European readers but the larger *barasingh*, native to the Himalayan foothills. The cow is not the Milking Shorthorn breed that is common in Europe but the emaciated breed of the Gangetic plain (its ribs can be counted) to whose defence JLK had risen in his 1891 study, *Beast and Man in India.* The blacksmith is dressed as a poverty-stricken Hindu artisan. A favourite compositional detail of Ruskin, a trellis of tendrils, or 'dependent climbers', is used as background. Throughout however, the characters of the folktale, animal and human, are intended to conjure up North India specifically. Thus the illustration reminds the readers—as the central text of the folktale does not—of its location in India. It is not entirely free of exoticism. The frame is clichéd in its evocation of a synthetic Saracenic enclosure that is completely at odds with the content. Nonetheless there is an essential realism and specificity to JLK's work here.

A more complicated involvement with India may be seen in JLK's many illustrations of village life. A recurrent theme in British representations of India in the nineteenth century is the insistence that 'the real India' lives in the villages, wishes to be governed by Britain, and does not wish for political engagement as educated townsfolk do. It is an idea that has been expressed in an earlier text. 'The average Oriental cannot be brought to look beyond his clan. His life, too, is more complete and self-sufficing, and less sordid and low-thoughted than you might imagine. It is bovine and slow in some respects, but it is never empty.'[5] In his illustration to 'Little Anklebone,' a melancholy story of an orphan who dies at the behest of a cruel aunt, JLK constructs a rural setting that is idyllic to the point of being millennial. It is a direct translation of Isaiah's prophecy into what he considers Indian terms (see Figure 15).

> The wolf also shall dwell with the lamb, and the leopard shall lie down with the kid; and the calf and the young lion and the fatling together; and a little child shall lead them. And the cow and the bear shall feed; their young ones shall lie down together… and the sucking child shall play on the hole of the asp, and the weaned child shall put his hand on the cockatrice' den. (Isiah:11:6.6-8)

The folktale is about a youngster who is eaten by a wolf so that his aunt's flock may be spared. He asks only that his anklebone be hung on a tree. As a spirit, he pipes magical tunes and conjures up a world of enchantment and tranquillity. This world is the subject of JLK's illustration (see Figure 15). It is clearly a dream world, neatly divided down the centre between the sun (given the face of the Hindu sun-god Surya, complete with regal moustaches) and the moon (represented as the Islamic crescent). Above the banyan-like tree that dominates the picture is a star rather like that set atop a Christmas tree. The piper is not the clichéd figure of Blake's frontispiece for 'Songs of Innocence' (common in illustrations for children) but a little boy wearing the turban and playing the *been*, or pipe of an Indian snake charmer. A tiger and a wolf flank the tree, with an apparently mild cobra between them. Uncharacteristically brave rabbits crouch in the foreground. The scene is presented from the point of view of a village-woman, who is a part of the illustration, not the folktale. She backs the viewer, but faces the scene, so that we see from her position, even though we do not see her face. It is clearly a stylised scene, based on wished-for illusion, and not reality. Despite the realistic human characters though, the idyll is annoying. The tranquil Indian village may seem tempting, but the contrary forces in the picture do not go away. Religious symbols, as the story about Pagett, M. P., suggests, divide rather than unite, and make nonsense—according to the governing class—of India's nationalist aspirations. Regional and communal hatreds rule out any kind of tranquillity except under British rule. The speaker here seems to be very far from the millennial and apolitical Indian village.

> There's the Afghan, and, as a highlander, he despises all the dwellers in Hindustan—with the exception of the Sikh, whom he hates as cordially as the Sikh hates him. The Hindu loathes Sikh and Afghan, and the Rajput—that's a little lower down across this yellow blot of desert—has a strong objection, to put it mildly, to the Maratha who, by the way, poisonously hates the Afghan. Let's go North a minute. The Sindhi hates everybody I've mentioned. Very good, we'll take less warlike races. The cultivator of Northern India domineers over the man in the next province, and the Bihari of the Northwest ridicules the Bengali. They are all at one on that point. [6]

Only when we look at representations of apolitical and millennial rural India, such as JLK's work here, do we realise that these are apologias for imperial rule. Rural debt, famine and fragmented land-holdings, as much a part of village life, do not usually figure.

A noticeable quirk in JLK's work is his use of a clichéd Persianised idiom for the representation of high life in folktale. Frame, costume and indoor setting collaborate in this equation. In distinct contrast, the same three markers are used with a wealth of realistic detail to suggest—as has just been shown—village life as specifically Hindu. An entertaining example of his representation of high life (not reproduced here) may be seen in his work on the folktale 'Sir Buzz'.[7] The story is a variant on the Puss-in-Boots theme in which a shrewd servant helps the younger son to love and fortune. The frame is of an onion-like bulbous shape, traditionally associated with Saracenic architecture. The setting is that of the boudoir of Princess Blossom, with whom the soldier's son anxiously pleads his case. A *jali* or fretted screen dominates this— the top left—of the illustration. In the lower right, the midget-like genie gloats over his cleverness. The way in which JLK revels in detail is contagious. The genie's costume, for instance, is that of the hero in miniature. A stray comic aside places him in a pair of fiercely upturned *mojaris* (embroidered shoes), next to which are placed the (comparatively) gigantic *mojaris* of the soldier. Yet the genie preens himself on his cleverness, which lets him stand tall in his estimate of himself. The soldier's tunic, the toe-curling footwear of both prince and genie and the drapes of the princess, suggest a setting that could have come from *The Thousand and One Nights*. The cluster of illustrations to which Richard Burton's text gave rise in the late nineteenth-century has clearly influenced JLK's work. This influence is costly. It teeters on the edge of cliché. Yet it is noteworthy that when JLK has to describe an exotic never-never-land and its people, he should choose a Middle Eastern setting, but when he has to describe Indian reality, he sketches real North Indian villagers, even if he mutes the landscape beyond credibility or endurance. JLK never loses sight of the fact that he has to develop and sustain an interest in the Indian empire for two sets of readers: administrators who might grow into folklorists, and children who might grow into administrators.

Sometimes, as with *The Arabian Nights* mentioned above, the influence of other traditions of book-illustration enters JLK's work. A striking example of this is his depiction of a conversation between a farmer and a bear. The story, 'The Bear's Bad Bargain,' is a variant of the paradigm in folklore called 'The Biter Bit', that deals with the outsmarting of a trickster. In the accompanying illustration (not reproduced here) a Himalayan black bear is standing on his hind legs in apparent conversation with the farmer.[8] Two points may be noticed. The first is that the bear's muzzle is remarkably like that of Reynard the Fox. Reynard, from the days of mediaeval *fabliaux*, is represented as a trickster who can be outmanoeuvred. It is as if JLK is playing for the reader's recognition—not of a particular animal—but of a particular trait. Again therefore, his love of detail is important, this time as a clue not to political but to literary traditions of representation. Moreover, the illustration anticipates what have since become two important principles of comic-book illustration. If conversation is to be depicted, it has to move from left to right. Therefore, the farmer plays the trick, and the bear is cheated. Further, if an animal is shown to speak, it has to be depicted as standing on its hind legs, and not, as a rule, on all fours. In such an illustration, JLK anticipates the comedy and the conversation of later graphic art.

Perhaps the most long-lived—and the most disturbing—image created by JLK is the figure of Mowgli. Mowgli enters in Rudyard Kipling's short story, 'In the Rukh,' from the 1893 anthology, *Many Inventions*.[9]

The calligraphic alphabet 'Y' which begins the tale is a remarkable choice. JLK uses the Roman letterform to considerable effect. Mowgli is presented as a longhaired adolescent slumbering in the nude, a fact that is half-concealed and half-revealed by the two upper serifs. He is positioned in the fork of the letter. At its base are two wolves, Mowgli's fellows from the Pack that has reared him from his infancy. The birds he feeds, and the wealth of convoluted tendrils in the background, indicates jungle life. The sexual challenge in this figure is something that does not reappear in the illustrations for Rudyard Kipling's *Jungle Books* that are published in 1894 and 1895. The later Mowgli is very much more like the early Kim, a cross between an imp and a waif, charming but not sexually awakened. It is as if Empire can handle the challenges of jungle life more than it can those of human life. Growing up is a reality that is better evaded. At any rate, it is a risk JLK does not care to run again.

Unsurprisingly then, JLK's Mowgli does not have a long life. When Mowgli is next represented, long after *The Jungle Books*, it is by Walt Disney's sketch of a lovable little urchin, carefully dressed in a brightly coloured loincloth.[10]

The Disney Mowgli is instantly recognisable. He is street-smart, but not in the least likely to transgress any codes of representation. He is independent of text, in a way JLK's Mowgli cannot be. For the Disney Mowgli is available across the world in comic books and animated cartoon serials dubbed in a wide range of languages. In a sense, the Disney Mowgli is available even to the pre-literate, who hear and watch him without having to read accompanying printed text. Literally and metaphorically, JLK's Mowgli lives within the saving serifs of a letterform. JLK's achievement thus has to be considered within the constraints of a language, a printed text and indeed an alphabet. As a cardinal saying of calligraphy goes, 'The greatest thing in the world is the alphabet, as all wisdom is contained therein—except the understanding of putting it together.'[11] There is a limit to how unfettered an image JLK can construct. As illustrator he responds to the text: he is not its first creator.

One illustrator who uses the idea of a virile young wolf-man and experiments further with it is Stan Vinson.[12] Vinson paints the oil on canvas 'Tarzan and Jane' (*c.* 1940) in response to the Edgar Rice Burroughs creation of a man reared from his infancy by wolves, and kept deliberately in ignorance of his birthright as a belted Earl. Burroughs retains the idea of the Mowgli-figure, a human being brought up as a wolf in a jungle. He changes the ethnic origin, however, of his character. Mowgli is an Indian, discovered by an Englishman in the forests of Central India. Tarzan is an Englishman, who grudgingly shares jungle-space with African tribes, when he meets a shipwrecked American girl. Jane, the Baltimore Belle of Burroughs' text, is drawn immediately to Tarzan, as he is to her. The painting is the best-known romanticised representation of Tarzan swinging through the trees with Jane. The attraction of Frazetta's oil owes much to Johnny Weismuller's depiction of Tarzan on film. As a former Olympic swimmer, Weismuller's Tarzan was a screen icon, and Frazetta captures this glamour. Again however, glamour comes at a price. Ethnic complexity and the challenge of adolescence are absent in this representation.

Such examples as Disney's Mowgli and Frazetta's Tarzan have travelled more widely than JLK's work. In the world of popular culture they have attracted phenomenal audiences and investment. In contrast, JLK's efforts to sustain England's interest in Empire seem politically incorrect today and limited in terms of ambition and achievement even for their time. Nonetheless, he brings to illustration the ability to conjure up a world even while it is fading, and breathe life into it all over again. Colour wipes out such an option. Only a world of black and white can evoke a response in shades of grey.

Notes

1 Henry Maine, *The Effects of Observation of India on Modern European Thought*, London, 1875, 10.

2 Richard Temple, 'The Value of a Training in Anthropology for the Administrator,' *Man*, 14 (1914): 34–6, in Talal Asad, (ed.), *Anthropology and the Colonial Encounter*, (London: Ithaca P), 1973, 139.

3 JLK's admiration of Ruskin's aesthetic is recalled by Rudyard Kipling throughout his autobiography *Something of Myself*, and specifically in 'Slaves of the Lamp', *Cosmopolis,* April 1897, later collected in *Stalky and Co., (*London: Macmillan, 1899), where a bright schoolboy is shown as enjoying *Fors Clavigera* despite his form-master's derision.

4 John Ruskin, 'The Elements of Drawing: Letter III, Of Colour and Composition,' (1871-87) collected with *The Crown of Wild Olive*, (Boston: Colonial P, n.d.), 379.

5 Flora Annie Steel, 'The Sparrow and the Crow," *Tales of the Punjab*, (illustrated by John Lockwood Kipling) (London and New York: Macmillan, 1894) 3 Apr. 2007 http://digital.library.upenn.edu/women/steel/punjab/punjab-11.html. For similar borders, see JLK's illustrations to 'The Death and Burial of poor Hen Sparrow,' and 'The Grain of Corn'.

6 'The Enlightenment of Pagett, M.P.,' *The Contemporary Review* 58 (September 1890), 333-55, 340, is more like a pamphlet against the Indian National Congress (founded in 1885) than like a short story. It was entered under the name of Rudyard Kipling in the above journal because it was originally published as the last story in the latter's 1888 collection, *Under the Deodars*. Scholars working on Kipling manuscripts have always attributed it to JLK. Rudyard Kipling did not republish it in his lifetime and allowed it to go out of print. It has been re-included in the Project Gutenberg text of *Under the Deodars* as Rudyard Kipling's work as the project has used the first edition of the text. However, I stay with the standard attribution of this piece to JLK.

[7] 'Sir Buzz,' Flora Annie Steel, *Tales of the Punjab*, (illustrated by John Lockwood Kipling) (London and New York: Macmillan, 1894). 3 Apr. 2007 http://digital.library.upenn.edu/women/steel/punjab/punjab//html. For a similar point, see JLK's illustration to 'The Close Alliance: A Tale of WDC,' where, when a poor woman dresses up as a man and rides a horse to terrify a tiger, she is given the accoutrements of a 'Persianised' Prince.

[8] Steel, *Tales of the Punjab*.

[9] 3 Apr. 2007. http://en.wikipedia.org/wiki/Mowgli

[10] From an old German bookplate, calligraphy by Raymond F DaBoll, *Speedball Textbook for Pen and Brush Lettering*, (1960) 20th (edn.) (Philadelphia: Hunt Manufacturing Co.), 36.

[11] www.World of Animation.com

[12] http://www.erblist.com/erbmania/bobz/bobzartcom.html

10. Captive and/or Captivating Bodies: The Collapse of the Aesthetic and the Political in the *People of India*

Sonali Pattnaik

Of Noor Khan, whose photograph has the caption 'Mussulman, Thug, Sangor', we are told the following: 'This man is a prisoner for life and approver in the jail at Jubbulpoor. [...] His confessions record five cases of thuggee, in which twenty-one persons were strangled...He was apprehended and tried in 1835, and has been in confinement since then. His age, if he is still living, may be about seventy-eight.' The biological age of Noor Khan seems of little significance now that the dangerous bandit has been apprehended and can pose no threat to the lives and property of the imperial government. It is also peripheral for one other reason and that is his encapsulation within the pages of this volume and the frame of the photograph for an eternity. His captivity is doubly enforced as he is simultaneously produced as subject of colonial law and object of aesthetic pleasure. Perhaps the photograph performs a function that is auxiliary to penal power here, reduplicating, through the visual, the signs of capture and confinement that the linguistic signs perform. In any case, the visual is meant to be supplementary to the writing, there to stand not for itself but to exemplify, substantiate and testify to the truth of the linguistic signs. This excerpt belongs to the encyclopedic eight-volume collection of photographs titled *People of India*, 'a series of photographic illustrations with descriptive letterpress of the races and tribes of Hindustan' edited by John William Kaye and J. Forbes Watson (1868–75), the text that this essay will be primarily interesting in analysing.[1] The task of this paper will be to throw light on this odd function that the 'image' has been accorded by the ethnographers and editors of this pivotal text to ask after twin issues; the function of photography in the latter half of the nineteenth century within colonial governance, and the relationship of this newly acquired status of objectivity by photography to the construction of the human body. The latter question, that of the camera's peculiar production of corporeality, I wish to argue, is critical to unravelling the subtle operation of power and administration in the new colonial state. My argument will be incomplete however, and will therefore return to the business of art time and again, as it is this altered aspect of art no more just for art's sake but at the service of the state that appears as the site of emergence for the hundreds of disparate images that are placed together under no single rubric or system except that they all re-present the 'people of India'.

The story of the collection's emergence is crucial in my analysis of the role of visual signs in the punitive disciplining and governance of natives in the aftermath of the 1857 sepoy mutiny and its place within modern governmentality as envisioned by one of the leading theorists of the liberal State, Jeremy Bentham.[2] The initial request for the volume came from Lord and Lady Canning to 'carry home with them at the end of their sojourn in India, a collection...of photographic illustrations which might recall to their memory the peculiarities of Indian life.' The Cannings shared a fascination for photography reflected in their patronage to the Bengal and Madras Photographic Societies during their stay in India. The project, although born from such aesthetic interest, soon assumed larger proportions spurred, as confessed in the preface, by the 'convulsion' of 1857 that swerved the focus of the volume from innocuous dappling in aesthetics to stringent governmental pragmatics. The dichotomy between art and governmentality is sustained not just by the editors of the volume but subsequent post-colonial analysis of photography, such as in Christopher Pinney's *Camera Indica*,[3] a brilliant exposition of the function of colonial photography.* The paper will attempt a complication of this binary to exhibit the collapse of aesthetics into governmentality as not only an instance of Orientalist constructions of other but a problem of the place of art in modern society, tracing out a politics of resistance born out of the contradictions that emerge from this alliance. The preface merits quotation at length as it presents the business of governmentality disguised as disinterested art, but indicates a *new* ardour in art that lends itself to greater political significance. The interest created in Europe by the development of photography, it states, 'communicated itself to India and originated the desire to turn it to account in the illustration of the topography, architecture and ethnology of that country' but rapidly transformed into an interest of another kind after the event of the 1857 sepoy mutiny.

---

* Pinney's argument that the object and subjects of the colonies were turned into art objects by a colonial idelogy that worked towards producing the Orient as exotic, different and other systematically in order to rule it better takes for granted that all colonial art must be viewed within the framework of the colonial split. While this Saidian position is crucial it does not address the question of what is it in the nature of the photographic medium that makes this transition by art from the realm of pure pleasure to that of governmentality possible and what are the moments that are unsustainble by this split which, I wish to argue, is due to the ability of art to elide institutionalism.

> The great convulsion of 1857–58 while it necessarily retarded for a time all scientific and artistic operations, imparted a *new* interest to the country which had been the scene of, and to the people who had been the actors in these *remarkable events*. When, therefore, the pacification of India had been accomplished, the officers of the Indian Services... encouraged and patronised by the Governor General, went forth, and traversed the land in search of *interesting subjects*. In this way the design soon exceeded the dimensions of a mere private collection... [my italics]

The dimensions now set are those of identifying the so-called 'actors' in the event of rebellion, which is portrayed as some sort of tableau whose disguised actors are of interest to an amused colonial audience who must now go with their disguised weapons to 'shoot' down these interesting but errant players. The camera would provide a horrified British with the means to guise its fears and hatred under the drama of interested art and enslave them without resorting to barbaric bloodshed. The purely ethnographic tendencies of photography are erased so that a new script of political exigency can be inscribed onto the photographic medium and ultimately onto the bodies of colonial subjects based on an axis of fidelity. As has been demonstrated by post-colonial critics such as Bernard Cohn and Edward Said, one of the immediate changes in the British attitude after the mutiny was of ruling the Orient through violently producing the Orient as a familiar other.[4] The project of historiography and artistic representation was hereafter predicated on the same rapacious desire to rule but by recording, detailing and familiarising the foreign and effacing that which could not be rendered familiar under the garb of objective knowledge. Within this scheme of re-casting the Orient by enslaving all that was unfamiliar and fierce, the masterful eye of the camera was deployed to replace the naked eye of the ethnographer. The representation of reality that the camera offered appeared to be free from individual intervention which endowed it with an unassailable authority. It produced an environment that did not carry the traces of the artist herself thus satisfying the criteria of what Pierre Bourdieu has called 'complete art'.[5]

This of course is the dilemma of photography as both Bordieu and Walter Benjamin have identified.[6] By negating the presence of the artist's toil it lost, ironically, its artistic value producing through extensive technological involvement, in the words of Benjamin, an 'equipment-free reality'. The camera gained aesthetic value in this traditional sense by the social function it fulfilled. In the colonies this function was immense as it silenced the complaints of ethnographers about the difficulty in mapping Indians. The visual, Christopher Pinney has argued was privileged as a guarantor of accuracy over the written which was seen as allegorical and unreliable in the representation of the by now well-established unpredictable and duplicitous Oriental, and the camera provided, this (falsely) objective vision. The bias of the coloniser over the visual against the verbal explains Kaye's (who was working in the Secret and Political department of Bengal when he decided to intervene in the project) remark that 'to represent India by mere word painting is an almost impossible task' (Pinney 18).[7] Ironically all of the photographs in his volume are not only framed by the blank whiteness of the pages (appearing as signifier of their objective truth) but by words that seek to order the visual imagination of the viewer according to a pre-determined narrative betraying the anxiety over the free play of signs that makes up visual language more than the verbal. I shall analyse five photographs to argue that far from telling an objective truth about the identity of the subject, the photographs are able to produce an identity of the colonised as colonial subject by locating them within the verbal framework that orients the viewer's reading of the visual image.

The first is a photograph of Duleep Singh who, we are told, is a 'landholder of Allyghur', where the family has been located for five to six hundred years. Further, that they are cultivators with settled habits, subsisting on the produce of their lands. Since this is part of the third volume, a pattern in these narratives has emerged and the first few lines are indicative of this. The fact that Duleep Singh is not a nomad but rather someone who has a long ancestral history signals a purity of lineage and a right to property. It also allows him a history, which many of the nomadic tribes described and photographed are denied. The opposition between those who are 'settled' and those who are roaming is only one of the many binaries (such as a real and pretender, true hindoo/muslim as opposed to a convert, etc.) that denote the value of an individual in the text. Duleep Singh, turns from individual to type in the space of two lines. Their religion is hindoo, we are told, 'Soorujbunsi, or children of the Solar race, and are perhaps haughtiest and most exclusive of all the great Rajpoot families which derive their existence from original Aryan stock.' Racial purity of the Aryans operates as the index of their superior status just as the lack of mixed breeding within the race signifies high moral character. Phyletic structures are evoked less for tracing out the origins of races through the quagmire of miscegenation as in early ethnography and more for the purpose of constructing a social hierarchy that would be fully cognisable to an administration inclined towards subjugation through productive power. Sexuality is given increased significance in order to cast the existing indigenous hierarchies of castes and tribes according to a Victorian self-image. That the Rajpoots are suspicious of mixture of races and guard their exclusivity through invigilating marriage alliances and through the practice of female infanticide is a marker, according to the ethnographers, of their social superiority. 'In contracting marriages, the pedigrees on both sides are investigated with curious interest; nor is the slightest family taint, wittingly passed over. The extreme exclusiveness and sensitiveness of the Chohan Rajpoots'... in this matter... 'led, previous to the British rule, to the practice of female infanticide.' The clinical and apologetic tone with which this is described is a consequence of the epistemological slippage such an identity structure of self-sameness engenders: while circumscribing female sexuality confirms a Victorian image of the patriarchal household; infanticide must be othered and produced as object of reform for a colonial image. The image of Duleep Singh must testify to this duality, produced as civil and yet in need of civilising.

As Foucault has argued in the first volume of the *History of Sexuality*, contrary to the misplaced belief that Victorianism shrouded an otherwise sexually loquacious Europe, the emergence of the discourses of psychoanalysis and medical science proliferated talk about sex, seeking to discover and codify it according to a heteronormative ideology.[8]

Eugenics and Darwinian theories of race also sought to place the onus of civilisation on sex. Leela Gandhi has demonstrated in her book *Affective Communities*, the links that emerged between heterosexuality and civilisational success. Darwin's *Descent of Man*, she argues, shifted the onus of civilisation from nature to culture, placing it, literally, in the lap of women. Civilisational success lay not in the survival of the fittest but in sexual difference, sexual selection and the faculty of reproduction.[9] The sexual other was represented as the civilisational other, savage, immature and incapable of contributing to socio-cultural progress. In this context, the Hindu's pride in caste results in aggressive heterosexuality which is contrasted with the sexual profligacy and abandon of the aborigines or shudras whose lack of strict sexual conduct is read as analogous to their lack of aesthetic appeal or use-value. The photograph of Duleep Singh must be seen through this lens, against the way in which those of lower castes are constructed. The materiality of the Rajpoot body is produced by a visual and verbal discourse of colonial ideology that sought to enforce the body as natural cause of disobedience while producing it as effect of a coercive discourse of sexuality and progress. The caption reads 'the respectable individual represented in the photograph wears no arms, and appears, according to his vocation, in an ordinary dress of quilted silk or chintz…yet it is impossible to mistake the resolute expression of the countenance.' Mark that costumes which are being read as signs of difference betray the sytematisation and this contradiction is casually dismissed by a reassertion of the natural body. In the absence of the rambling verbal caption, Duleep Singh may not have appeared naturally aggressive, loyal and monogamous. Although not so evident in these volumes, the link between physical characteristics and social superiority that are being established here will become a necessary feature of colonial rule. The next photograph is of a mussullman which makes the identity politics at work rather evident. 'Shair Ali Syud is a Mohomedan of the Syud sect, or descendants of the Prophet, and of the Soonnee belief…His features are peculiarly Mahomedan, of the Central Asian type; and while they vouch for the purity of his descent, exemplify, in a strong manner, the obstinacy, sensuality, ignorance, and bigotry of his class. It is hardly possible, perhaps, to conceive features more essentially repulsive.'[10]

The connection drawn between Shair Ali's features, unfamiliar to the British viewer, and the immorality that he is accused of appears arbitrary, to say the least. And yet, it is significant that social hierarchy and loyalty be naturalised and the body be produced according to institutional demands. While the photograph shows an individual, the verbal narrative coerces the viewer into reading the visual as testimony of the verbal, as a symptom of the degeneracy of an entire group of individuals, muslims. The body, it seems, renders visible the hidden features of Mohomeddan treacherousness. It is called forth to bear witness for the crimes of the soul, its materiality acting as the blueprint of its interiority. The use of photography for forensic evidence and its adoption along with dactylography by the whole of Bengal Police in 1891 as a means of preventing crime makes apparent the potential for accuracy in representation that it was believed to possess. It is not descent or sexual practice that makes Shair Ali's body 'repulsive' but a resistance to co-option into a productive workforce within the colonial administration. For following the statement on lack of corporeal beauty is the following; 'On the classes to which Shair Ali belongs, time and change, with all the adjuncts of modern civilisation, make little progress. Such as his ancestors were, he is, and desires his descendants to be, rigid Mohomeddans, religious after their fashion, but attempting no change, and tolerating none.' Another Muslim, Izzat Ali Khan is similarly described which is conclusive in his case, of the fact that 'their fidelity as a class is very questionable, and their sympathies are more perhaps with the ancient powers...' The interesting point about this photograph is that the individual looks rather similar to the Hindu individual, Duleep Singh and there is little in the facial features, the costume, or the posture in which the two are sitting, to suggest innate difference.* This is when discourse confronts its own limits, an instance of the body being produced in excess of the discursive idealisation that hegemonic power deploys to denounce the working of that very power structure.

The images I have studied appear within oval shaped frames, placed within blank pages covered with a page of tissue, the kind of design that would become popular in depicting family photographs both in the metropole and the colonies rather than in the police department of the colonial government. Interestingly enough, read against the caption they suggest objectification of another kind: images of people with 'peculiarities', captured not for purposes of identification but as objects to be exhibited in homes—fascinating and exotic. Time does not permit me to examine the politics involved in an aesthetics of exoticism and whether, as I suspect, this indicates a desire for accepting difference rather than subsuming it under an ontological split but I do wish to indicate that the frames, the surrounding blankness and the postures of individuals are markers that place the images in a moment of historical transition where the moment of recognising and being fascinated with difference gives over to regimenting and coercive ordering of such differences. That the photographs document this shift is significant as art does not here simply mimic historical reality but rather evinces the ruptures in perception that such a historical event engenders.

The question of loyalty is gauged by the use-value of individual bodies. To return to the earlier discussion of the convergence of a Darwinian narrative of sexual selection with heteronormative productivity, what we find mediating between aesthetics and loyalty is a politics of utility. Sexual reproduction is valuable not only because it vindicates the significance of heterosexual alliances but because it is productive and thus contributes to social progress. Whether sexual or otherwise, labour which leads to production defines the body as relevant or irrelevant to society and so the homosexual is outside the field of progress as they lack productivity, while women's social function is reduced to their

* I am indebted to a colleauge for pointing the similarity between the two individuals to me after watching the slides of the photographs I presented with this paper at the seminar. Similarly, I am thankful to the keen observation by Prof S. Chakraborti that while the caption beneath the image of Shair Ali Syud reads 'Shia Mussulman', the description refers to him as belonging to the 'Soonee' sect. Such a gross error may be explained by the overwhelming desire among the editors to make the photographs adhere to an easy categorisation of the muslim as 'other'.

reproductive faculty. While at the heart of the binary opposition between civilised and savage lay the principal of heteronormativity, I am arguing that another grid that the discursive production of bodies is interlocked with is the discourse of utility.

Many individuals are photographed with their traditional tools of trade and most are described in terms of their existing social functions and the potential force of their bodies that may be utilised. So, while the Tharoos of Rohilcund are nomadic and do not possess 'sufficient intelligence' they are 'most useful from their capacity…of not only living but thriving in the most malarious situations', the Nagas despite being a 'marauding tribe' have great martial skills and the Gurungs, although civilised because of their 'freedom from the shackles of caste, unadulterated military habits' show 'perfect subjectibility to discipline'. Of Sookha Kunjar who has several wives and lives on petty thievery the writers maintain that they will 'remain as they are: thieves dacoits…What are railways and telegraphs and education to him? Sookha Kunjar (a lower caste Hindu) isn't photographed with any tools and with very little clothes on his body creating an immediate opposition with the extensive descriptions of costume engaged with in most other cases. The discourse which renders him useless/abject seems to find itself in the gaze of the camera as the individual seems to have internalised that denigrating categorisation of him.

Foucault reminds us in *Discipline and Punish* that power relations have a hold over the body; 'it is largely as a force of production that the body is invested with relations of power and domination; but, on the other hand, its constitution as labour power is possible only if it is caught up in a system of subjection…the body becomes a useful force only if it is both a productive body and a subjected body' (Foucault 26).[11] Visuality had an important place in modern mechanisms of power and was what informed the principle of Bentham's contribution to the modern state, the Panopticon. Behind the construction of this mechanism of ideal governance of prisoners lay the principal of optimisation of resources, both human and non-human which would reform illegal individuals into productive citizens. Panopticism rendered governance unverifiable and pervasive, controlling individuals by subjecting them to its gaze perpetually, collapsing the distance between individual and authority. The well-governed individual was a productive and self-vigilant individual who could contribute to the state's progress. Panopticism would re-order constructions of time, space and corporeality to shift focus from an evolution in terms of genesis to an evolution in terms of progress. The text being discussed, I submit, is in principle an exercise in panopticism; a new mechanism of subjection which grants the overseer power over the seen, by remaining visible yet unverifiable. Moreover, as a work of art, it brings into play an aesthetic of the body that finds its justification in an adaptive labour force, the body's materiality is produced upon an axis of utility and adaptability to the forces of change.

The cameraman, according to Benjamin, is like a surgeon who 'greatly diminishes the distance between himself and the patient by penetrating into the patient's body, and increases it but little by the caution with which his hand moves among the organs' (Benjamin 29).[12] An erasure of shared ground between the subject of the photograph and the cameraman renders the latter invisible in the operation. The decay of aura is the result of a desire for bringing things humanly and spatially closer which the camera fulfils. This is simultaneously accompanied by a loss of the uniqueness of the object as it gives itself over to infinite reproduction. The body which is rendered familiar through the lessening of distance between viewer and subject is also simultaneously alienated from its audience and alienation may operate as a value in the face of an aesthetics that is predicated upon reception rather than the spiritual connection of artist with her work.

The human body becomes differently organised as art moves from auratic stasis to infinite reproducibility, losing its objective truth to appear as an effect of the performative politics of visual practice. The alienation of the body, born from the new social function of art, which although political, de-naturalises, robs the body of its auratic presence but in the process upsets the aesthetics of labour that has produced it as naturally relevant or irrelevant. I shall end with the image ofWazeerun who's countenance carries an expression of penetrating defiance which is at odds with the generalising description (or lack there of) of courtesans provided, as one instance of the body alienated from its narrative captivity which seeks to portray it as naturally vile. It is not incidental that Wazeerun's profession which cannot be acknowledged as labour and yet remains crucial for the survival of the British administration up until latter half of the nineteenth century leads to the slippage between verbal and visual narrative forcing the ethnographers to produce her through exclusion. Their profession is unspeakable and the courtesans, we are told, 'debar description'. Perhaps the anxiety of the ethnographers holds the clue: art could operate, in the age of mechanical reproduction, as anti-colonial thought, if the images were to be read against their socio-political function, produced through and against these objectifying frames. As an individual commanding a certain acceptance from the viewer, Wazeerun's expression is a reminder of the disappearing aura in the exhibitionist quality of photography. The object of art can no longer be read as only that for the politics of imperialism wills that separation of art from its political context. However, the expression on her face, is also a reminder of a resignification operating in the visual signs that produces the image in excess of its political function and carrying the possibility of resisting the colonial framing of her body.

Notes

1 *The people of India: A Series of Photographic Illustrations with Descriptive Letterpress of the Races and Tribes of Hindustan Originally prepared under the authority of the Government of India and Reproduced by order of the Secretary of State for India in Council* eds. Watson J. Forbes and John William Kaye. 1868–1875. Delhi: B.R Publishing Corporation 1987. Plates 137, 138, 139, 146, 165. The original collection of 8 volumes of photographs is to be found in the India Museum, London.

2 L. J. Hume, *Bentham and Bureaucracy* London: Cambridge UP, 1981

3 Christopher Pinney, *Camera Indica: The Social Life of Indian Photographs* Chicago: Chicago UP, 1997

4 Edward W. Said, *Orientalism: Western Conceptions of the Orient* New Delhi: Penguin Books India, 2001.

– Bernard S Cohn, *Colonialism and Its Forms of Knowledge: The British in India* Princeton University Press, 1996

5 Pierre Bourdieu, *Photography: A Middle-brow Art* Trans. Shaun Whiteside. Stanford, California: Stanford UP, 1990.

6 Benjamin, Walter 'The Work of Art in the Age of Mechanical Reproduction'. *Media and Cultural Studies* Ed. Meenakshi Gigi Durham and Douglas M. Kellner MA, USA: Blackwell, 2006 (revised)

7 Christopher Pinney

8 Michel Foucault, *Discipline and Punish: The Birth of the Prison* New York: Vintage 1995. (second edition)

9 Leela Gandhi, *Affective Communities: Anticolonial Thought and the Politics of Friendship* Delhi: Permanent Black, 2006.

10 *The people of India: A Series of Photographic Illustrations with Descriptive Letterpress of the Races and Tribes of Hindustan Originally prepared under the authority of the Government of India and Reproduced by order of the Secretary of State for India in Council* eds. Watson J. Forbes and John William Kaye. 1868-1875. Delhi: B.R Publishing Corporation 1987. Plates 137, 138, 139, 146, 165. The original collection of 8 volumes of photographs is to be found in the India Museum, London.

11 Michel Foucault

12 Walter Benjamin

11. Of Lines and Letters

Divya Dwivedi

O.V. Vijayan is known in 'North India' largely as a cartoonist, and he is relieved that at least in Kerala he will be remembered as the author of the novel, *The Legends of Khasak*.[1] Although he was never a journalist, he has been a columnist, a temporarily cardholding member of the Communist Party of India (Marxist), and of course, to begin with, a lecturer in English literature.[2] It could be said that he is a man of letters and lines.

The caption of one of his cartoons where a diptych shows some animal-politicians says: "The cartoonist gives up when his subjects turn into cartoons themselves'—ancient saying' (see Figure 16). The satirical significance of this caption is obvious, but not its primitive availability. In that case, cartooning would have been given up long ago, because the cartoon might be said to have broken down as a medium of satire and wisdom, with its very demise offering the sole possible wisdom. Vijayan's cheek is his ability to offer it to us in nothing less than a cartoon—the last cartoon on the end of cartooning. What qualifies, as cartoon according to Vijayan's cartoon is the cartoon that has cartoons as its subject. In saying so Vijayan's cartoon is the primitive cartoon, the pure cartoon, for the cartoon which is its subject is not just within it but is all of itself. I will discuss ahead this primitive quality, which is already not historical.

Vijayan's cartoons come across as primitive drawings, an unrefined and uncontrolled meandering of line, uneven—sometimes lean, sometimes excessive. The archaic diction, deliberate (rather than naturalistic or representative) and metaphysical (especially in his novel *The Saga of Dharmapuri*), of his writings, compares with the primitive lineation, equally deliberate and highly stylised, of his cartoons. Where do we find a measure of style in order to evaluate Vijayan?

I have mentioned drawings on the one hand and novels on the other. The cartoon consists of both lines and letters. It is also historical and topical, the cartoon of the day, a daily editorial commentary. These two elements count the ingredients of cartoon as its object and its medium—the understanding of occurrence and the representation of this. Even if it is argued that this representation is already an understanding of the topical, it retains the task of distinguishing the incident and its understanding, and glossing them both. The incident is re-presented and its understanding, as understood from the point of the cartoonist, is incorporated under the name of distortion, generating parody, burlesque, ruthless satire, or gentle ridicule— cruel or genial laughter in any case. The method of distortion provides the definition of style; a cartoon has a moral style.

In the cartoons of Vijayan, this structure of representation as the measure of style, of moral, of the distance between incident and understanding whereby the cartoon might expose or criticise shared understanding, only producing or assuming a truer shared understanding, is marginalised. It is stood up, sidelined. His lines and letters stand up. They critique the regime of representation.

First of all this is not a Platonist uprising, it is not a prohibition or destruction of art as representation leading to the mal copy. The moralism here will be found in any indignant cartoon; the topical or a particular attitude to it being the mal copy of truth and the measure of its malady, which, in cartoon, satirical humour would cure.

It is at least Kantian. The pure, *a priori* part of sensibility is raised in the first part of the transcendental doctrine of elements. Noumenon is a limiting concept that restricts knowledge to sensible intuition, which itself is *a posteriori* in its matter but a priori in its form.[3] This form, the transcendental condition of aesthesis and aesthetics, of the finitude of objectivity and subjectivity, namely space and time, and time more than space, under which subject and object immediately relate, has moreover its own *a priori* content – itself.[4] Time is 'infinite given magnitude' that contains its own manifold, and yet never alters, but only what is in time.[5] It can be formalised in non-empirical representations but it is their intuition as well, and hence more primitive as a form.[6] It is the subjective condition in the peculiar Kantian sense, and not in the psychological sense; it abstracts nothing from experience but precedes it everywhere, every time[7]—we could say it is the primitive in experience. Not absolutely real, but transcendentally ideal, it is a one-dimensional form that is radically undeterminable,[8] that, we would find, can be determined in many ways, as circle, as line, as a mad spiral that eats its own tail. This pure intuition of time is the *a priori* knowledge we have in order to come across the world, and therein across ourselves. Time separates this *a priori* subject of knowledge, the 'I', from us.

Time does not of itself afford us judgment or nostalgia. The cartoon could rely on any image of time by implicating us in measuring or mourning the past, and predicting or cursing the future. But Vijayan cannot be easily assigned to any one of these because he keeps proliferating such images: the milestone, the wheel, the uprooted pre-independence politician with rotting straw-limbs. The most astounding comment on the image of time and cartoon is offered in the phrase 'updating a cartoon' (see Figure 17). A cartoon, though topical, does not simply update us or deploy the trope of updation to contrast 'now' and 'then'. It is itself updation. Vijayan shows the logic of updation to be the replacement at positions in a plain structure of politics whose relations are backdoor alliance, extra-electoral influence, corruption and seat-control. This is another cartoon on cartoon, whose predictability, as well as that of its subject, is no longer a method but a theme; and what kind of past or future could be adjudged for its predictability or lack of it?

I would not agree with Bruce Petty that Vijayan's cartoon is a commentary that is 'relevant to human future in a way Western cartoonists may never be.'[9] Ashis Nandy gives us a profound insight into Vijayan's art, calling it 'a powerful and captivating commentary on the past of India's future.'[10] This past does not determine or cause the future, and Nandy adds that Vijayan 'is certainly not a clown forced by circumstances to nurture a tragic vision of life.'[11] He is not, any more than time is, affected by temporal entities. His cartoon is not a commentary owing to an ontic conception of time, and hence is not an ontic tragedy, that is, tragic vision. This means the lines and letters are not inexorably led to a representation of the tragic any more than of black humour. But his cartoon is also not a pictorialisation of *The Critique of Pure Reason*. According to Gilles Deleuze, 'empiricism truly becomes transcendental and aesthetics an apodictic discipline only when we apprehend directly in the sensible that which can only be sensed, the very being of the sensible.'[12] Time is not independent of entities, although it does not derive from them. Here are the lines; lines are thick; and they have to be drawn.

In art, unlike in geometry, lines are not ideal but always thick or thin. What is thickness and thinness? There is no form of thickness, just as of largeness and smallness. In Kant, the moral subject is noumenal, in sharp separation from the phenomenal lines. It is in Heidegger that nothing remains of noumena: the noumena is phenomena. He even reads *The Critique of Pure Reason* in such a way that it 'threatens the supremacy of reason and the understanding', so that 'the comprehension of Being must be projected on time'; Kant can only pull back from this threat and 're-establish the supremacy of the understanding' in the Edition B of CPR.[13] Heidegger himself undertook this projection of the comprehension of Being on time by showing in *Early Greek Thinking* that time is the fourfold of past, present, future, and their gathering in being: the past as what is already past, the present as what is present, the future as what is still future.[14] This gathering is 'a while,' the fourth dimension of time that holds the whole of time, each time, with each dimension belonging to the others simultaneously.[15] 'A while' provides the sense of time. Time in Heidegger is four-times thick, rather than the transcendental line of succession. In each while, time remains more primitive than any chronometry. Primitivity does not imply some immemorial past but the non-historical primality of Time and Being with respect to every possible being and every future.

The primitivity made available by Vijayan's cartoon is the thickness of lines and the concatenability of letters, the surface tension of these two elements. Like news, cartoon is topical. Yet, we might for unusual reasons pick up the newspapers of old but unusual cartoons of old are there to survive their time. It cannot be owing to its universal concerns or anything like 'human future', but something else about lines and letters. Put simply, it is the wonder that lines and letters are utterly different elements of the magical cartoon world of picture and meaning. Vijayan's own definition of cartoon is that

> Cartoon is, ideally, word and picture, with words chosen with poetic exactness. Even when the cartoon is a mere visual, deep down within it there is the experience of the word, and it is this experience that it ultimately communicates.[7]

Ontologically speaking this is only half the truth, the other half secreted away in his cartoons themselves, albeit for all to see. Lines do not have something like a language coded into them, for example, a code that can match the judgment that there is a deformity in our economy or in our politicians. We do not have a linear language that supplies the alphabet for a pictorial communication. They have to be concatenated with letters to form words and pictures, messages in short, for example, 'poverty line' written along a line from which the tent of a poor boy hangs. In Vijayan's cartoons letters no longer provide the representation of world as news, nor lines that of world as figure. Yet there they are, nudging out on the page, next to news. They do not constitute for that reason an alternative space or vision. But through the surface tension of their lines and letters they cast a new light on this neighbouring news and even further on the world neighbouring the newspaper. This is however not equivalent to confusion and Vijayan's cartoons do not operate to that effect by means of incoherence, obscurity or messy draughtsmanship. They are all too sharp, precise to the letter, and to the line. In the Indira Gandhi–Charan Singh cartoon (see Figure 18), the newsprint, a recurring item in Vijayan, spells confusion about the status of Indira's support to Charan, with words like 'unconditional', 'terms', and 'if' militating against each other above a non-plussed close-door meal-sharing among the concerned parties. If the graphics have a message, the letters spell it out in other words than the news: 'the creatures outside looked from pig to man, and from man to pig, and from pig to man again; and already it was impossible to say which was which.' We are the creatures, we are in the cartoon trying to read the news and detect our leaders and we cannot tell the difference although it is calmly spread before us. The drawing is there but meaning has taken flight.

This tension does not derive from moral assessments of the world, not even the third world which Vijayan thought distinguished him from first world cartoonists. It is explained by the fact that a cartoon is an assemblage, that is, a set of items that mutually determine one another, without any member being privileged. Vijayan titled his note to a publication of his cartoons, 'a cartoonist remembers'. This statement captures his cartooning. Cartoon is an assemblage of lines and letters, an assemblage or a well-arranged manifestation that is sense. It shows us the agitation of lines and letters, the agitation of sense, the thickness of sense rather than transparency, or clear message. The message along with its decipherer is lost somewhere in the thick of things, and we pour over these old masterpieces trying to find ourselves in it. In Vijayan's, at least, we are also one of those subjects turned into cartoons.

Vijayan describes a cartoonist's workshop thus:

> Between historical pessimism and imbecile revolution, there is a stretch of arid territory where the cartoonist retires to. It all begins in a lot of violence and subsides as ingloriously—as it had come. That is history—the cartoonist views it from his arid space and catches its absurdities and contradictions.[8]

This arid space is the primitivity of lines with respect to history, almost like the amoeba catching food by the quick uneven thickening and de-thickening of their pseudopodia— the modifications of their own thick existence. The cartoonist's eyes are his lines and letters, and the view, that is, the sense of the cartoon is in the cartoon. We have to lose ourselves in it to find it. His cartoons, whose captions make the deformation of the cartoon simulacral, swallow us. The cartoon does not wait for us to read off its distortion and satire by moral comparison. It reads it out to us. But the letters that are part of it, are not for that reason a verbalisation of the drawing. They team up with lines and explain matters only by making them more enigmatic, but without losing their meaning or pertinence. In numerous father–son cartoons the child interprets the state of affairs draughted in the cartoon as though he were reading the world off like a cartoon. Here we find him destroying the very rules of reading newspapers (see Figure 19). The news in his father's hands is made to contrast with the news-pastiche above in reverse proportion to what common sense (enshrined in newspapers and supposedly in cartoons) dictates. The subject is not just the finance ministry but 'The people'; the proportion of pettiness and greatness stands disturbed.

Disproportion in Vijayan's cartoon is a theme and not a method. It is *techne* in the Heideggerian sense. It is a disclosure manifest only in the disclosed—we are shown the disproportion itself, and not something else by means of disproportion. Most of all not proportion. The resemblance of the subject with the cartoon is a more primitive disproportion. Hence, Vijayan's cartoons disclose not the historical culminations of the past, present and future, but the primitivity peculiar to cartoon.

Vijayan frees lines and letters as elements of cartoon by turning them inside out as elements of the regime of representation. He manages a line that stretches and yawns beside signification and marginalises meaning. Repeatedly we meet this thick line, hardly line, a dash of black ink, a thick uneven stroke. It is the asignifying contour of signification. It caresses the contours of the other lines and their intervals like the sky touched by the earth at every point. It manifests the outside that is its own inside. However, it should not at all be mistaken for a sign of a theoretical thickness. It is thick and that is all. Here (see Figure 20) it is the both the line with which a white cloud has been almost drawn, and the black night in which a white cloud floats. Nevertheless, white clouds do not bring rain, nor can rain drops be drawn out of white ink. Perhaps, the black dab is the laden cloud from which a piece of the sky looks in. Vijayan mostly signed on the other side of this line, nothing more than a scrawl, as though the darkness had spilt.

Notes

1 O.V. Vijayan, *A Cartoonist Remembers* (Delhi: Rupa & Co 2002) 20.
2 *A Cartoonist Remembers.* This selective reproduction of Vijayan's cartoons is accompanied by Ashis Nandy's foreword and Vijayan's own recollections of his career as a cartoonist.
3 *Immanuel Kant's Critique of Pure Reason* trans. Norman Kemp Smith, (London: Macmillan, 1963) A20/B34, 65–66.
4 Kant A21/B35, 66.
5 Kant A32/B48, 75.
6 Kant B49, p. 76.
7 Kant A33/B49, 76.
8 Kant A33/B50, 76–77; A36/B53, 78.
9 Sundar Ramanathaiyer and Nancy Hudson-Rodd eds. *The Tragic Idiom: O.V. Vijayan's Cartoons and Notes on India*, (Kottayam: D.C. Books, 2006) 8.
10 *A Cartoonist Remembers* xi.
11 *A Cartoonist Remembers* x.
12 Deleuze 68.
13 Martin Heidegger, *Kant and the Problem of Metaphysics* trans. James S. Churchill, (1929; Bloomington: Indiana UP), 1962, 252.
14 Martin Heidegger, *Early Greek Thinking*, trans. David Farrell Krell and Frank A. Capuzzi, (San Fransisco: Harper 1975), 34.
15 Heidegger *Early Greek* 41, 48.
16 *The Tragic Idiom* 153.
17 *The Tragic Idiom.*

Art and Philosophy

Art and Philosophy

In this last section of the book the essays, unlike those in the preceding sections of the book, are not a chronological and/or geographical discussion of the ways in which nature and time operate in verbal and visual culture. Moreover, at first sight, the two essays do not seem to share a common ground, one being abstract-philosophical and the other concrete-autobiographical. But Hofmann's abstract speculation is animated by the observing subject's experience of art while the developing self-observation of Button is firmly anchored in recent theoretical debate. There is a deeper link. Both the essays are preoccupied with the problem of temporality, of transience—thereby interlinking the categories of nature and time—in the genesis and experience of art. Unlike the other essays in the collection, these two do not seem to locate themselves within the broadly academic disciplines of history of art and history of literature. But here again there is an underlying link, of contemporaneity: the self-reflexivity and self-engagement that constitute the crux of the essays are historically conditioned by modernity.

Gert Hofmann in his essay discusses Nietzsche's analysis of Raphael's painting *The Transfiguration* and notes that Nietzsche in his philosophical commentary on the painting grasped its performative quality, its theatre-like presentation. The painting forces the viewer to take up a double perspective in time and space, thereby making self-reflexivity unavoidable. The rupture of the perspective within the painting corresponds to the theatrical effect on the viewer. Not only does the viewer have to grasp two scenes simultaneously, he/she also has to be aware of his/her own perceptual interference. The viewer is both a part of the performance of the painting as well as part of the audience.

Loris Button, the only practising artist among the contributors to this book, introduces the dimension of artistic experience that lends a note of poignancy to the themes of nature and time. Here we encounter an artist recording her lifelong preoccupation with time and identity captured in sustained self-portraiture through the years. She contextualises this conversation with herself and her artistic forebears and peers through time within the debate about a specifically visual, as opposed to literary, mode of autobiography. By focusing on the autobiographical element in the oeuvre of past masters like Dürer or Rembrandt and contemporary artists like David Hockney, she is able to challenge the widespread prejudice about the fixity of visual imagery.

12. Syncopes: Fractures in Time and Space Demonstrated through Nietzsche's Interpretation of Raphael's *Transfiguration*

Gert Hofmann

Since Nietzsche's reinvention of philosophy as a Dionysian adventure which rises from the praxis of theatre, time ceases to be interpreted as a transcendental continuum of empirical awareness. It rather appears to be an inexhaustable potential of transformation which underlies all intellectual and cultural processes. It seems, however, that this process of transformation is always rooted in a rupturing event, splitting apart the continua of time and space, fragmenting the philosophical vision of identical truth. This dramatic event puts the 'self' into a complete eccentric situation. It ruptures the identity of self-consciousness and forces the 'self' to succumb to the double event of being-transformed-into-the-other and reflecting-on-this-other-by-myself at the same time. The ultimate refuge of the human self, and the actual potency of artistic practice, lie in the tears and fractures of human time and space experience, in the undefined and non-identifiable clefts and caesuras, syncopes and absences of a fragmented stream of consciousness—the either aesthetic or pathological condition of being non-identical with oneself. In this way Nietzsche recreates philosophy as a theatrical 'art of transfiguration'. Here truth is a trope and can only be perceived as the eventful *mise en scène* of a never-ending masked performance. The Dionysian non-topos of theatre provides the paradigm for the particular dynamics of the philosophical process between annihilation and identification.

Nietzsche's concept of 'transfiguration' is originally inspired by Raphael's painting with the same title. In its religious context the Christian phenomenon of transfiguration (or metamorphosis) promises redemption through the transcending power of imagination. Raphael however discovers and demonstrates its intrinsic ambivalence: promising sublimation on the one hand, it casts abjection on the other. Raphael's *Transfiguration* (see Figure 21) is well known as the painter's last work and perhaps *magnum opus*. The exceptional fame of this painting is not only motivated by its aesthetic brilliance and originality, but also enforced by the peculiar circumstances of its public emergence on the day of Raphael's death, Good Friday in 1520, which happened to be his 37th birthday. Obviously affected and literarily inspired by these coincidences, Giorgio Vasari gave us a myth-like narration of the scene:

> ...Raphael came to the end of his life's journey on the same day that he was born, which was Good Friday of his thirty-seventh year, and we can believe that just as his talents embellished this world, so he himself will adorn heaven.
>
> As Raphael lay dead in the hall where he had been working, the painting of the Transfiguration he had done for Cardinal de' Medici was placed at his head, and the sight of his dead body and this living painting filled the soul of everyone looking on with grief. ...Oh happy and blessed soul, for every man gladly speaks of you, celebrates your deeds, and admires every design you left behind! When this noble artisan died, painting too might as well have died, for when he closed his eyes, painting was left almost blind.[1]

Vasari tells us the historical scene of Raphael's death, but also transforms its coincidences into a meaningful configuration that even involves the scriptural theme of the painting, the *Transfiguration* of Christ: a gesture of redemption in the eve of destruction, and a corporeal vision of transcended mortality.

What Vasari intended by his literary transformation of the scene seems to be clear: to prove the immortality of the work as a kind of artistic 'transfiguration' of the mortal individual. The narration of the scene should be perceived as a *mise en scène* which is performing the very act of transfiguration by configuring the historical datum of Raphael's death with the completion of his opus. In this vision, the artisan's death, his perishing corporeal existence, transfigures itself in the light of his unique work of art into the immortal existence of his artistic genius. This is invested with the power of the imaginaire, the power to create an alternative reality, a second nature, which is not subject to death.

Vasari's narrative *mise en scène* of Raphael's death performs the split of human presence and divine transcendence as a crucial moment in the rhythms of life and art. The ambivalences of a sublime and hermetic capacity for existential redemption and artistic creation due to a mortal passion and fatal devotion become apparent. However, compared to the chiliastic optimism in the religious concept of transfiguration, taken as a symbol of redemption, Vasari's literary enactment of the transfiguration-scene—as a model for an artistic configuration of life—suffers a certain undermining tendency of irritation. Finally and ultimately he pays attention not to the artefact, which manifests the eternal genius, but to the corpse, representing the time-bound human existence, that is still lying there in front of the painting. The dead body is obviously the actual focus of all compassion, love and honour. Bound to decompose in due time, it manifests itself as a rather obscure nuance of the transfiguration-phenomenon: it does *not* promise the transcendent bliss of redemption but the fatality of decay and sorrow about inevitable loss.

Vasari creates a hybrid image of the human artist and emphasises through his dramatising perspective the essential *split* in the transfiguration-event: it means completion of the artist's mortality-transcending genius (in the artefact), but also death of the person (as of the body), both of them—eternal life and temporal death, presence and absence—signed and identified by the same name: Raphael.

So much for Vasari's text. What about Raphael's painting? Vasari's narrative and its hybrid performative structure is essentially inspired by the particular composition of the painting. The split reference of Vasari's narrative perspective—to the mortal corpse, and on the eternal artefact—is in accordance with Raphael's decentred pictorial focus on two different scriptural scenes in one picture. One is the glorious 'Transfiguration of Jesus' on the Tabor mountain, and the other is the presentation of the 'possessed boy' to the distressed Apostles. As it has been Raphael's ingenious and provoking idea not to paint what is actually narrated in the Bible—the healing of the boy by Jesus after his return from the mountain —but what is on this occasion only reported,[2] namely the previous failure of the Apostles' cure, we perceive in Raphael's pictorial configuration as well as in Vasari's narrative a presentation of the double-faced human condition with its inseparable aspects of glory and misery.[3] The synopsis of the pictorial performance can reveal what the diachrony of the scriptural narrative always hides: the synchronism and mutual reference of glory and misery, of redemption and abjection. The fragmented, contradictory character of this synchronism is fatal and traumatic, but it seems intrinsic to the lived experience of human time. It can never be conceptually integrated as the underlying continuum of human self-consciousness, but it can be performed, it can be aesthetically repeated and multiplied, and the ultimate paralysis, which is always imminent within it, can thus be deferred in time, but never be transposed into an eternal sphere of transcendence.

The biblical symbolism of the 'Transfiguration' scene is meant to provide us with the signet on the truth of the redeeming as well as healing power of Christ. This signet is broken through Raphael's synoptic presentation of the spiritually sublime corpus of Jesus together with the spiritually tortured body of the possessed boy in the double scene of his pictorial composition. Enacting it on a two-storied theatre stage, he forces the viewer to become a spectator or even a witness, as he will be projecting himself among the chorus-like groups of apostles and relatives who are framing both scenes. The unframed openness of this stage-like presentation, the broken signet of the scriptural meaning, and the provoking split in its aesthetic (narrative and pictorial) composition design all together the performative and also temporal signature of the crucial moment of transfiguration.

This irritating of corrupted references within a traditional framework of symbolism is constantly interfering with the hermeneutic discourse about the painting through centuries. Here we could highlight names such as Wilhelm Heinse,[4] Johann Wolfgang Goethe,[5] Jacob Burckhardt,[6] and, of course, Friedrich Nietzsche.[7] Without exploring in details the genesis of the painting's literary and philosophical reception I have to say that in spite of the formal and substantial complexity of the painting and against the critical mainstream of the eighteenth century, all of them emphatically confirm the conceptual[8] unity of the work. They establish a rather theoretical school of perception that culminates indeed with Nietzsche's philosophical analysis in '*Die Geburt der Tragödie*' (*The Birth of Tragedy*) of 1872.

The theatrical signature of human existence and truth, understood as the performative and time-bound event of transfiguration, which becomes visible in Raphael's painting, becomes for Nietzsche the fundamental structure in his Dionysian philosophy. To Nietzsche, philosophy meant performance. The performance of philosophy is intended as 'the art of transfiguration', designated by the philosopher's corporeal existence and his ludic or tragic presence between agony and healing: The philosopher is always 'der Genesende' (convalescent):

> *er kann eben nicht anders als seinen Zustand jedes Mal in die geistigste Form und Ferne umzusetzen, -* ***diese Kunst der Transfiguration ist eben Philosophie****. Es steht uns Philosophen nicht frei, zwischen Leib und Seele zu trennen, wie das Volk trennt, es steht uns noch weniger frei, zwischen Seele und Geist zu trennen. … – wir müssen beständig unsre Gedanken aus unsrem Schmerz gebären … Leben—das heißt für uns Alles, was wir sind, beständig in Licht und Flamme verwandeln, auch Alles, was uns trifft, wir können gar nicht anders.*[9]
>
> (he can't help but to transform/convert his condition (=his illness) each time into the most spiritual/intellectual and remote form—**this art of transfiguration *is* indeed philosophy**. As philosophers we are not free to distinguish/discern body and soul, as the mob does, we are even less free to distinguish body and mind…. We always have to give birth to our thoughts out of our pain… Life, that means for us to transform everything what we are into light and flames, everything too, what hits us, we *cannot* do it differently).[10]

The philosophical act of transfiguration is not corporeal mediation of a transcendental/universal meaning, not a written representation of a substantial *a priori* and thus not physical articulation of the metaphysical reference of human thought in a continuous process of signification. It claims on the contrary the total 'self-expenditure' of human life to an abyss of temporality, of illness and decay, because the philosophical process of cognition (and 'life') is due to the burial of its given intellectual conditions and their eternal metaphysical resort. In that sense philosophical truth, with Nietzsche, reveals itself only to an act of 'tragic intelligence' which relies on the imaginary fascination of time as a process of passing away. Such tragic cognition is an existential and imaginative step[11] that could never be hermeneutically enforced by the consequent historical application and textual exposition of a metaphysical reference. It rather happens as a split of it: 'the split as reference, so to speak, a suspension of all mediation.'[12] This means the discouragement of all kind of dialectical, hermeneutical and systematic philosophy of identity as well as of the perception of time as a transcendental form and integrative continuum of all living experience. It inspires, however, the human capacity of the imaginary. The truth of philosophy is only given with the theatricality of its performance, with the non-topical tropical blur of its scene-like and tragic presentation. The purely temporal phenomenality (you could also say 'corporeality') of theatrical presentation is the eternal signature of truth itself, of its non-identical, fractured and eccentric characteristics. The aesthetical face of truth is coincident with its philosophical substance. It is not a deficient representation of something else but an actual incident: '*Nur als ästhetisches Phänomen ist das Dasein und die Welt ewig gerechtfertigt*.' ('Existence and world are only justified as an aesthetic phenomenon.')[13] The face of truth is the double face of the theatre mask. It is initiating performative art neither as mere naturalistic imitation nor as idealistic sublimation of reality, but, in fact, as a kind of 'metaphysical supplement' of it in experiential reality. It is based, as a kind of imaginary emergence, on the rupturing experience of time as an abyss of extinction, as a caesura, a syncope in the proved rhythms of the regular, traditional, and conventional.

The coincidence of aesthetics and metaphysics and the supplementary character of intended and pretended reality lead us again to the focus of artistic transfiguration ('*die metaphysische Verklärungsabsicht der Kunst überhaupt*').[14] In *Die Geburt der Tragödie* the two contradictory aspects of human life become apparent as the two sides of the theatrical mask: the tragic backside, the face of extinction, of time as loss, of disappearing authenticity and hiding performing intention, and the ludic front, the face of appearing/apparent identity and performed pretence, of time as a promise of future. Both are one, but without synthesis. Both are generating the third, the theatrical scene of transfiguration as only supplementary and deferred entity. The philosophical theatre of truth is the performance of actual (metaphysical) non-identity:

> *Die Welt, die uns etwas angeht, ist falsch d. h. ist kein Thatbestand, sondern eine Ausdichtung und Rundung über einer mageren Summe von Beobachtungen; sie ist 'im Flusse', als etwas Werdendes, als eine sich immer neu verschiebende Falschheit, die sich niemals der Wahrheit nähert: denn—es giebt keine Wahrheit.*[15]
>
> (The world *that concerns us* is false. I mean it is not factual, but fiction and assumption about some meagre amount of observations. It is flowing, something moving, a kind of again and again deferred falsity which is never approaching truth: for—there is no *truth*.)[16]

Due to its theatrical signature, philosophical truth is like a dramatic event exposed to the perspectivism of the spectators 'perception (his '*Summe von Beobachtungen*') on the one side and to the figments ('*Ausdichtung*') of the world's masked encounter on the other. The case of truth is the incident of a masked encounter, it is the irreducible fictitiousness inherent in such a moment of theatrical metamorphosis. It is also, on the level of philosophical reason, the interruption and tragic confusion of the temporal stream of consciousness and its conceptual foundation. True is only the articulate transgression and confusion of any assertive opposition of true and false, of intention and pretence, and of past and future in the way of the theatrical play. According to Paul de Man, the 'assimilation of truth and trope' and the 'homology between concept and figure'[17] make up the intrinsic potential of Nietzsches Dionysian understanding of philosophy. Any traditional philosophical concept or category will always be unveiled as 'Residuum of a metaphor' founded in an illuding act of 'artistic transference'. In this will coerce the philosopher to conduct by his searching for truth nothing less but

> '*die Metamorphose der Welt in den Menschen.*'[18] (the metamorphosis of the world in human beings)

This process of metamorphosis, which is to be released from its constraint under human morale and any other authority of 'assimilation' is the true mandate of philosophy in terms of Nietzsche's 'art of transfiguration'. It tries to establish a preponderance of the figure over the concept, of performance over reference, and of time as an abyss over time as a process of continued identities.[19] Truth does not seem to be completely annihilated, but the moment of annihilation is true. Therefore truth does not refer to the domain of episteme, but to the playgrounds of art. 'Truth is a trope'; therefore, the trope cannot transport any substantial meaning, but has to perform the metaphoricalness, i.e. the temporality and mortality of truth itself.[20]

Philosophy, what has been so far a mere metaphysical '*Missverständnis des Leibes*', misunderstanding of the body has to be turned into the physical and theatrical 'art of transfiguration'.[21] Another metaphor for this metamorphosis of philosophy is '*Genesung*,' 'convalescence' which is as ambivalent as the theatrical play of the tragedy, always showing an ironic smile in the human face of agony. Nietzsche presents us this as the epitome of absolute art: '*eine Kunst für Künstler, nur für Künstler*!' 'Art for artists, for artists only!'[22] Obviously Nietzsche wants to stress both: the corporeal character of his philosophy as an act and incident of physical transformation which is completely immersed in the sphere of time as the sphere of passing identities ('*Genesung*') and its artistic character as '*Kunst für Künstler, nur für Künstler*' ('art for artists, for artists only'). An 'art for artists' is also opening the theatrical situation, interpreting the moment of transfiguration as a momentous encounter of performer's intention and spectator's perception, creating together the doubled reality of an irreducible theatrical pretence, presenting reality itself as being fictitious ('*fingierter Naturzustand*' 'fictitious state of nature').[23]

The symbolism of the human body is the true matter of Nietzsche's philosophical art of transfiguration. The human body, known to die and decompose in due time, is the focus of life's antagonism, the coeval creation of two antagonistic powers, the Apollinian power of figuration (the 'principle of individuation') and the Dionysian power of extinction and defiguration (the 'abyss of annihilation'). But the symbolism of the body, does not suspend or mediate the antagonism; rather, it expresses it by enacting it, forcing the individual into a de-centred situation of self-metamorphosis and self-reflexion. Nietzsche called this '*das dramatische Urphänomen*' (the dramatic ur-phenomenon):

> *sich selbst vor sich verwandelt zu sehen und jetzt zu handeln, als ob man wirklich in einen andern Leib, in einen andern Charakter eingegangen wäre. Dieser Prozeß steht am Anfang der Entwicklung des Dramas. (...) hier ist bereits ein Aufgeben des Individuums durch Einkehr in eine fremde Natur.*[24]

> (to watch yourself being transformed in front of you and to act as if you would have really entered another body, another character. This process is the beginning of the development of drama. (...) here is already giving up of the individual through entering the being of another.)[25]

The dramatic phenomenon puts the 'self' into a complete eccentric situation timewise. It ruptures the identity of self-consciousness, splits the continuity of the time stream, and forces the 'self' to succumb to the double event of being-transformed-into-the-other and reflecting-on-this-other-by-myself at the same moment. It is not just the binary opposition of inside and outside (and its reflecting mediation) but the aporia of identity and difference, self-confirmation and self-sacrifice conjoined into the masked performance of the tragic theatre. The time condition of the tragic theatre is however the experience of a suspended time experience: the experience of a caesura or syncope, where the antagonistic time streams of passing away to death and going out to giving birth, can be brought together in multifarious, unconditional ways.

Let us finally return to Raphael's *Transfiguration*. After all, it is becoming quite clear what could have been Nietzsche's concern with Raphael's painting.[26] He realised and appreciated not so much its pictorial but rather its performative quality and the theatre-like presentation of its subject. The religious idea transformed under his artistic hands into a pure aesthetical event. Nietzsche realised, that the painting unfolds a kind of theatrical situation towards everyone who is looking on it, for it is actually putting on stage what the usual painting could only show: it forces the viewer to cope with its double scene by taking up himself a double perspective in time and space, thus performing willingly the split of his own perceiving identity. The breaking of the pictorial central perspective within the painting corresponds with the theatrical effect on the viewer in front of it, for it compels him to get involved in the two scenes and to assure their conjunction only by his own perceptional interference. So the viewer/spectator has to perform a change in his perspective twice in one action: as a spectator he has to be involved in the artistic event as a genuine part of the performance (what makes up the shift from mere pictorial to actual dramatic art), and as a spectator-performer he has to execute again the split within the performed coincidences of Jesus' Transfiguration, paying attention to both of the scenes and necessarily to their 'unconciliatory antagonism.' Here he is eventually aware of some

Widerschein des ewigen Widerspruchs, des Vaters der Dinge.... [27]

(reflection of the eternal antagonism, which is the father of everything.)[28]

'Changing the perspective' (*Perspektiven umzustellen*) is another formula to design the procedure of the philosophical art of transfiguration, even for the very late Nietzsche:

> *jene Psychologie des 'Um-die-Ecke-sehens' ... ist das eigentliche Geschenk jener Zeit, in der Alles sich bei mir verfeinerte, die Beobachtung selbst wie alle Organe der Beobachtung. ... Ich habe es jetzt in der Hand, ich habe die Hand dafür, Perspektiven umzustellen: erster Grund, weshalb für mich allein vielleicht eine 'Umwerthung der Werthe' überhaupt möglich ist.* [29]

> (that psychology of 'gazing around the corner' (...) is the actual benefit of that period, when everything with myself became more sophisticated, the observation as such as well as all its organs. Now I have the power to *change perspectives*: this is the first reason why only for me the 'transvaluation of values' may be actually possible.)[30]

It is not the alternative of changed perspectives: it is the momentous incident of changing the perspective in time and space—an incident of splitting time, of time not as the categorically secured continuity of presence (*nunc stans*), but as the abyss of mortality —that creates the art of transfiguration, opening, bearing, executing and iterating infinitely an antagonism of possibilities, of health and illness, of concentration and dissipation, and of time as the one and only abyss of disappearance and emergence. Time is perceived not as a transcendental continuum of intellectual identities, but as an artistic configuration of unforeseeable aesthetic images. Here we do not find the normative opposition of right and wrong (that would allow any dialectic or chiliastic solution), but the minute nuance, the syncope of a de-centering self, which blurs the focus of any perceptive identity and unleashes the demons of the imaginaire[31]

> *denn alles Leben ruht auf Schein, Kunst, Täuschung, Optik, Nothwendigkeit des Perspektivischen und des Irrthums.* [32]

> (for all life is founded on appearance, art, deception, optics, necessary perspectivism and error.)[33]

Notes

1 Giorgio Vasari, *The Lives of the Artists* trans. Julia Conaway Bondanella and Peter Bondanella (Oxford: Oxford UP 1991) 336f.

2 Malhew 17,16; Mark 9,18, Luke 9, 40.

3 Cp. Konrad Oberhuber, Raphael's 'Transfiguration'. Stil und Bedeutung, Stuttgart 1982: '*Obgleich frühere Künstler die beiden aufeinanderfolgenden Begebenheiten schon in Zyklen miteinander verknüpft hatten, hatten sie immer den Augenblick dargestellt, in welchem Christus*

den Knaben selbst heilt. (…) Raphael hingegen (…) wollte vielmehr darstellen, wie die Apostel außerstande sind, dem Kranken unmittelbar zu helfen. Christus erscheint als eine ferne und doch auf geheimnisvolle Weise gegenwärtige Kraft (…) Diese außergewöhnliche Beziehung zwischen den beiden Szenen war etwas völlig Neues.' (Even though earlier artists had already linked these two events in cycles, they had always represented the moment when Christ cures the boy himself. (…) Raphael, however, (…) rather wanted to show, how the apostles are unable to help the boy immediately. Christ appears as a distant but nevertheless in a mysterious way present power. (…) This unusual connection between the two scenes was something completely new. Trans. mine.) (10, 12)

4 Wilhelm Heinse, *Ardinghello und die glückseligen Inseln*. 1975 (publ. at first 1787), 216f.

5 Johann Wolfgang Goethe, *Werke* (Sophien-Ausgabe), *Weimar 1887-1919* 1.32 (*Italienische Reise*), 172f.

6 Jacob Burckhardt, *Der Cicerone. Eine Anleitung zum Genuß der Kunstwerke Italiens*, Vol. 2, Heinrich Wölfflin (ed), Stuttgart, Berlin, Leipzig, 1933, 283–85.

7 Friedrich Nietzsche, *Sämtliche Werke. Kritische Studienausgabe*, Vol. 1 (*Die Geburt der Tragödie*), (München 1980), 39f.

8 See Goethe's remark: '*Die Gleichgesinnten berstärkten sich auch diesmal in ihrer Überzeugung; Raphael, sagten sie zueinander, zeichnete sich eben durch die Richtigkeit seines Denkens aus, und der gottbegabte Mann, den man eben hieran durchaus erkennt, soll in der Blüthe seines Lebens falsch gedacht, falsch gehandelt haben? Nein! er hat, wie die Natur jederzeit Recht, und gerade da am gründlichsten, wo wir sie am wenigsten begreifen.*' (Those who were of the same mind also here reconfirmed their conviction: Raphael, they told each other, excelled by the correctness of his thought. This god-chosen man should have had wrong ideas in the blossom of his life? No! He is, like nature, always right, and especially there where we comprehend him the least. Trans. mine.) L. c., p. 173.

9 Friedrich Nietzsche, l. c., Vol. 3 (*Die fröhliche Wissenschaft*), 349f. Emphasis mine.

10 Translation mine.

11 See Gisela Dischner, '*Die Mauern stehen sprachlos und kalt*'. *Tragische Erkenntnis in der Moderne*, Bielefeld, 1999, who shows the links between Nietzsche and modern existentialism moderated by the literary traces of 'tragic intelligence'. Cp. also Walter Kaufmann, Nietzsche. *Philosoph—Psychologe - Antichrist*, Darmstadt 1982: He confirms a principle of 'existential unity' within the pluralism of Nietzsche's 'experimental' philosophy.

12 Jacques Derrida, *Guter Wille zur Macht* (I). *Drei Fragen an Hans-Georg Gadamer*, in Philippe Forget (ed.) München, Text und Interpretation, 1984, 56–58 (58). Derrida belongs to the protagonists conducting the performative turn of Nietzsche interpretation after Martin Heidegger. He emphasises the anti-metaphysical potentials in Nietzsche's way of thinking, exploiting them for his own philosophy of semiotics, articulating the performative release of the *signifiant* from its coercion by the metaphysically established *signifié*: '*Die Lektüre und*

damit die Schrift, der Text wären für Nietzsche 'ursprüngliche' Operationen (...) gegenüber einem Sinn, der nicht bezeichnete Wahrheit (...) oder apriori notwendige Struktur wäre.' (The reading and therefore the writing, too, the text would be for Nietzsche 'original' operations (...) towards a meaning which would neither be denotated truth (...) nor *a priori* necessary structure. Trans. mine.) He provokes the metaphysical tradition of Philosophy by claiming with Nietzsche a kind of physical *a priori*: the corporeal exteriority of any significance as scripture. S. Jacques Derrida, *Grammatologie*, trans. Hans-Jörg Rheinberger and Hanns Zischler, (Frankfurt a. M. ain 1988), 36f. For Nietzsche, Derrida and the French Nietzsche discourse after Heidegger see Ernst Behler, *Derrida - Nietzsche. Nietzsche - Derrida*, (München, Paderborn, Wien, Zürich, 1988).

13 The sentence appears even twice in Nietzsche's *Geburt der Tragödie*: l. c., Vol. 1, 47, 152. Translation mine.

14 l. c., Vol. 1, 151.

15 l. c., Vol. 12 (*Nachgelassene Fragmente*), 112, written in 1885/86 when he worked out the '*Versuch einer Selbstkritik*' about *Die Geburt der Tragödie*, annihilating decisively its apparantly 'metaphysical' tendency.

16 Translation mine.

17 Paul de Man, 'Anthropomorphism and Trope in the Lyric' in *The Rhetoric of Romanticism*, (New York: Columbia UP, 1984), 239–262 (239).

18 Friedrich Nietzsche, l. c., Vol. 1, 882f. (*Über Wahrheit und Lüge im außermoralischen Sinne* 1).

19 Dealing with Julia Kirsteva's psychoanalytically charged semiology, Cynthia Chase leads her deliberations about a 'performative model of language' to similar conclusions: 'Prior to the sign is a figuration *producing* that structure. A performative dimension of language exceeds its cognitive function.' Of course it is her main issue to explain, how this model could emerge in Kirsteva's 'reinterpretation' of the Freudian concept of 'primary narcissism' (conjoined with Paul de Man's rhetorical structure of 'prosopopeia'). Whether this kind of psychoanalytical challenge of semiology does maybe affect also Nietzsche's transcendental provocation of semiotic philosophy could be subject to further research. Cynthia Chase, 'Primary Narcissism and the Giving of Figure. Kristeva with Hertz and de Man', in: *Abjection, Melancholia and Love. The Work of Julia Kristeva*. Edited by John Fletcher and Andrew Benjamin. (London: Routledge, 1990) 124–136 (125f).

20 The consequence is the absolution of the metaphor. Cf. Paul Ricoeur, *Die lebendige Metapher*, trans. Rainer Rochlitz, (München, 1986) '*es gibt keinen Diskurs über die Metapher, der nicht mit einem Begriffsnetz arbeitet, das selbst metaphorisch hervorgebracht wurde. Es gibt keinen metaphernlosen Ort ...*' (There is no discourse about the metaphor, that wouldn't operate with a network of concepts which are not themselves metaphorically produced. There is no metaphorless place. Trans. mine.); 263. The metaphor is generating the concept. But the substantial meaning of the concept represents only the decomposed

remnants or sediments of the metaphorical dynamics, generating significance: '*wo die Metapher ausgelöscht wird, erhebt sich der metaphysische Begriff.*' (Where the metaphor is being deleted, the metaphysical concept is rising. Translmine.) (260) S. Nietzsche, l. c., Vol. 1, 880f.: '*Die Wahrheiten sind (...) Metaphern, die abgenutzt und sinnlich kraftlos geworden sind, Münzen, die ihr Bild verloren haben und nun als Metall, nicht mehr als Münzen in Betracht kommen.*' (The truths are metaphors, used up and sensually depleted, coins which have lost their embossing and are now being regarded as metal only, not as coins. Trans. mine.)

21 See note 26.

22 L. c., p. 351.

23 This is confirmed in Greek theatre by the comments of the *chorus* incorporating itself the double perspective of performer and spectator. Cf. Nietzsche, l. c., Vol. 1, 54ff.

24 L. c., p. 61.

25 Translation mine.

26 Nietzsche knew about the painting probably only through Jacob Burckhardt who gives in his *Cicerone* a quite detailed description of the work (see footnote 15). Burckhardt already stesses on the dramatic constellation and the 'enormous antagonism' of the double scene, even being aware of the spectator's moment: '*die Verbindung beider Szenen existiert nur im Geiste des Beschauers*' (The connection of both scenes does only exist in the mind of the onlooker. Trans. mine.) 283. Otherwise he still insisted on the totality of the painting, inaugurating a kind of metaphysical or religious salvation - but without working out any clear concept of it.

27 L. c., Vol. 1, 39 (*Die Geburt der Tragödie*).

28 Translation mine.

29 L. c., vol. 6, pp. 265ff. (*Ecce homo, Warum ich so weise bin* 1).

30 Translation mine.

31 '[R] eaching the point of no return, where science and philosophy '*in Kunst umschlagen muss.*' (have to turn into art. Transl. mine) L. c., Vol. 1, 99 (*Die Geburt der Tragödie*).

32 L. c., 18.

33 Translation mine.

13. Facing Time: The Evocation of Time in Visual and Literary Forms of Autobiography

Loris Button

This paper explores the interrelationship that I will argue exists between literary and visual forms of autobiography. I have approached this investigation from the particular perspective of a practising artist—a maker of images.

Fine portraits have always had the capacity to engage the imagination of the viewer about the nature and history of the person portrayed. As an artist who has particularly focused on self portraiture as a means of investigating the nature of identity and ageing in contemporary culture, I have taken great pleasure and inspiration from the ways in which creative writers have used the forms of biography and autobiography in particular, as a means of describing lives, cultures and times in both historical and contemporary periods.

Literary examples demonstrating the interweaving or juxtaposition of times and individual lives include the English writer A.S. Byatt. In particular, her novel *Possession* is a complex fictional tale which weaves the idea of late twentieth century biographers pursuing nineteenth century poets and lovers back and forth through temporal space. Also English/Australian writer Drusilla Modjeska's wonderfully poetic tale *The Orchard* and the memoir of her mother *Poppy,* each play games with the reader's understanding of the relationship between autobiography, biography and fiction. Furthermore the distinguished

Australian philosopher, Raimond Gaita's extraordinarily evocative and moving memoir, *Romulus, My Father* is a biography that contains a strong autobiographical thread.

These examples are just some of the writings which over many years, has informed and fuelled my creative imagination in much the same way that the work of other artists in my field such as Alice Neel, Lucian Freud, David Hockney and Maryanne Coutts have all done.

A search of the relevant literature in this area appears to indicate that there is a broadly held belief amongst art theorists and creative writers about the nature of the visual portrait in relation to written autobiography or biography that appears to suggest that a portrait has limited ability (or none at all) to give temporal insight about an individual, compared to a biography or autobiography.

In this regard, I examined a range of opinions from relevant theorists, historians and writers about their understandings of the nature of such written and visual images of the self. I began to see that many of the writers and scholars whom I admire, did not in fact share my belief that written and visual forms of autobiography could serve (at least partially) similar functions in their role of describing 'self' and 'identity' in culture.

Shearer West, Professor of Art History at the University of Birmingham, has written a comprehensive and thoughtful book about the history and practice of portraiture. West says that there are clear affinities between biography and portraiture and as such, the portrait may fulfil the role of a brief biography in that it may say things about the character of an individual. However, despite the clear links, she maintains that there are essential differences between the two forms in that the 'momentary nature' of a visual portrait and its tendency to portray the identity of the sitter as timeless or iconic, is very different to the ability of biographical writing to describe the character of an individual over a long period of time (*Portraiture* 50).[1] Developing this point she also claims that: 'The particular moment chosen for a portrait cannot be extended…it represents the individual's appearance at a specific point, and other aspects of his or her life can only be alluded to' (51). West uses the term 'momentary nature', to refer to what I believe she sees as the measured span of time in the life of the subject that is encompassed during the production of a portrait.

Three writers speaking at recent public forums support West's differentiation between autobiographical and biographical writing and self portrait and portrait images.

The English writer A.S. Byatt[2] is justly acclaimed for her complex and layered novel *Possession*, a fictional tale about biographical writers and their subjects. In her essay *Portraits in Fiction,* based on the Heywood Hill Annual Lecture, delivered at the National Portrait Gallery, London in 2000, Byatt says that portraits in paint 'exist outside time and record merely the time of their making, therefore they should be seen as opposites [of fictional portraits] rather than metaphors for each other' (*Portraits* 1).

The Australian writer David Malouf's autobiographical novels *Johnno* and *12 Edmonstone Street*, are seminal works in Australian literature for their evocation of time, place, the character of a particular era and the individuals who were part of that era. In a talk presented as a component of the exhibition *To Look Within: Australian Self Portraits* at the University Art Museum of the University of Queensland in June of 2004, Malouf discussed what he saw as the parallels and differences between portraiture and biography. He expressed the view that a self portrait may only refer to a fixed moment in time and is therefore wholly knowable; as opposed to an autobiography wherein the writer may allude to or refer, the reader backwards and forwards through the lifetime of the subject, or even beyond it, therefore encompassing a much larger span of time in the portrayal of identity (*Author's notes*).

At the 'Likeness Symposium' held at the Sydney College of the Arts in Sydney 2001, Australian historian and author of the memoir, *Tiger's Eye*, Inga Clendinnen suggested during her talk based around ideas relating to self portraiture and autobiography, that the key difference between the two forms lay in the fact that a painted portrait could be wholly 'known' in a moment's glance, whereas a written autobiography required time to read and understand (*Author's notes*). Clendinnen was arguing for the merits of imaginative readers of autobiographies, but seemed to me to lack the same type of sensibility as a viewer of visual self portraits.

Thus, there seems to be a considerable body of respected intellectual opinion behind the idea that the key difference between visual portraits and biographies may be seen to be the idea that a written biography (or autobiography) is able to convey a broad span of time in the life of the subject and investigate character in depth. Visual portraits are said to differ in that they may only refer to that specific time in the life of the subject during which the portrait was produced; their primary role, to convey a physical likeness and some general aspects of character (*Portraiture* 51).

Whilst this premise may indeed be true for many portraits, I wish to argue that recent changes in our understanding of identity in culture *are* reflected in the practice of some contemporary portraitists and, that it is indeed possible to use self portraits to allude to a life seen through time at various junctures.

The English artist David Hockney has been making art and writing about its production with great insight, since the 1970s. He provides a valuable support for the idea that has been germinating through my work and reflection that artists 'know' things about images and image making that art historians and theorists or writers do not (*Secret Knowledge* 13).[3]

A voice from literary and visual theory who does offer a differing opinion, which in part seems to support my own point of view, may be found in the writings of the distinguished theorist Meike Bal. In her book *Quoting Caravaggio,* Bal says that it is clearly apparent that visual images are able to '*evoke* or *represent* time—the past, the future, two or more moments simultaneously' (*Quoting Caravaggio* 165).[4] However, she then goes on to say that it is more difficult to see how they can unfold literally through the act of viewing or reading in the way that film and literature may be experienced (165).

I will argue that this literal unfolding is exactly what may happen, but over a briefer span of time, or perhaps in episodic periods of time, as a viewer returns again and again to contemplate the nature of a particular portrait or self portrait image and sees it afresh, consequently developing a temporal understanding of the person portrayed by the artist.

Australian art critic and writer Peter Timms offers some support for this concept of 'episodic looking' when he commences the chapter 'What can art do?' in his book *What's Wrong with Contemporary Art?*[5] by relating the tale of his own ongoing encounter with a particular work of art. What started as an unplanned but nevertheless powerful encounter with the National Gallery of Victoria's (NGV) eighteenth century painting *A lion attacking a horse* by George Stubbs, when Timms was 11 or 12 years of age, has developed into a lifelong pattern of regular visits to see the work again and again. Timms relates that after such a long period of repeated viewings 'I feel that I know every brushstroke, yet it never fails to surprise me' (145). Timms is clearly not discussing portraiture here; however it is his acknowledgment of the way in which images may continue to offer unfolding access to understanding through the act of repeated looking that is relevant to this argument.

Bal differs somewhat from this notion of the unfolding temporal possibilities of a 'static' visual image, when she says that many contemporary artists today are concerned to make time the focus of their work 'on a level that simultaneously acknowledges and challenges the fixity of the visual image' (*Quoting Caravaggio* 166–70). She is in fact referring to artworks that may be literally seen to change before our eyes, disintegrate, or simply begin to deteriorate physically. See for example the work of Jeannette Christensen, *The Passing of Time (Woman Holding a Balance,* 1994 and *The Passing of Time (Girl Reading a Letter),* 1995. These polaroid photographs which, whilst visually reaching back through time across four centuries to the iconic paintings of Vermeer, are literally snapshots which fix the moment in time of their creation and simultaneously, begin to fade (170).

I do count myself among those contemporary artists who intend to make time a focus of my work in order to both acknowledge and challenge the supposed 'fixity' of visual imagery. But my means can be seen to be less ephemeral and more bounded by the notion of painting as a visual language, one that has the capacity to translate empirical data (sensory input), to individual understanding and has a grammar, structure and continuity with a duration comparable to verbal language.

A clear example of the way in which artists visually 'read' pictures may be found in David Hockney's book, *Secret Knowledge*. In defiance of traditionally accepted timelines, Hockney makes a convincing argument for the use by a range of artists from the early fifteenth century, of lenses such as a camera lucida or a concave mirror, as a means for accurately depicting such things as physiognomy and elaborate fabrics and folds.

Hockney has argued from his position as a maker of images, an artist who is intimately involved in the practice and process of visual language, who 'reads' images differently from the way in which art historians or art theorists would. He notices and knows the level of difficulty, time and skill required to achieve the high level of accuracy that must have been brought to bear on the depiction of the portrait images he has considered in this enquiry. He says that: 'Like most painters, I imagine, when I look at paintings I am as interested in 'how' it was painted as 'what' it is saying or 'why' it was painted (these questions are of course related)' (*Secret Knowledge* 13). And that '... I'm sure that these things [how, what, why] could only have been seen by an artist, a mark-maker, who is not as far from practice, or from science, as an art historian' (13).

In her collection of essays entitled *Art Objects,* Jeanette Winterson makes the point that good artists, always work in the living language [textual or visual] of their time. 'Ours has been a century of rapid change, and if literature [or visual art] is to have any meaning beyond the museum, it must keep developing ...' (*Art Objects* 39). Writing in the last years of the twentith century, she argues that artists have a type of insight that enables them to grasp from a fluid moment, the unique present, or the 'psychic resonance' of a people at a particular time.

> [Artists] who seem to sum up their times are ... [those who are able to recognise and articulate] ... the ... living, breathing, winding movement that flows out of the past and into the future whilst making its unique present. This fixity and flux is never clear until we are beyond it and into further fixity and flux, and yet it seems it was clear, at least to one group of people ... who come to be absolutely identified with their day; the artists. (40)

Both Hockney and Winterson's views offer support for the notion that in part the relationship or ability to speak across or through time exists because of the continuity that can be seen to exist in the language of mark making as a means of communication. The ability to 'read' this language has been passed from one generation of artists to the next for hundreds of years and, as with all living languages, it is mutable. While some understandings clarify and deepen, new ones appear and others are lost or the readings may change.

For example, Andrew Forge[6] in writing about Claude Monet's painting technique, clearly articulates the process through which artists develop visual language. Forge says:

> Any way of working implies a philosophy, a position. Technique is the first embodiment of content ... Meaning accrues with manipulation. The painter sees this and responds. His [sic] recognition is added to the earlier content and informs further manipulation. A dialogue develops between the maker and the made that is unique to the conditions of making. It has its past and its future, its own limitations and hence its own unique possibility of freedom (Forge 76).

Ludmilla Jordanova[7] in her essay 'The Body of the Artist' in the exhibition catalogue, *Self Portrait: Renaissance to Contemporary,* uses the term 'visual intelligence' when she refers to 'the mental processing that is required for any work of art to be produced'. She goes on to say that the transformative process that artists use to produce the material objects of their particular genre, is embedded in the time and place of the production of that artwork, interpreted through social, historical and material knowledge of what has gone before (the work and methods of artistic forebears and peers) and yet, is specific to the time and place of its making ('The body of the Artist' 54).

The same types of changes in society's understanding of the nature of identity may also be seen to occur. The modern era notion that a person's identity is relatively fixed and stable has now changed.

Recent sociological and psychological theory has stressed that a person's 'identity' is in fact something multiple and potentially fluid, constructed through experience and linguistically coded (Bullock and Twombley).[8]

This clear dichotomy between concepts of the self as a fixed and knowable entity and contemporary understandings of the fluidity of identity has been clearly articulated in regard to written biographical and autobiographical works (for example in A.S. Byatt's essay *Portraits in Fiction),* but as yet, seems to be largely unrecognised as a practice of visual artists.

Just as biography is a specific technique of literary language, portraiture is a specific genre of visual language, a technique in its own right that painters have developed in referring to or revealing character and identity. The notion of identity being referred to is inevitably specific to the time that the writer writes, the painter paints, the subject is presented and the audience 'reads'.

Famously the first artist to produce self-consciously aware self-portraits, Albrecht Dürer was also the first to document his ageing self. From a precociously adept draftsman at the age of thirteen, through his young manhood, maturity and decline, shortly before his early demise at the age of fifty-seven, Dürer has left an absorbing record of his changing visage and engagement with his world.

No discussion of the ageing self could be complete without reference to Rembrandt von Rijn and his extraordinary series of self portraits documenting (like Dürer) his progression from a similarly gifted youth, through, to his rise and fall in the society of his time and, most poignantly, his unflinching scrutiny of the ageing process as it affected him in his later years.

Sofonisba Anguissola, who was active throughout a long life in both sixteenth and seventeenth centuries, provides a relatively rare glimpse of this same process from the point of view of a woman artist and in recent times, Alice Neel and David Hockney have contributed revealing insights into key rites of passage and the ageing process in the twentieth and early twenty-first centuries, through the process of developing a continuing record of their selves, families and friends as they progress through life in contemporary times.

All these above mentioned artists have worked episodically to produce over extended periods of time, a lasting and evocative narrative record of their lives. It is now becoming clear that more recently, some contemporary artists engage in a more complex process of self portraiture, evoking the fluid nature of the contemporary understanding of the concept of identity.

For example, Rachel Lachowicz with her 1992 sculptural self portrait, *Forensic Project 28, 58, 88 Years* (see Figure 22), visualised her own ageing process by imagining how she would look at thirty-year intervals.

The contemporary Australian artist, Maryanne Coutts regularly produces self portraits with a strong fictional, narrative content. These images are at all times strongly connected to the larger project of narrative imagery structures in visual arts practice that Coutts is working on at the time. Each one reflects a particular part of her working life and, as with writer Drusilla Modjeska, weaves a magical path between truth and fiction, which together may be seen to develop an extended concept of identity and time in the life of this artist.

Of particular interest in this discourse is the 2002 *Self Portrait*, where Coutts has incorporated several self portrait images into what initially appears to be a single large head. This visual acknowledgment of the simultaneous roles that contemporary society imposes on individuals is, I believe, an important indicator of the intricate ways that visual imagery may evoke the complex nature of contemporary identity and I argue, comparable to the ability of autobiographical writing.

My own work approaches this problem from a slightly different perspective and the series entitled, *Facing Time,* (see Figure 23) is perhaps most relevant to this discussion. Comprising a set of twenty drawings (some of which incorporate digital or lino prints within the drawn image), they together constitute one large work. All are self portraits, some contemporary, but the majority referring to older self portrait images. The earliest is from 1979. Repeated, reversed, cropped, scaled up or down, drawn, scanned, cut into lino, printed, redrawn and repeated again and again ... they are intended to act as a conversation through time with my 'self', my artistic forebears and with my peers (see Figure 24).

I have always regarded the many self portraits I have undertaken over the past thirty years as a means of laying down some information about a contemporary life and, as mentioned earlier, this idea has been formulated in part through my extensive reading of literary forms of autobiographies. *Facing Time* can be seen as a visual response to the issue of describing identity in contemporary culture by the means of using physiognomy (the effects of time and ageing), and character (images painted at various significant times in my life) over an extended period of time.

Therefore, my argument regarding this difference in interpretation between the ways in which literary and visual forms of autobiography may be 'read', turns on the belief that the apparent lapse in understanding of shifts that are occurring in art practice, as seen through the eyes of many art historians, theorists and creative writers, stems from a different perspective to that of practising artists. This perspective is from the dominant discourse of written language and so, may be seen to be a form of cultural imperialism. The discipline of art history and theory necessarily draws on works of art for its meaning and purpose and has considerable influence over, and in many ways drives, what is seen to be acceptable in contemporary art practice. Many speakers of the dominant written language do not see the necessity of learning a subordinate visual language. After all, they are speaking from the centre, from somewhere 'other' than the field of art practice in which visual language operates.

Ludmilla Jordanova offers a clear alternative to this point of view in her persuasive argument for artists' 'vivid awareness that can be termed 'historical' of what has gone before' ('The body of the Artist' 32) and their ability to make this knowledge manifest through the production of their artworks. It seems appropriate to sum up this discussion with a further quote from Jordanova which underpins my own position about self portraiture, when she says that:

> ...a genre that appears at first sight to be highly individual may turn out to be the most deeply social of them all, and that is why it should never be considered in isolation but imagined in deep conversation with other works of art, with texts, [and] with social processes ... (54).

Notes

Meike Bal, *Quoting Caravaggio: Contemporary Art, Preposterous History*. Chicago and London: The U of Chicago P, 1999.

A. Bullock and S. Twombley, *The New Fontana Dictionary of Modern Thought*. London: Harper Collins, 1999.

A.S. Byatt, *Portraits in Fiction*. London: Vintage, 2002.

Andrew Forge and Robert Gordon. *Monet* trans. John Shepley. 1983; New York: Harry N. Abrams, Inc., 1989.

David Hockney, *Secret Knowledge: Rediscovering the Lost Techniques of the Old Masters*. London: Thames & Hudson Ltd., 2001.

Ludmilla Jordanova, 'The Body of the Artist'. *Self Portrait: Renaissance to Contemporary*. London: National Portrait Gallery Publications, 2005. 43 - 55.

Peter Timms, *What's Wrong with Contemporary Art?* Sydney: University of New South Wales P Ltd, 2004.

Shearer West, *Portraiture*. Oxford History of Art. Oxford: Oxford UP, 2004.

Jeanette Winterson. *Art Objects: Essays on Ecstasy and Effrontery.* London: Vintage, 1996.

Artists cited

Sofonisba Anguissola (1532/5–1625)
Jeannette Christenson (1958–)
Maryanne Coutts (1961–)
Albrecht Dürer (1471–1528)
Lucian Freud (1922–2011)
David Hockney (1937–)
Rachel Lachowicz (1964–)
Claude Monet (1840–1926)
Alice Neel (1900–1984)
George Stubbs (1721–1806)
Rembrandt van Rijn (1606–69)

Notes on the Editors

Shormishtha Panja is a Professor of English, University of Delhi. She was till recently Head, Department of English and Dean, Faculty of Arts, University of Delhi. She is the President of the Shakespeare Society of India. She has taught at Stanford University. Her publications include *Many Indias, Many Literatures: New Critical Essays* (1999, second edition 2001, reprinted 2004), *Critical Theory Textual Application* (2002) *Signifying the Self: Women and Literature* (co-edited) (2004, reprinted 2007). She has published numerous essays on Renaissance studies, gender studies, literature and the visual arts and Indian literature in international journals and collections. She is the founder member of PEHEL: Delhi University Women's Support Group.

Shirshendu Chakrabarti is a Professor of English at the University of Delhi. He was an Inlaks Scholar at Trinity College, Oxford and has a D.Phil. from the University of Oxford. His interests lie in English literature from the Renaissance to the Eighteenth Century; European intellectual history, literature and the visual arts; modern English poetry; modern Bengali literature; translation. He has published on Jonathan Swift, Montaigne, George Herbert, Shelley, T.S. Eliot, Tagore and done Tagore translations for the *Oxford Tagore*. He has published two volumes of poetry in Bangla from Ananda Publishers and an annotated edition of Congreve's *The Way of the World*.

Christel Devadawson, Reader in the Department of English, University of Delhi, was a Cambridge Nehru Scholar for her Ph. D. She has studied and taught at St Stephen's College where she went on to head the English Department. As Westcott Memorial Lecturer at the University of Cambridge, she has lectured at the universities of Cambridge, Birmingham, Leicester and Warwick. Her writings include *Reading India, Writing England: The Fiction of Rudyard Kipling and E. M. Forster*, an edited versions *A Passage to India*, *Jane Eyre* and (with G K Das) a collection of critical essays on *A Passage to India*. She has just directed a film on the history of South Campus, Delhi University.

Notes on the Contributors

Davinder Mohini Ahuja is a Reader in the Department of English, Ramjas College, University of Delhi, and has been teaching since the past thirty-five years. Her interests include the Renaissance and Contemporary Literature. She is working on the Romances of Ludovico Ariosto and Philip Sidney for her Ph.D. Ahuja is currently a Fellow at the Institute of Lifelong Learning, University of Delhi.

Megha Anwer is a Lecturer at Lady Shri Ram College, University of Delhi. In 2007 she completed her M.Phil. with a short dissertation on the James Bond phenomenon. Her doctoral research area is crime and modernity in fictional and cinematic representations. She has published papers/articles on identity politics, cinema, the French Revolution and reviewed books for the journals *JSL* and *In-Between*.

Loris Button grew up in Melbourne, completing undergraduate studies in painting and drawing at the Phillip Institute of Technology, followed by a Master of Fine Arts degree at the University of Tasmania. Her Ph.D. thesis employed self- portraiture as a means for reflecting on identity, time and ageing in contemporary culture. Loris works with prints, paintings and drawings on handmade paper. She is Painting Coordinator at the Arts Academy, University of Ballarat, teaching into undergraduate, honours and postgraduate programmes. Loris regularly exhibits in both solo and group exhibitions throughout Australia. Her work is represented in public collections including the National Gallery of Australia, Artbank, the Ballarat Fine Art Gallery, the University of Ballarat and Loreto College.

Divya Dwivedi is pursuing her doctoral studies at the Department of Humanities and Social Sciences, Indian Institute of Technology, Delhi. She has completed her M.Phil. in English from the University of Delhi.

Gert Hofmann teaches German and Comparative Literature at the National University of Ireland in Cork. He has been a faculty member at the Hankuk University of Foreign Studies in Seoul and at the University of Hanover. His publications include *Schweigende Tropen. Studien zu einer Ästhetik der Ohnmacht* (Tübingen Basel 2004); *Dionysos Archemythos. Hölderlins transzendentale Poiesis* (Tübingen Basel 1996); *Figures of Law: Studies in the Interference of Law and Literature* (ed.) (Tübingen Basel 2007).

Maria Antonia Martí Escayol (Terrassa, 1972) has a Ph.D. from the Autonomous University of Barcelona 2004, and is a tenured assistant professor. She is a Renaissance and Early Modern historian. Her research and teaching interests include environmental thought, cultural identity, personal diaries and climate history, natural disasters, the Palladian tradition of agricultural writing, agriculture development and early modern science fiction.

Sonali Pattnaik is a lecturer at the Department of English, Kirori Mal College, University of Delhi. She has completed her MPhil in English from the University of Delhi. Her reviews and articles have appeared in the online academic journal *Intersections: Canada and the World. Theory, Literature, Cinema*, and in *Yearly Review*. Her articles on gender and cinema have appeared in the electronic news journal *Tehelka*. Her poetry can be found on Sonali-s-musings@over-blog.com.

Stuart Sillars is Professor of English at the University of Bergen, having previously been a member of the Faculty of English, University of Cambridge. His extensive work on the relations between literature and visual art includes books on their importance in two world wars, and on Victorian book illustration. His most recent books are *Painting Shakespeare: the Artist as Critic 1720–1820* (Cambridge UP, 2006) and *The Illustrated Shakespeare* (Cambridge UP, 2008). He is a member of the Norwegian Academy of Arts and Letters, a Visiting Fellow of Sidney Sussex College, Cambridge and an Honorary Research Fellow of the Shakespeare Institute, Stratford-upon-Avon.

Vincent Villafranca is a working sculptor. He has a strong appreciation for long-standing sculpture traditions, particularly those found in India. He has made several trips to south India and Nepal to observe the living history which still exists in many of the traditional sculpture-making communities. He believes that, in some instances, the unbroken practices being implemented to produce art in these communities can act as windows to the past. Vincent currently resides in Texas where he actively produces bronze sculptures revolving around a variety of themes. In 2008, he was the recipient of the Chesley Award for Best 3-D Art.

James Yoch teaches classes in Shakespeare and Drama, best known for the student teams who stage creative productions at the University of Oklahoma. In a triad of books he has explored the role of domestic place in the American scene: *Landscaping the American Dream: the Gardens and Film Sets of Florence Yoch, 1890-1972; A Guide to Villa Philbrook and its Gardens;* and *On the Shore of Empire: Phineas Banning and the Development of Southern California*. He is currently writing about friendship in the *Aeneid*, subversive elements in the entertainments and gardens of Versailles, and scenery in *The Tempest* and current video games.

Index

D

Q

R